RETIREMENT COUNTDOWN

TAKE ACTION NOW
TO GET THE LIFE YOU WANT

FT Prentice Hall
FINANCIAL TIMES

In an increasingly competitive world, it is quality
of thinking that gives an edge—an idea that opens new
doors, a technique that solves a problem, or an insight
that simply helps make sense of it all.

We work with leading authors in the various arenas
of business and finance to bring cutting-edge thinking
and best learning practice to a global market.

It is our goal to create world-class print publications
and electronic products that give readers
knowledge and understanding which can then be
applied, whether studying or at work.

To find out more about our business
products, you can visit us at www.ft-ph.com

Pearson
Education

RETIREMENT COUNTDOWN
TAKE ACTION NOW
TO GET THE LIFE YOU WANT

DAVID SHAPIRO

FT Prentice Hall
FINANCIAL TIMES

An Imprint of PEARSON EDUCATION

Upper Saddle River, NJ • New York • London • San Francisco • Toronto • Sydney

Tokyo • Singapore • Hong Kong • Cape Town • Madrid

Paris • Milan • Munich • Amsterdam

Library of Congress Cataloging-in-Publication Data

Shapiro, David
    Retirement countdown: take action now to get the life you want / David Shapiro
        p. cm. -- (Financial Times Prentice Hall books)
        Includes index.
        ISBN 0-13-109671-0
        1. Retirement income--Planning. 2. Retirement--Planning. 3. Investments. I. Title. II.
Series.

    HG179.S452 2004
    332.024'014--dc22
                                                                    2004047219

Editorial/production supervision: *Techne Group*
Cover design director: *Jerry Votta*
Manufacturing buyer: *Alexis Heydt-Long*
Executive editor: *Jim Boyd*
Editorial assistant: *Linda Ramagnano*
Marketing manager: *Marten Litkowsky*
Full-service production manager: *Anne R. Garcia*

FT Prentice Hall
FINANCIAL TIMES

© 2004 David Shapiro
Publishing as Financial Times Prentice Hall
Upper Saddle River, New Jersey 07458

Financial Times Prentice Hall books are widely used by corporations and government
agencies for training, marketing, and resale.

For information regarding corporate and government bulk discounts please
contact: Corporate and Government Sales at (800) 382-3419 or email to
corpsales@pearsontechgroup.com.

Printed in the United States of America

First Printing

ISBN 0-13-109671-0

Pearson Education Ltd.
Pearson Education Australia Pty., Limited
Pearson Education South Asia Pte. Ltd.
Pearson Education Asia Ltd.
Pearson Education Canada, Ltd.
Pearson Educación de Mexico, S.A. de C.V.
Pearson Education-Japan
Pearson Malaysia S.D.N. B.H.D.

FINANCIAL TIMES PRENTICE HALL BOOKS

For more information, please go to www.ft-ph.com

Business and Society

Douglas K. Smith
On Value and Values: Thinking Differently About We in an Age of Me

Current Events

Alan Elsner
Gates of Injustice: The Crisis in America's Prisons

John R. Talbott
Where America Went Wrong: And How to Regain Her Democratic Ideals

Economics

David Dranove
What's Your Life Worth? Health Care Rationing…Who Lives? Who Dies? Who Decides?

Entrepreneurship

Dr. Candida Brush, Dr. Nancy M. Carter, Dr. Elizabeth Gatewood, Dr. Patricia G. Greene, and Dr. Myra M. Hart
Clearing the Hurdles: Women Building High Growth Businesses

Oren Fuerst and Uri Geiger
From Concept to Wall Street: A Complete Guide to Entrepreneurship and Venture Capital

David Gladstone and Laura Gladstone
Venture Capital Handbook: An Entrepreneur's Guide to Raising Venture Capital, Revised and Updated

Thomas K. McKnight
Will It Fly? How to Know if Your New Business Idea Has Wings… Before You Take the Leap

Stephen Spinelli, Jr., Robert M. Rosenberg, and Sue Birley
Franchising: Pathway to Wealth Creation

Executive Skills

Cyndi Maxey and Jill Bremer
It's Your Move: Dealing Yourself the Best Cards in Life and Work

John Putzier
Weirdos in the Workplace

Finance

Aswath Damodaran
The Dark Side of Valuation: Valuing Old Tech, New Tech, and New Economy Companies

Kenneth R. Ferris and Barbara S. Pécherot Petitt
Valuation: Avoiding the Winner's Curse

Personal Finance

David Shapiro
Retirement Countdown: Take Action Now to Get the Life You Want

Steve Weisman
A Guide to Elder Planning: Everything You Need to Know to Protect Yourself Legally and Financially

Strategy

Edward W. Davis and Robert E. Spekmam
The Extended Enterprise: Gaining Competitive Advantage through Collaborative Supply Chains

Joel M. Shulman, With Thomas T. Stallkamp
Getting Bigger by Growing Smaller: A New Growth Model for Corporate America

Contents

PART III
TAKE ACTION NOW TO GET THE LIFE YOU WANT

APPENDICES

Foreword

A freight train is bearing down on middle-aged Americans. That train, carrying with it true peril for tens of millions of millions of citizens, is retirement. As difficult or as easy as it is for the 77 million Americans in the Baby Boom generation, born roughly between 1946 and 1964, to get along on what they earn, it will be a whole new ball game, played at night and without lights, for those Boomers when they reach the end of their working lives. At that point, in addition to having to deal with boredom, health issues, and—worst of all—mortality, they will have to address financial issues totally different from what they have ever faced before.

Retirement Countdown does not have any brilliant thoughts about mortality as far as I can tell, and it is not a health guide. But as a comprehensive guide to preparing for the financial challenges of retirement, it is in the stratosphere of highest quality.

In lucid, easy-to-follow steps, expressed with a maximum of levity and a minimum of cant, author David Shapiro shows you how to start thinking about the financial aspects of retirement planning, how to set realistic goals, and how your various retirement goals and plans must mesh. He does this with a modesty and self-deprecating humor that makes *Retirement Countdown* inform and amuse at the same time.

He then takes you into the various worlds of investments that are available to help prepare for retirement—stocks, fixed income, bonds, annuities, immediate and deferred (my own favorites for their unique feature of being guaranteed to live at least as long as you do), real estate and collectibles, and mutual funds as a way of diversifying and benefiting from professional investment management, especially when they are not index mutual funds. In a catch-all, he explains how to manage all of these investments together.

Shapiro then goes back to the beginning to help guide you to a plan that will make your retirement comfortable. And that is what this book is all about: making your retirement comfortable. That is about as big a challenge as most Americans will ever face unless they have been in combat or lost a loved one. Yet it is a challenge of desperate importance.

It is hard to imagine a worse fate in peacetime than having to live in old age and failing health with inadequate money on hand. To have to leave your home, to have to live without decent food, to have to live without unlimited access to good medical care—these are frightening prospects. Reading and heeding the words in Shapiro's book will keep them distant prospects. To have to live in old age in fear and worry, to have to cower at the prospect of unexpected bills—medical bills, repairs on one's home, a new Mercury—these are consummations *not* devoutly to be wished, to paraphrase Hamlet of Denmark, a man who did not live to retirement.

You can get far away from the prospect of spending your old age in fear and worry by the simple (and pleasant!) expedient of reading and following the advice of Shapiro. He has done all of the legwork and the heavy statistical and legal lifting. (He has also provided his uniquely clever insights into modern life. I love his point that it's not worth taking your kids to ball games any longer because today's athletes are not good role models—the money would be better saved for their education.)

But you have a still more difficult challenge. You have to pay attention, and you have to make plans, and then—far more tricky—stick to them. You have to restrain your spending in the face of a society that commands you to spend, and, instead, you have to save and save and then save some more. And you have to give serious thought to how you deploy your savings, both before and after retirement. But this book is your guide and your trainer as you do the financial bodybuilding you need to do to get ready for retirement and then to cruise happily through retirement.

How important is it to pay attention to this book? That depends. How important is it to get a good night's sleep? How important is it to live without fear? How important is it to be able to help your children and grandchildren? How important is it to be able to enjoy yourself after you retire instead of living in terror? How important is it to live on the golf course instead of in a single room of a retirement hotel? How important is it to be able to go south in the winter?

To put it another way, this book is important, and rarely has a book so important been so much fun to read.

Read it. Laugh along with it, but learn from it. *Retirement Countdown* is amusingly written, but it is vital. In every sense, if you are a preretiree—and so many of us are—you cannot afford to be without this book on your shelf and in your head.

Ben Stein

Introduction

Congratulations on taking the first step toward reaching your retirement goals by making this timely purchase and finding your way to the starting line. My commitment to you is to "tell it like it is" without sugarcoating the message and yet deliver the message with a strong sense of encouragement and a touch of humor. Granted, your retirement is no laughing matter, but I've always found humor to be a great source of realism and perspective in life, so let's get to work. We can solve some problems and share a laugh or two. I promise that some will be at my expense.

I think it's important for you understand why I'm writing this book and what you can expect from it. My primary reason for writing *Retirement Countdown* is a fairly simple one: I feel that with all my experience in the financial services investment industry, I have something to say that could help you achieve your retirement goals. That's why I hope that as you read this book, you feel the sincere spirit in which it is offered. I've seen a lot of good and bad over the past 25 years, and my fear is that 77 million Baby Boomers and a lot of others are heading into a harsh winter retirement storm.

For me to be successful, I need to convince you that I have something of value to offer, and if you don't trust the advice I've provided, I will have failed in my goal. I need your trust to be able to help you. You need to know that I don't sell financial planning services, nor do I provide individual advice to anyone for a fee—the occasional apple fritter or a new-release DVD, perhaps, but never a fee. Not that there is anything wrong with fees or commissions; I think that the role for professionals is a vital one in helping you meet your goals. However, I've always enjoyed leveraging my skills, and writing, speaking, and building businesses create the kind of leverage that I love and have excelled at over the years.

You also need to know I haven't spent the majority of my years in a corporate ivory tower and that my experience is not purely from teaching others. The experiences I reflect on in this book are the result of thousands of meetings I have had with financial planners and their clients to discuss the benefits of retiring on *their* terms. I have worked with people of all ages, and I've conducted seminars in luxury hotels, trailer parks, schools, and conventions. One of the books I co-authored has been used in research for a Supreme Court decision and was quoted by Justice Ruth Ginsburg in her majority opinion. But what I've found is that people are simply people—some more informed, some less informed, some more trusting, and some less trusting. And the reason that I *have* to tell it like it is in this book is that so many people lack the information necessary to develop a dialogue of substance with a professional who truly engenders trust in a relationship. And the result of that lack of trust is likely to be procrastination or a splintered approach to financial planning without balance, without vision, and without a plan.

I can also say that financial planning in general and retirement planning specifically are difficult subjects to speak broadly to because we all have unique goals and obstacles to deal with. So, as you read this book, keep in mind that you'll have some work to do along the way—actually, a lot of work, because it's *your* retirement and no one else's. I hope that *Retirement Countdown* becomes the most tattered book on your bookshelf, and I hope that my supporting Web site, *www.retirementcountdown,* is saved as one of your favorites.

You'll need to be introspective and honest with yourself about where you are in your own planning cycle and how much time and effort you have to devote to fostering the kind of retirement that will make you happy. You need to approach saving for retirement or managing income in retirement as a task. I always find it helpful at the outset of any task to establish the game plan. That means:

1. Define the need or task.

2. Set reasonable goals and expectations.

3. Create a framework for achievement.

4. Establish a methodology for assessing progress and modifying your game plan.

5. Execute, *do it,* and don't quit. This is not a failure you can afford!

Let's talk about the game plan briefly before we move on. Successful people come in all sizes, shapes, and colors. They share certain common attributes such as determination, a desire to succeed, a natural or time-honed talent, and a sixth sense that guides them to the right shot at the right time or the right strategic decision at the right time. They also know that as good as they are, they need to have a game plan and others to assist them in achieving their task or goal. It's no secret that less gifted people can outperform those more gifted than if they have a better game plan or a stronger will.

I can't tell you how important it is for you to plan your retirement and make it a priority in your life. Reviewing your retirement plan needs to become second nature to you. Throughout this book, you will run across all kinds of statistics, but look at the message carried by the words and not the implication of the statistic itself. Although statistics can be impersonal, I'm asking you to look inside and see if they might apply to you or your situation. You cannot be successful in achieving your retirement goals without a plan, and most of us cannot do it without help from a professional. So many of us feel that we can do it ourselves, but in the end, we simply do nothing. We lack the same commodity that drives our ability to meet the retirement challenge—time. This book will help you sort through the financial and emotional issues and establish some guidelines for selecting and working with a financial planning specialist if you choose to enlist help.

Choosing the right professional or professionals for your needs is perhaps one of the most important decisions that you'll make. In Chapter 13, I'll help you find someone who has the right skill sets and a complementary style, and most important, I'll help you find someone who understands that meeting your needs is the number one goal.

You will find a variety of professionals, from stockbrokers to insurance agents to attorneys and accountants. Virtually all of these professionals are also salespeople, so you have to make certain that they have properly balanced your needs with their needs. If it's not a win-win proposition, someone is will be unhappy. To borrow a line from one of my favorite musicals, *Man of LaMancha*, "Whether the pitcher hits the stone or the stone hits the pitcher, it's going to be bad for the pitcher." You don't want to be the pitcher in this analogy.

Balance is incredibly important in everything that we do and is a consistent theme throughout the book, as are references to musicals and movies as my personal passion bleeds into the book's character. One final note on the planning aspect of this book relates to setting reasonable goals and not giving up. I believe in reaching for the stars, so using the word "reasonable" can make my stomach knot up. Overachievers don't like the word reasonable, but I have to say that for the vast majority of us, if we don't set reasonable goals, we create an environment in which failure becomes easier than success to achieve. Once we establish reasonable goals, it's easier for us to get some wins and feel good about the planning process.

The greatest challenge to achieving your goal will not come from bad investments or from bad advice, though these can certainly contribute to an unwanted outcome. No, the greatest challenge will come from within, from *procrastination*. People procrastinate for all kinds of reasons, but as it relates specifically to retirement and money management, most people procrastinate because the subject is simply too much to digest and too much to manage. It can often be too difficult to face issues like mortality, possible loss of personal health, and the fear that you may not have sufficient assets to support the retirement of your choice. Procrastination thrives on the adage "Ignorance is bliss."

So let's get down to work and set expectations. *Retirement Countdown* is not your everyday book on retirement; it is an *action-oriented* book designed to get you to recognize the importance of being an active participant in the retirement process. There are dozens and dozens of books on retirement that focus on everything you wanted to know about retirement and investment products. These books tend to be offerings that appeal to the "do-it-yourself" investor. Although a do-it-yourself investor can certainly gain great value from reading this book, *Retirement Countdown* is designed to hit you right between the eyes with the harsh realities associated with reaching your retirement goals and managing your retirement assets. And one important fact is that a very small percentage of Americans have the right combination of time, skill, and discipline to manage their own retirement assets effectively. Think of how many times you have started a project on your own only to abandon it before completion. That may be fine if you're building a doghouse or knitting a scarf, but if it's your retirement, your procrastination can have a catastrophic impact.

Retirement Countdown will take you on this journey in small steps, separating the concepts from the actual investment products so that the issues at hand don't suffocate you or leave you feeling helpless and paralyzed. Most people don't understand that managing your retirement is a three-dimensional task requiring great focus and discipline. The first two dimensions are time and performance, but the third dimension is represented by all the external forces that play on your goals, such as risk, market volatility, and life events. These are all defined and discussed in later chapters. *Retirement Countdown* is all about process, not products, and about empowerment, not procrastination. In reading this book, you can expect a splash of drill sergeant and a dash of humor woven into my concept of "chicken soup for your retirement."

You will find that the book is divided into three basic sections. In the first section, we take a broad look at the problems associated with accumulating assets for retirement and managing assets to create and sustain retirement income. Perhaps the greatest challenge facing retiring seniors and aging Baby Boomers today is the lack of adequate financial resources to support their retirement choices. *People want to enjoy their retirement at a standard of living that does not compromise their preretirement lifestyle.* Unfortunately for many Americans, that is not an option. In this section, I want to lay the groundwork for you to be one of the fortunate Americans who do not have to compromise their lifestyle after retirement. At the end of this section, we will begin to plan for retirement and set up the "goal-oriented" approach to retirement planning.

The second section of *Retirement Countdown* takes a look at the various investment products available to you in your quest for retirement security. But what is much more important, this section looks at the risks associated with any investment and discusses your options relative to these risks. This section also does a thorough job of looking at what the financial services industry refers to as packaged products, including mutual funds, annuities, and insurance products.

Many of the current texts on retirement gloss over the issue of risk management in general and insurance as an option to protect assets in particular. My own belief is that many of the authors of these books just don't have the depth of knowledge in this area to be comfortable in making insured risk management a part of the retirement process. For better or for worse, I have worked with insurance companies, banks, and stock brokerage firms for the past 25 years, and I understand how these products work and how they can be of benefit to you in your retirement planning. I also can help you understand the difference between products that are properly designed to meet your needs and those that might be better suited to someone else. I can also show you the products to avoid and products that lack the balance of being good for you and for the company that sells them.

The final section of *Retirement Countdown* is about action and resources. In this section, we review the need for action, provide additional resources, and prepare the road map that will guide us to success. I don't think that many of you have the time or discipline to climb this mountain without a guide and without a safety rope. This section of the book will help you to find the right safety rope (professional) to assist you in your planning, and I have strong opinions on what you should be looking for in such an individual or company. That said, if you have the time and discipline and want to do it yourself, I'll provide you with resources and tools, including the Web, that will aid you on this retirement climb.

Be aware that the Internet has made so much information available that you can easily overload and become paralyzed by having too many options and too little time to effect change. To aid you on an ongoing basis, you're welcome to visit *www.retirementcountdown.com* and enjoy the Web site that I have set up to provide you with an ongoing kick-in-the-butt and the latest information on retirement trends and products. You'll find that some of the tasks you will have to perform to develop and monitor your plan are better accomplished through use of a computer and not pen and paper. On the *Retirement Countdown* Web site, you'll find helpful calculators and online tools to aid in developing your goals.

I hope you're ready to join me on this journey. With the protracted bear market at the start of the century and the movement away from income-oriented defined benefit retirement plans, people are searching for answers and too often can be misled into believing that they can climb the retirement mountain with no guide and no ropes. Let me help guide you up the right path and encourage you to stay on that path. No one else can do this for you; you have to be the climber and you have to take charge of your path to security in retirement. We're about to head up the mountain, and we won't stop until we've reached our goal, so turn to Chapter 1, and let's get started.

I Am So Grateful

Not many people stick around for the rolling credits at the end of the movie, which is why I'm glad that acknowledgements are placed at the front of a book. As the author, I like to think that people will read this special page and that all the people who contributed to this project will get their just recognition in print.

This list represents the names of those who helped with the book and those whose impressions on my life have been profound.

To my parents, Harvey and Popie: I am what you made me, and I am more grateful with every breath.

To my wife, Judy: You ground me. You're my inspiration and you epitomize the word "perseverance." (See Chapter 14 to understand how much of an impact this trait has on our lives.)

My thanks to the following wonderful people for being literary guinea pigs and providing their personal perspectives on *Retirement Countdown: Terry Barger, Cathie Enjaian, Joe Lamberson, Stuart Phillips, Judy Shapiro, Tom Streiff,* and *Tom West.*

Thanks also to *Mary Shapiro* for helping me find Financial Times Prentice Hall, to my editor *Jim Boyd,* and to *Frank Hill,* a wonderful illustrator who brought the cartoon ideas to life.

And my heartfelt thanks to *Naomi Holland* for her generous contribution of countless hours, providing terrific insight and making me look as if I have grammar skills.

How to Use This Book

As you read *Retirement Countdown,* I hope that you'll find the added features helpful to you. Keep in mind that with regard to Web sites, addresses can change frequently and companies do go out of business (you'll read about that later in the book). If you have trouble with a Web address that has additional letters following the slash (/), put your cursor in the browser address window right after the slash and erase all but the core address. For example, if the complete address is *www.abc.com/calculator.htm* and the site does not load, try just *www.abc.com* instead and see if the particular link has moved or is no longer offered. You can also visit *www.retirementcountdown.com* where I'll keep up-to-date links and useful information.

Book Navigation Tools

 More information or tools available online

 Savings tip

 Common mistake made

 Interesting information

 Be careful

 Wake-Up Call

 Key point

PART I

UNDERSTANDING THE PROBLEM AND THE SOLUTION

CHAPTER 1

Tick Tock Goes the Retirement Clock

Thomas Edison was quoted as saying that genius is 1 percent inspiration and 99 percent perspiration—prepare to be inspired and to sweat. Congratulations on taking this step toward empowering your retirement. You've gotten your hands on this book, and you're ready to partner with me as your guide to climb this retirement mountain.

You will find this book very conversational. Imagine me as the little guardian angel on your shoulder whispering into your ear (and occasionally shouting benevolent words of encouragement). My goal in writing this book is simple and straightforward: I want to educate and empower people who are struggling with their own retirement issues.

There's an old Chinese proverb that basically goes like this: *"Tell me something and I'll forget it, show me something and I may recall it, but involve me in something and I'll understand it."* I want you to understand the consequences of your action or inaction, and I want to provide you with a path to achieve your goals. This first chapter is all about overcoming inertia and establishing the proper mindset as we prepare to learn about retirement issues and build a framework that will ultimately provide you with the retirement of your choice. This won't happen without a lot of hard work; the hardest fought victories always feel the best.

Carrying forward our Far East references, 2,500 years ago, there lived a military expert by the name of Sun Tzu. He and his father before him were renowned across the land as being not just great warriors, but great military strategists. Those who have studied Sun Tzu understand that one of his core principles was avoiding conflict, not forcing conflict. He was also well prepared for achieving any goal, and I've always been able to apply his principles during my career. Imagine that achieving your retirement goals is a war and listen to Sun Tzu's thought: "Conquerors estimate in their temple before war begins. They consider everything. The defeated also estimate before the war, but they do not contemplate everything. Estimating completely creates victory; estimating incompletely causes failure".

The Retirement Countdown Plan

For you to be able to retire on *your* terms will require a concerted effort. Only a small percentage of Americans have the luxury of not worrying about how they will meet their post-retirement income needs. The rest of us must either be lucky or take action to establish, monitor, and achieve a plan that will result in meeting our goals. The process we will go through to establish your retirement framework is called Goal

Oriented Retirement Planning, or GORP for short. GORP is the energy for your retirement plan.

GORP breaks down the process of planning for retirement into small digestible steps that create a feeling of hope and empowerment, not fear and procrastination. But hope and empowerment can only create the proper mindset for doing the work that needs to be done. Once you recognize you have to work to achieve these goals, you need to develop a plan to implement change. On a step-by-step basis over the course of this book, you will learn what is required to establish and meet your retirement goals. The following is a brief discussion of the framework from which we will work. Much greater detail can be found on GORP and applying its principles in Chapters 5, 12, and 13.

Step One: Commit to the Process

Retirement planning is a process, not an event. To achieve your goals will require a commitment of time on a regular basis. You will have to decide if this is a task you want to tackle on your own or one that requires you to enlist the help of a professional. If you choose to go it on your own, you must remember the key limitation is time, and 100 percent of the workload rests on your shoulders. If you work with a professional, you can choose the extent to which you want to seed control of certain elements of the process and take a management role. In Chapter 13, you will find a grid that will help you decide when and how to use a professional.

Step Two: Collect Information

The second step involves pulling together all kinds of data you will need as you begin to conceive and develop your plan. Included here would be information on the following:

- Income and assets
- Expenses and liabilities
- Insurance
- Legal documents
- Tax documents

Step Three: Develop a Plan (Strategic)

Once you have collected all of the necessary information, you can start to lay out a strategic plan. It's important at this stage to keep the tactical aspects of the plan at bay until you have completed the strategic aspect. In other words, this is *not* the stage to start looking at mutual funds or any other investment vehicle, regardless of whether you have listed them as assets or feel compelled to buy them. This is the stage of the process at which you articulate your retirement goals and determine the cost of the individual goals.

Step Four: Implement the Plan (Tactical)

In this fourth step, you are ready to implement the plan. This is the tactical element of GORP where you match assets to goals and look at repositioning assets that have no place in your plan. One of the benefits of GORP is that there is no place for an asset that is not assigned to meeting a goal. This is also the step at which you'll take action on implementing an estate plan and you'll develop a plan for managing the various elements of risk that can impact your goals.

Step Five: Monitor and Update the Plan

The final step is to monitor and update your plan. This involves periodically reviewing your goals and the assets assigned to meeting those goals. It also involves looking at how your life may have changed and how changes affect both your goals and other elements of the plan such as tax, estate, and insurance planning. As you change jobs or are promoted within an organization, your life can change and your goals may be affected by those changes. What if your original plan assumed both you and your spouse or partner would be full-time wage earners and you chose to modify the plan to allow for one of you to stop working for 10 years to raise a family? Or, what if your lifestyle were altered in such a way that your estimate for retirement income was either too high or too low? By continuing to review and modify your plan, you increase your odds of achieving success.

Timely Tidbits

Professional and recreational climbers use GORP too. Whereas GORP in *Retirement Countdown* is the fuel you use to sustain your retirement, GORP to a mountain climber is a trail mix for energy. Originally, GORP was granola, oats, raisins, and peanuts, but today the term refers to any energy boost mixture.

Facing the Facts

In early 2004, the Congressional Budget Office (CBO) released a report stating that approximately 50 percent of baby boomers will likely face a reduced standard of living at retirement. The CBO goes on to say this assumption may even be too optimistic based on the projected financial status of government-administered retirement programs like Social Security. The report points out that the CBO assumptions are based on no future cuts in Social Security benefits, which many people feel is unlikely. The Social Security Administration itself freely admits the Trust fund is likely to be able to support current benefit levels only until 2040, at which time it suggests that benefits will need to be reduced by 37 percent for the system to maintain its integrity.

With Social Security waning in its ability to support retirement for the vast majority of Americans, the responsibility for achieving retirement security falls squarely on the shoulders of the individual. For you to be able to maintain your current or desired lifestyle in retirement, you need to take action now. That means that you have to get moving and create some momentum so that you can enjoy your retirement years.

Let's Physically Climb the Mountain

The laws of motion, as defined by Sir Isaac Newton and the great astronomer Galileo Galilei, provide us a framework for understanding momentum, or inertia. Their wisdom simply suggests that a body at rest will remain at rest until moved by an outside force. Now, let's try to apply physics rules to finances. The law of motion applied to your retirement planning would suggest that if you do nothing to prepare for your retirement, you are destined to get what you prepare for: nothing. So we need an outside force to move you along. That's where I come in. I'm the outside force pushing you to engage in this process, to take action, to let inertia carry you to retirement security at a level that meets your needs.

info

Interesting Information

An interesting fact about Sir Isaac Newton is that he could bench-press 275 pounds and was the three-time Calculus World Champion. He was Charles Atlas and brains combined.

I can't think of a better analogy than that of climbing a mountain to use as the foundation for our journey. As a recreational mountain climber, I have read numerous books on the subject and have yearned, like so many other recreational climbers, to one day test my physical and mental discipline on a noted climb in the Himalayas, Africa, or some other exotic location. By general definition, a mountain has a broad base, tapering to a peak. The goal of climbers is to reach the peak. In doing so, climbers typically have any number of routes they can take in pursuit of their quest. Each route carries with it different challenges and a unique landscape to navigate.

In general, the easier the mountain terrain, the less need for assistance in the climb. Most people can walk up a hill without ropes and a guide. But as the terrain becomes more challenging, the risk of injury increases dramatically, and climbers must then make certain decisions that directly impact their personal safety and their ability to achieve their goal. For the most difficult mountains, climbers may need a professional guide, various ropes and ladders, special clothing and equipment, and even oxygen to sustain their life at higher altitudes.

INFORMATION

Web Sites

If you enjoy the analogy of mountain climbing, you may want to check out these Web sites:

www.mountainzone.com

www.mountaineers.net

The road to a secure retirement is much like the mountain that stands before us with its lofty peak and snow-capped ridges beckoning us to achieve the ultimate goal of standing at its highest point. And as with choosing the best route to ascend the mountain, there are any number of ways to reach your retirement goals, each with its own risks and rewards. There are also certain actions you can take without any direction from a guide and others that I believe will require that you either achieve a level of understanding equal to that of a guide or enlist the help of a professional to climb your retirement mountain.

But whichever path you take, either alone or with a guide, you need to make a decision. We live in a free society, and it's up to you to control your retirement destiny. Yes, *you* are the ultimate decision maker and *you* can choose to climb the mountain yourself or to enlist someone to help you in achieving your goal. I just urge you take action and do something because paralysis is likely to result in failure. Let me add here that when I refer to "you" throughout this book, I'm referring to either an individual or to a couple. If you're one voice in a decision that will ultimately affect two people, I strongly suggest that your spouse, partner, or significant other either read this book as well or at least read Chapters 1–6, Chapters 13–15, and the Power Checklist at the end of each chapter.

A Lesson from a Great Corporate Leader

From 1986 to 1989, I had the distinct pleasure of working with the former CEO of the ITT Corporation, Harold Geneen. Geneen was the CEO of ITT for 18 years, and during his tenure, he invented the international corporate conglomerate by acquiring over 250 companies, including Avis, Sheraton, and Hartford Life, to name a few. He had hired my former partner and me to help build some investment and insurance products for a life insurance company that he purchased after retiring from the ITT board of directors at age 76.

When I visited Hal's office in New York's Waldorf Astoria, I was always humbled by the photographs hanging on the walls of his conference room. In front of me were pictures of Hal with every president dating back to Harry S. Truman. But it wasn't the pictures on the wall or the incredibly rich corporate legacy Hal left behind that impressed me the most. It was how Hal broke information down into small digestible pieces that wowed me. He had an uncanny thirst for understanding, not just a thirst for knowledge.

For a two-year period, I met with Hal twice monthly at the insurance company in Chicago and at the holding company in New York. The meetings at the insurance company were with all the heads of the various departments and the senior management of the company. I was always impressed by the way Hal ran these meetings. Since Hal did not grow up in the insurance business, he only had a cursory understanding of how products were designed, priced, and managed. To compensate for his lack of industry knowledge, he would ask a lot of questions. If a manager gave a report on a subject that Hal was not informed on, he would not let the manager proceed with the presentation until Hal clearly understood enough of the subject matter so he could make an intelligent decision.

| info | **Interesting Fact** |

Harold Geneen was a feared corporate leader. His toughness was legendary, and in the famous 1976 movie *Network,* Ned Beatty played a character patterned after Geneen. A famous scene from the movie is actually filmed in the ITT boardroom, the only boardroom at the time that could seat over 100 people.

I learned a fundamental lesson from Hal that I will never forget: There is no such thing as a stupid question. I also learned you can't let your ego get in the way of understanding what you need to know to make an informed decision. Let's take this a step further because we often think to ask the immediate question on our mind, but we may not grasp the entire concept. If you don't have an understanding of the concept, the answer to a specific question may be of little value to you in the long run. It's not that people ask the wrong questions; typically, they don't ask enough of the right questions. There is a fine line we have to manage between collecting information pertinent to the subject and collecting information that is superfluous. Don't be afraid to ask what all good reporters ask: who, what, why, when, and where! We'll cover specific questions as they relate to your retirement plan throughout the book.

Procrastination

I've been in the financial services industry since 1979, but I've really never been in direct sales to consumers; rather, I have always trained others and assisted them with their clients. That means that although I have earned a variety of professional designations within the financial services industry, I have never chosen to make a living by providing advice directly to consumers for a fee or for a commission. I have, however, done just about everything else in the industry, including training tens of thousands of financial planners, stockbrokers and insurance agents.

I think it's important for me to explain to you why I have never done what is commonly referred to as personal production, or consumer sales. I have always been one to leverage my skills, whatever they may be. To that end, I've felt that I could do the greatest good and better leverage my time by working with financial planners and their clients. I have done this through my writing, through my training of financial planners, and

through the one-on-one contact that I have had over the years working with people just like you. To continue with our analogy, I have spent much time on the mountain covering all types of terrain and every conceivable situation.

During those times when I was fortunate to meet face-to-face with consumers and their financial planners, I got to see, hear, and feel the concern over the issue of not having enough money to live comfortably in retirement. I've seen the aftermath of bear markets when people have lost 40 percent to 60 percent of their life savings and, as a result, lost the ability to choose when and how to retire. And during the process, quite frankly, I've seen some horrible mismatches between clients and planners.

I've also learned that we all live incredibly full lives, which makes it difficult for us to focus on and follow through with tough decisions. With family, work, hobbies, and other social and athletic activities, we tend to put off decisions and dealing with issues that require consideration of one or a combination of the following criteria:

◆ Complex issues

◆ Issues not immediately important

◆ Issues that deal with health or mortality

◆ Issues that two parties don't immediately agree on

Wake-Up Call

The number one reason people fail to meet their retirement goals is:

   A. Their investments don't earn enough

   B. They don't save enough in their 401(k)s

   C. They don't do anything

   D. They don't have enough time

And the answer is:

   C. Procrastination is the single biggest reason people fail to reach their retirement goals.

When the topic of retirement planning comes up, it's no wonder that people choose to procrastinate—all four of the criteria laid out above could well be factors in postponing action. Let's look at these individually as they relate to accumulating or distributing retirement assets and try and find a way to put each issue into a perspective so that you can feel empowered, not paralyzed.

Complex Issues

Complex issues, by definition, scare many people. The word "complex" summons up images of the investment of large amounts of time and a tremendous amount of concentration to understand a given issue. We often further complicate the matter by wanting more information than is necessary to make a decision. As I mentioned earlier, I don't want to dissuade anyone from doing research and making fully informed decisions, but you must keep the issues in perspective or the task gets out of control and the result is procrastination.

Let's illustrate this with the purchase of a new watch. If your objective is to be able to have an accurate timepiece, do you really need to know exactly how the watch is made, or do you just need to know it tells accurate time? If you were choosing a surgeon, would you be more interested in the doctor's credentials and experience or in understanding every step of the surgical process? Granted, in some cases you may want to understand both.

Retirement planning is a very complex topic, with many different strategies to meet your goals and tens of thousands of products to apply once you have chosen your strategy. The best way to climb this mountain is by taking one step at a time, just as the professionals do. Actually, in mountain climbing, climbers often acclimate to a given altitude by repeating the same leg of a climb again and again and again. In retirement planning and in *Retirement Countdown,* we'll take one step at a time and encourage you to repeat it until you're "acclimated" to the topic. That's how we will eliminate fear and empower you to take action. You have to make the goal achievable or you'll never get started.

Issues Not Immediately Important

"Oh, we have plenty of time!" We all have to prioritize our workload, whether it's personal or business. In that process, we engage in what I call "life event triage." Triage is the French word made popular by medical and war television shows and movies. It means to sort or prioritize and is the process that emergency rooms and field combat medical operations use to determine the order in which people are treated. The more serious the illness and the greater the risk of death, the higher the patient is in the order of treatment. From a personal perspective, we use life event triage daily. It's called time management.

Key Point: The Rule of 72

An interesting tool you can use to illustrate compounding and inflation is the Rule of 72. Simply divide 72 by any number and the quotient will be the amount of time takes to double your money. Example: divide 72 by 10 and it will take 7.2 years to double your money at 10 percent (72÷10=7.2). Or assume that inflation is growing at 3 percent a year. Divide 72 by 3 and you'll see that the cost of goods or services doubles every 24 years (72÷3=24).

The problem with retirement planning is that most people think they have so much time before they retire that it's a low priority and they keep pushing it off in favor of issues with more critical timing. This is a very dangerous position to take because your ability to accumulate assets for retirement is based primarily on time and investment return. Without both of these working in concert, it will be difficult to achieve your goal. If you start too late, you'll be counting on a high rate of return to make up the difference, leaving you exposed to much greater market risk. The less time, the more difficult it is to take advantage of compounding. You'll learn more about this later in the book, but one of the key elements to achieving financial independence is compounding your returns.

It might be helpful for you to know that interest is applied two basic ways: simple and compound. The difference is significant. Simple interest is interest on a principal sum of money only, and not on the interest itself that is being earned. Let's say you put $10,000 into a certificate of deposit at the local bank earning 3 percent simple interest each year. The first year, and each year after that, you'll earn $300 in interest.

Compound interest is interest on interest, so the interest is being applied to both the principal and the earned interest. In the same example, interest in the first year would be $300, or 3 percent of $10,000. In the second year, however, your interest would be $309, in the third year, $327, and so on.

In Table 1–1, we see an example of how compounding impacts money over time. We use a principal sum of $10,000 invested in an interest-bearing account for 20 years. Column two shows us 6 percent simple interest, column three shows us 6 percent compound interest, and column four shows the difference in dollars with the percentage difference in parentheses. You'll note that in the first five years, compounding generates only a 3 percent improvement over simple interest. But 20 years out, the difference is a staggering 31 percent. Now imagine the impact of starting your retirement planning 10 years late!

Issues That Deal with Health or Mortality

When HBO launched *Six Feet Under*, it took a big risk by wrapping a prime time show around a family-owned mortuary. Although the show has been a critical success, the subject matter is one most people embrace cautiously. When the mortality in question is our own, we often run as far

Table 1–1   Value of a $10,000 Investment with Simple and Compound Interest

End of Year	Total ($) with 6% Return		Improvement with Compounding (Difference)
	Simple Interest	**Compound Interest**	
1	10,600	10,600	None
5	13,000	13,382	382 (3%)
10	16,000	17,908	1,908 (11%)
15	19,000	23,965	4,965 (21%)
20	22,000	32,071	10,071 (31%)

as we can in the opposite direction. Therefore, people tend to procrastinate on decisions that involve facing mortality or our own human weakness. This tendency presents very real problems when we are trying to prepare for funding our lifestyle choices after our retirement.

Life expectancy tables are simply an actuarial projection of the years that we have remaining in this life. Your own life expectancy may be shorter or longer than what a table might suggest based on your gene pool. If you had parents who lived into their 90s, your projected life expectancy would be different from that for someone whose family history is less favorable.

Life expectancy and quality of life are two topics that I ask you to openly and honestly consider. They are critical pieces to the retirement puzzle, and you just can't ignore them; you must be honest with yourself about them. The simple fact is that we are living longer, which means that our retirement assets need to carry us further. If you retire at age 65, you are likely to live another 20 years. In addition, we must also look at the ongoing costs associated with our healthcare. I won't get into too much detail here because we will cover this area exhaustively in Chapter 3, but we can't let the fear of these issues paralyze us and keep us from preparing for retirement.

Key Point

This life expectancy table shows that the average male at age 65 will live another 15.75 years, and the average female at age 65 will live another 18.6 years

Life Expectancy

Age	Male	Female	Joint[a]
35	75.77	80.21	84.19
45	76.69	80.79	85.66
55	78.24	81.8	86.19
65	80.75	83.6	87.28
75	84.62	86.53	89.34

[a] Joint Life assumes both same age.

Issues That Two Parties Don't Immediately Agree On

According to a 2002 study done by the Administration on Aging, 17 percent of men over the age of 65 live alone and 40 percent of women over the age of 65 live alone. While the difference between the numbers may speak to issues of biological life expectancy, stress, and lifestyle, the vast majority of retiring households have two or more people to support at retirement and for some number of years thereafter.

Financial planning for couples is much different from financial planning for one person. With two people you can have two opinions, two levels of risk taking, two health profiles, and so on. It also makes it more difficult to choose the right financial planner because of the two unique personalities at work along with the new dynamic of a third person. Sometimes procrastination sets in as couples find it easier to do nothing than to meet this challenge head on. You need to face the facts and develop common ground so that compromises can be established. If one party has a very low tolerance for risk and the other party is very aggressive, you're going to have to find a common ground or reach an agreement on whose perspective will be used without alienating the other party.

Perfection and Procrastination

Before leaving the topic of procrastination, I'd like to make one final point. Early in life, we are taught to embrace concepts like "a job worth doing is worth doing well" or "if you can't do it right, don't do it at all." This focus on perfection can be empowering to some and incapacitating to others. Perfection is always a goal to reach for, but in my opinion, it should not be seen as the only acceptable result. Without seeking perfection, we can find ourselves left without adequate motivation to accomplish our goal. But if we set perfection atop the highest pedestal, admiring it and becoming frozen by its challenges, we often do nothing. With regard to your retirement planning, you are well advised to seek perfection and accept reality.

What If I Don't Reach My Goal? Facing Compromise

One of the goals of *Retirement Countdown* is to minimize the circumstances in which you are faced with compromising your lifestyle after you retire. The younger or richer you are today, the easier that task will be. For some, it may be time to discuss the areas where you want to consider compromising or trading off one need for another. Remember at the opening of this chapter, we discussed the recent study showing that about half of retiring baby boomers will have to find ways to make compromises in their post-retirement lifestyle.

Many aging baby boomers, rapidly approaching retirement, will have to determine if they want their style of retirement to be financially passive or financially active. A passive retirement is one associated with predominantly managing assets and distributing income. In an active retirement, there is a need to continue to earn income to supplement assets used to create retirement income. With the current and historical savings rates in America, many retirees will have to face reality and recognize that they will likely have an active, not a passive, retirement.

Once you accept the fact you may be faced with an active retirement lifestyle, I would encourage you to embrace it. There are so many ways to contribute post-retirement that can be both financially and emotionally rewarding. We'll discuss some of those in Chapter 3.

Meet the Glovers

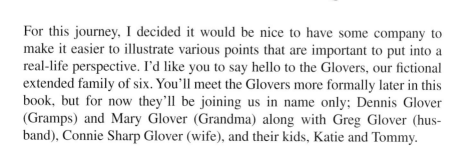

For this journey, I decided it would be nice to have some company to make it easier to illustrate various points that are important to put into a real-life perspective. I'd like you to say hello to the Glovers, our fictional extended family of six. You'll meet the Glovers more formally later in this book, but for now they'll be joining us in name only; Dennis Glover (Gramps) and Mary Glover (Grandma) along with Greg Glover (husband), Connie Sharp Glover (wife), and their kids, Katie and Tommy.

You're Not Alone

As you begin to better understand the issues affecting your retirement, you will likely want to reach out for help. The most convenient and comfortable place to find assistance will typically be the warm environment of your friends and family. When you get beyond that small circle, you can also find help with establishing, monitoring, and achieving your goals through other reference sources as well as paid professionals. The key to working outside your comfort zone is being able to trust the source or sources you come into contact with.

The Internet most certainly offers a wide variety of both resources and information, but you need to be selective. Trust only sources you can verify and be mindful of those who are a little too willing to offer up advice tied directly to a product and not necessarily the solution to achieving your goal. To harness the power of the Internet requires discipline because so much information is available online.

A tremendous source for both pre- and postretirement is the AARP. Founded in 1958 by retired California educator Ethel Percy Andrus, the AARP represents the interests and needs of those over the age of 50. While membership in this nonprofit organization may be limited to those 50 and over, the Web site at *www.aarp.org* offers considerable information that can be used by anyone interested in life as a senior citizen. The site offers some basic retirement planning tools and loads of information on healthcare, Social Security, and much more. Today the AARP has over 35 million members, over half of whom are still working.

I'm also proud of the work being done by a coalition of nonprofit organizations that have embraced a concept that I came up with in 2001 called National Retirement Planning Week. Each year, the organization grows and the message gets out to more and more consumers on the importance of funding their retirement. For more information on National Retirement Planning Week, go to *www.retireonyourterms.org*.

Summary

Alan Greenspan, the chairman of the Federal Reserve Board and certainly one of the most respected sources for economic trends and impact, was quoted as saying, "We need to start teaching financial literacy in our schools." Such is the expected plight of future retirees that we must begin this educational process as early as possible.

At this point, you should be mentally prepared to start this journey. Up until now, I haven't dealt deeply with the retirement planning process, nor have I shared with you all the frightening statistics that show most people must compromise their postretirement lifestyle. The intent of the Introduction and Chapter 1 is to prepare you for the reality of what is to follow and to make sure as you approach this topic, you do so with the proper mindset.

Retirement is not a sprint; it is a distance race. To reach your retirement goals, you will need to have the perseverance to stick to the course and take one chapter at a time. If you do that, your chances of success will be greatly enhanced. Your need to succeed and the value you gain from that success must be greater than the emotional disappointment of failure, or you'll fail more often than you'll succeed. Remember Thomas Edison's words of wisdom: "Genius is 1 percent inspiration and 99 percent perspiration." Before we're done, you need to experience that sensation.

Power Checklist

- ✔ A body at rest will stay at rest unless pushed by an outside force. You must push yourself and create positive inertia in your retirement planning.
- ✔ Tackle complex issues by breaking them into smaller tasks.
- ✔ Ask yourself if you need to know how the watch was built or if you just need to know it tells time accurately.
- ✔ Perseverance *must* be part of your plan; don't accept less than what is required to meet your goal in preparing for your retirement.
- ✔ Just as a mountain climber has the proper equipment, you too need to be sure you have the proper help in achieving your retirement goals. Be honest with yourself and seek help when you need it.
- ✔ Couples should engage in the planning process together and establish a method for resolving differences and managing choices throughout the process.
- ✔ Procrastination with regard to retirement planning may result in your making compromises to your postretirement lifestyle.
- ✔ Time is your friend only if you use it wisely.
- ✔ There is truly no such thing as a stupid question. If you understand a point but not a concept, go back and get comfortable with the concept too.

- ✔ Your need to succeed and the value you gain from that success must be greater than the emotional disappointment of failure, or you'll fail more often than you'll succeed.
- ✔ With regard to your retirement planning, you are well advised to seek perfection and accept reality.

CHAPTER 2

Saving for Retirement

If we boil things down to a simple two-part equation, retirement planning is all about managing inflows (income) during your earning years and outflows (expenses) during your retirement years. Of course, retirement means different things to different people at different points in their lives. Rather than a static state, retirement is a dynamic state, changing with life events, financial events, and even your own education as you learn more about concepts and products. The more information you absorb, the more comfortable you feel in being an active participant in the retirement planning process. Your plan for accumulating assets for retirement has to take all of this into account and be flexible enough to adapt to all kinds of changes.

If all that isn't complex enough, our confusion is compounded by the fact that retirement isn't left up solely to our own devices. We have corporate retirement plans, individual retirement plans, and Social Security that all must be factored into our goals for achieving financial independence. The good news is that much of this can be quantified, meaning we can measure our ability to achieve any goal we set. What we can't easily measure are the qualitative issues that drive your retirement income needs and your ability to save for those retirement goals. The qualitative issues are the more emotional issues driving decisions both pre- and postretirement.

Common Mistake

Most people grossly underestimate the amount of income they need to live on postretirement. Sports like golf can be very expensive, even with senior citizen discounts. And you need to realize that in retirement, you'll have more time on your hands, which means more time for projects and hobbies that cost money.

You'll need to ask yourself questions like how many vacations you want to take each year during retirement. (Yes, even retired people take vacations, trips, or other diversions.) How often will you go to the movies, how many presents will you buy for the kids, and what impact will all this have on your ability to ensure that you have enough money on which to retire? Will you take up any new and expensive hobbies that will have to be accounted for in your postretirement budget? You'll also find yourself wrestling with trade-offs that may require you to postpone the immediate gratification associated with an act today so that you can afford to define your own terms for retirement.

At this point in the book, it might be a good idea for you to keep a pad of paper handy for your notes and thoughts. You need to begin to define just what retirement will look like for you. What would a typical day, week, or month offer? This is how you can begin to frame out the amount of money needed to fund your retirement. If it helps you to think in socio-economic terms instead of absolute dollars, go ahead and define your retirement by the number of cruises you want to take each year, the number of times you want to play golf each week, and the number of times you'll eat out during a given week. Someone can always convert those to absolute dollars for the purpose of projecting your income needs.

Why don't you pause here and take some time to reflect on these questions? If you have a spouse or significant other, get together with that person and talk about how you want your retirement to look and feel. Make lists and brainstorm ideas; you'll be much better prepared to read the balance of this chapter if you have begun the process of better understanding your retirement needs.

Another way of viewing the difference between saving for retirement and managing your assets in retirement is by going back to our mountain. As you ascend the mountain, you are faced with the challenge of climbing and achieving your goal. In many cases, you don't know what to expect and you have to be prepared for anything that comes your way. Saving for retirement is much the same as climbing the mountain. You can't predict the economy, the stock market, or personal events that affect your life and your ability to save. Around each corner you may have to alter your strategy; you may have to take two steps backward to go three steps forward.

Savings Tip

Conserve. There are numerous ways to make conservation work for you; regardless of whether you conserve on energy or recycling, you can save money. With the cost of gas and electricity, a 25 percent reduction in use can mean savings of $50–75 a month for a family. Multiply that by 12 and add a few years of compound interest growth, and you have paid for a child's college education.

You've dealt with this in other facets of your life, so it shouldn't surprise you to know that retirement planning is no different. When companies fail, the employee's retirement plan can be affected, particularly if the company invests its matching portion of the retirement plan into its own stock. The colossal failure of Enron forced thousands of people to basically start their planning process over with regard to assets in the Enron 401(k) because the plan consisted almost solely of Enron stock. That's why it's so important to maintain a balanced approach to your retirement, looking at your personal savings, your corporate or personal retirement programs, and Social Security to get the complete picture.

Experienced climbers will tell you that descending the mountain is no less treacherous than ascending the mountain. Though it may be physically less demanding, it is just as challenging mentally and emotionally. However, you have the wisdom of the experience of climbing the mountain, and your experience will go a long way toward your safe return home. After you reach your goal of accumulated assets for retirement, your focus shifts to managing your assets in retirement. That discussion, coming up in Chapter 3, will focus on how important it is to preserve your assets and ensure that they last as long as you do. But don't be fooled into believing that distributing assets and managing your income is an easy task; for many people, that process could extend to 30 years or more. You have to be just as careful spending your money as you were saving your money, and you have to be even more conservative managing your assets after you retire than you were accumulating those assets for retirement.

Reflect on the statistics that I share through this book with you in a reflective light. Ask yourself, "What does this statistic mean to me?" If it isn't applicable to you, quickly put it into perspective, digest it, and move on to the next point. But don't use this as permission to avoid making a difficult decision. Take the time to look at the statistic or the point I'm making and walk all the way around it, see if any part of it fits and could be modified to provide you with some value or insight. Let's use an example to illustrate my point.

A study was recently sponsored by the National Retirement Planning Coalition on retirement readiness. This study targeted 500 individuals between the ages of 40 and 65 with incomes in excess of $50,000 per year. In this study, 41 percent of the respondents surveyed have never tried to figure out how much money they will need to save for their retirement. Another 23 percent tried but could not figure out how much they needed. This means almost two-thirds of the respondents have not a clue as to how much money they will need to retire.

You can accept this statistic and count yourself as one of the two-thirds and do something about it, or you can dismiss it as not being applicable to you. If you dismiss it, just make sure you are dismissing it for the right reasons. If you dismiss it because you are 39 years old and make $49,999, you're dismissing it for the wrong reason. If you're dismissing it because you don't think 500 people is a significant enough sample, just see how it fits on you personally and forget about everyone else. Making hard decisions is never easy, but ask yourself which is more personally gratifying: A leisurely walk through an alpine meadow or a more challenging ascent on a mountain? And I'll ask you again to pause, if you haven't done so yet, and consider what retirement means to you.

Wake-Up Call

A study done by Plansponsor.com revealed that in 2003, there was a 3.6 percent drop in 401(k) participation to 72.6 percent.

The Current State of Retirement Savings—We're Just Not Saving Enough!

By some estimates, the personal savings rate in America has dropped to as low as 1 percent of income in recent years. This is down from approximately 8 percent in 1980, 5 percent in 1993, and 2.2 percent in 1999, and it is a frightening statistic. We save half as much as the Europeans and one-third as much as the Japanese. Not only is the trend bad in relative terms, in absolute terms, it means most people today will have to either work longer to achieve their retirement goals or sacrifice quality of life during retirement. Some will have to do both.

In November 2002, the *USA Today* lead story in the Money section was titled "More Workers Say No to 401(k) Plans." In the article, the writer pointed out that fewer employees are participating in their employer-sponsored plans, and those who are participating are contributing less and less. This is partly because of the problems resulting when Enron loaded up its employees' 401(k) plan with Enron stock and partly because of the economic conditions during this period. Either way, it is impacting people's retirement, in terms of when they can retire and the quality of their life in retirement.

We can look at retirement savings from other perspectives, but the conclusion is still the same: We aren't saving enough.

One last statistic and then we'll move on. A study done by the Congressional Research Service in late 2002 took a look at employer-sponsored retirement plans such as a 401(k)s. Its findings show that for workers

between the ages of 55 and 64, the average value of their households' employer-sponsored plans was a mere $107,000. For all ages, the number was $71,040. These statistics should scare you, but don't let them paralyze you. In the next several paragraphs, you will get some perspective on how little $107,000 is when we are talking about providing income for 30 years or more.

For most of us, retirement income sources consist of personal savings, corporate retirement savings and/or individual retirement savings, and Social Security. A recent study[1] by the Social Security Administration suggests that 48 percent of your retirement income will come from Social Security and retirement plans such as pensions and 401(k) plans, leaving the majority of your income to come from personal assets. Later in the book I'll show you how to calculate your Social Security benefits and project your pension benefits so that we can quantify the amount you'll need to supplement those two income sources.

Relative Versus Absolute Comparison

During the course of understanding products and services, you may need to look at their relationship to one another. This is called a relative comparison. Other times, you need only understand how the product or service performs on its own. This is called an absolute analysis.

Let's say three people named Joe, Nancy, and Bill set a goal to retire in 10 years with $1 million in assets. In 10 years, Joe has $900,000,

---

1. *Fast Facts & Figures About Social Security,* Social Security Administration, June 2001.

Nancy has $1.1 million, and Bill has $1.3 million. They are all close on a relative basis, but on an absolute basis, Joe can't retire. Sometimes you can make the mistake of looking at yourself relative to others when you should be looking at things absolutely. This doesn't mean you shouldn't look at things relatively as well; you should. You just need to be careful at the underlying issue and apply the proper perspective.

You'll find other examples of where this difference between relative and absolute is critically important. For example, as you look at the different investment products you can use to fund your retirement goals, you'll see that each has characteristics that allow you to compare it with the others. As you compare characteristics, you'll have to determine which should be evaluated on a relative basis and which on an absolute basis. For example, safety is a characteristic you want to look at absolutely.

Several ratings companies evaluate the solvency of the insurance industry in general and insurance carriers specifically. All but one of these ratings companies provides opinions using absolute standards. This means that as long as a company demonstrates its solvency, it gets a rating consistent with that level of safety. The safety of one carrier relative to that of the next may not be as important as the absolute safety of your money.

Which Generation Group Do You Fall Into?

In 2002, the U.S. Department of Labor sponsored "The National Summit on Retirement Savings." During this summit, both government and non-government attendees focused on the retirement challenges facing Americans. During the summit breakout sessions, they discussed the four generational groups that make up our population. I think it's important to briefly look at these generations to make sure you can put yourself into one of the broad categories. It will be helpful for you to identify with these groups as we move forward in the book. One note of caution is that there are not hard and fast rules about where you belong and that because these groups are broadly defined, the birth dates may overlap and vary from source to source. Each group has its own savings characteristics, but you should make certain that they apply to you.

Generation Y (Born 1982 to Present Day)

Generation Y is obviously the youngest group, and quite frankly, I doubt that many 21-year-olds will be reading this book, which is a shame because they are in the best position to begin this process with the least amount of financial commitment. If you have children in the group and want to help them get off on the right foot, you need to impress on them how important this topic is. You may want to share with them the cost of waiting because this generation is very goal oriented. Its members also grew up on computers, which puts them in a very strong position with regard to accessing information and knowing how to use technology to their benefit.

The following are characteristics of Generation Y as determined by the Corporate Executive Board:

- They number 76 million.
- Their spending power is estimated at $600 billion a year.
- Signs point to a strong generation of savers, but there is some concern about the number (over 100,000) of those under age 25 who have already declared bankruptcy.
- They are very Internet savvy and value the online experience.
- They identify with Bill Clinton, the WB network, Stone Cold Steve Austin, and *The Truman Show.*

Generation X (Born 1961–1981)

The Gen Xers, as they are called, had a totally different experience framing their lives. They grew up in world of profound social and economic change, not all of which painted a pretty picture in our country or in the world around us. Gen Xers tend to be much less trusting of people and therefore less loyal. But the Gen Xers also have a better sense of how to define their retirement. If you're in the Generation X group, you will be cautious about selecting a financial planner to deal with and you'll be lest trusting of that person than other generations would. There is also a risk with Generation X members who think that they can do things themselves, but they get caught up in the same emotional quagmire that we all do when things get too complex or too difficult to deal with emotionally. Procrastination is something to be careful of if you're in the Generation X group.

The following are characteristics of Generation X as determined by the Corporate Executive Board:

- They number 53 million.
- They have average annual household earnings of $40,200.
- This generation is cautious about spending and has not saved very consistently or effectively.

- Internet use is high, but they don't trust the Web as much as Generation Y does.

- They identify with Michael Jordan, Ronald Reagan, "Just Say No" campaign, Fox Network, The Cold War, and cable TV.

Baby Boom Generation (Born 1946–1964)

The largest group of them all is the Baby Boomer generation. This group, totaling roughly 77 million people and of which I'm a member, consists of well-educated risk takers who, while financially literate, have done a terrible job of saving for retirement. According to Ken Dychtwald, a leading author and speaker on generational marketing, the average Baby Boomer has $1,300 in his or her lifetime savings account. If you're a Baby Boomer, you're already starting to realize you may be forced to work longer or make sacrifices in your postretirement lifestyle.

The following are characteristics of Baby Boomers as determined by the Corporate Executive Board:

- They number 77 million.

- Average annual household earnings are $53,000.

- Predictions are the average boomer will retire with $500,000 to $1,000,000 in assets.

- They are skeptical of the Internet, and although 61 percent use the Internet daily, only 34 percent use it for online purchasing.

- Two-thirds do not feel confident in their ability to choose a mutual fund.

- They identify with JFK, "Let it Be," Mohammed Ali, the NBC Peacock, Vietnam, and feminism.

Wake-Up Call

The number of Americans saving for retirement has reached record lows, and the biggest drops have been found in the category that can least afford it, the Baby Boomers. In a study done in 2002, the percentage of those between the ages of 45 and 59 saving for retirement dropped to 41 percent, down 17 percent from 2001.

Silent Generation (Born Before 1946)

Many members of the Silent Generation survived the Great Depression and World War II. If you relate to this group, you are likely to be more cautious, having a broader range of life experiences to draw from. You also have learned your lessons; most members of the Silent Generation have done a reasonably good job of saving for retirement. The cautionary remark here is that with increased life expectancy, many of them didn't count on living as long as they have and many are operating on a fixed income.

The following are characteristics of the Silent Generation as determined by the Corporate Executive Board:

◆ They number 33 million.

◆ A quarter of the households over age 65 have assets of $250,000 or more.

◆ They have over $1.6 trillion in buying power.

◆ Silent Generation members are not passive about their wellbeing or their lives. They question policies and demand to be heard.

◆ Most are on a fixed income and do not have time for elaborate financial planning

◆ They identify with Social Security, World War II, The Great Depression, and the GI bill.

Gap Analysis

As we begin to quantify your retirement, we have a number of tools we can use for goal setting and for monitoring. The best place to start for those groups that have not yet retired is the gap analysis. This type of analysis defines the gap between your goal and your current state. Let's say you tell me you need to have $100,000 a year in income when you retire, which you're planning on doing in 20 years. You expect to live at least 25 years after you retire. Once we agree on an assumed interest rate to guide our growth rate and an agreeable rate of inflation to compensate for the future cost of goods and services, we can solve for the amount of money required to meet our goal. We can solve for the amount you would need to invest today, or if you like, we can solve for the amount you would need to save on an annual basis for the next 25 years.

Savings Tip

Take advantage of discounts. Another area where you can save is in using discounts. Discounts mean you pay less, and the difference can help to fund your retirement. I was recently at a grocery store and was about to check out without entering my frequent shopper ID. I did so at the last minute and ended up saving over $4 on that visit alone. These may seem like insignificant amounts, but they represent a mindset that you need to start to incorporate into your life if there is any doubt about your ability to meet your goals.

Not to further frighten you, but we can, and should, also look at the cost of waiting. Using this type of calculation, we can see what happens if we wait five or ten years before beginning the process. Those types of calculations are not for the weak of heart! Overall, these are *easy* calculations to make today thanks to technology. There's no excuse for you not to know what the requirements are for meeting your retirement goal. And there is certainly no excuse for any financial services professionals you deal with to not have these tools at their fingertips. You can do anything you want with the assumptions, including making a partial lump sum investment today and then making the periodic investments required to meet your goals. But let's keep our eye on the mountain we have to climb, not the route we will take. The Tables 2–1 and 2–2 may help us look at these numbers as we apply different factors to consider.

Don't Get Discouraged

Don't let the numbers in the tables frighten you too much. Some element of fear can be a great motivator, but too much fear can paralyze you. Look at your own situation and use *Retirement Countdown* to help you with the step-by-step process of breaking your goals down into digestible pieces. To do this, we'll make extensive use of Goal Oriented Retirement Planning (GORP). If you use GORP to help you define and maintain your goals, you'll be able to modify a goal so that you can still gain value from achieving the goal, albeit under different assumptions.

Let's say Greg and Connie Glover want to take two trips each year in retirement. As they use GORP, they will define a cost for those vacations in today's dollars then inflate those dollars based on the number of years until they retire. Finally, they will bring that result back to a lump sum amount or an annual amount required to provide for that goal. In making their vacation assumptions, they will have to look at how they are spending their vacation to quantify the cost. If the goal costs too much money, they can go back to their assumption and make changes to reduce the cost and hence the amount they will have to save. Remember that they can modify the goal at any time should their circumstances change.

By using GORP, we can begin to make decisions based on their importance and their cost. If we find that Social Security payments at retirement are only 75 percent of what we expected and planned for, we have to find income somewhere else by reducing other goals or replacing income postretirement through part-time work, a hobby, or a small business that generates enough income to replace the shortfall.

Table 2–1 applies to anyone intending to retire 20 years from now on an income of $100,000 and expecting that income to last for 25 years. It also shows what changing the investment return does to the single sum and/or annual contributions that would be required to meet these retirement goals.

The assumptions for Table 2–1 are as follows:

◆ Years to retirement: 20

◆ Amount of annual income needed: $100,000

◆ Inflation rate: 3 percent

◆ Life expectancy postretirement: 25 years

Table 2–1   How Investment Return Impacts Your Goal

Return on Investment	5%	6%	8%	10%
Amount needed at retirement ($)	2,252,635	2,065,559	1,752,569	1,504,332
Lump sum to fund today ($)	1,110,441	886,515	571,803	374,497
Annual contribution needed, assuming no initial investment ($)	78,840	67,093	48,885	35,901
Annual contribution needed, assuming $250,000 initial investment ($)	61,091	48,173	27,512	11,935

The numbers are daunting to say the least. If you're looking at a conservative long-term investment return of 6 percent, you'll need to have
almost $900,000 earmarked for retirement today, or you'll have to be put-
ting in annual deposits of $67,000 to reach your goal. But calm down—
there's lots we can do to avoid falling into a financial crevasse.

Savings Tip

Turn a hobby into income. Many people have skills they can market
on a part-time basis in retirement. Find something you love so that
it's not a burden and see how much fun it is to make money doing
something you love.

Table 2–2 looks at delaying the decision to fund your retirement by
just three years. It also assumes the following:

◆ Years to retirement: 20

◆ Amount of annual income needed: $100,000

◆ Inflation rate: 3 percent

◆ Life expectancy post retirement: 25 Years

Table 2–2   The Cost of a Three-Year Delay (AKA Procrastination) on Investment Return

Return on Investment	**5%**	**6%**	**8%**	**10%**
Amount needed at retirement ($)	2,252,635	2,065,559	1,752,569	1,504,332
Lump sum to fund today ($)	1,234,738	1,006,442	676,411	461,352
Annual contribution needed assuming no initial investment ($)	98,370	84,794	63,450	47,911
Annual contribution needed assuming $250,000 initial investment ($)	78,453	63,731	40,000	21,949

Look at just the 6 percent column and compare funding retirement now with waiting three years. A three-year delay in funding our retirement increases the lump sum cost to over $1 million and the cost for the next 17 years by over $17,000 each and every year. Time is everything when it comes to retirement savings, as Table 2–3 shows.

Table 2–3   Factors That Can Impact Your Retirement Nest Egg

Return on Investment	6% Now	6% in 3 Years	Difference
Amount needed at retirement ($)	2,065,559	2,065,559	–
Lump sum to fund today ($)	886,515	1,006,442	119,927
Annual contribution needed, assuming no initial investment ($)	67,093	84,794	17,701
Annual contribution needed, assuming $250,000 initial investment ($)	48,173	63,731	15,558

By now, you clearly understand that this chapter is dedicated to establishing the importance of retirement saving and to creating the discipline necessary to achieve our retirement goals. We also need to talk about trade-offs you can make to be in a better position to save for your retirement goals. These trade-offs will be incredibly important as we consider having to compromise our retirement goals because of a lack of time or a lack of financial resources. The following can have an impact on achieving our goals:

- ◆ **Time.** The more time you have, the more risk you can take and the less money you have to commit to a regular savings plan. Conversely, the less time you have, the more you need to look at increased risk or changes in lifestyle to meet your goals.

- ◆ **Health.** Health impacts our retirement in a couple of ways. Poor health impacts our ability to earn and therefore our ability to achieve our goal. Our health in retirement is also an issue. The healthier we are, the longer we live, and the longer we need our savings to last.

- ◆ **Risk Tolerance.** The greater the risks, the greater the potential reward, but you must have the time to wait for the reward. In addition, you'll need to note that risk tolerance, like retirement goals, is not a static state; it's dynamic and changes with your age and life experiences.

♦ **Inheritance.** Any inheritance you receive then becomes an investable asset that can be applied to a retirement goal. For Baby Boomers, more than $10 trillion will be passed from your parents to your generation.

Of course, our goal is to effectively manage our invested assets and income in a manner that allows us to retire comfortably. That means we have to know which investments are earmarked for our retirement and how much we can save from each paycheck and bonus. We need to have a plan to monitor and adjust these to meet our goals. This is all about creating choices and protecting your ability to be in a position to make lifestyle decisions in retirement without compromise. The real work on this subject will be done in Chapter 5.

Summary

In this chapter we dealt with the harsh reality of saving for retirement. The underlying point of this chapter is that every day you wait to save for your retirement makes it more difficult for you to achieve your goals. And it won't get better if you do nothing. If failing to save for retirement were an illness, it would be bacterial, not viral. A viral infection will go away over time; a bacterial infection will get worse and worse. The medicine you need to take is called *action*, and you'll need a large dose of it now as well as a steady course of treatment until you retire and start living off what you have saved … but that's a segue to the next chapter.

Power Checklist

✔ Retirement planning is all about managing inflows (income) during your earning years and outflows (expenses) during your retirement years.

✔ There are three elements to your retirement nest egg: your personal savings, corporate or personal retirement plans, and Social Security.

✔ Start thinking about what your retirement looks and feels like so that you can then quantify the cost.

✔ When you look at a statistic and your inclination is to say, "This doesn't apply to me," walk all the way around the statistic and try and find some value in its message.

✔ The rate of personal saving in the United States has dropped as low as 1 percent in recent years.

✔ Performing a gap analysis can help you see any shortfall in your retirement planning.

✔ The following factors can dramatically impact your ability to retire on your terms: time, health, risk tolerance, and inheritance.

CHAPTER 3

Establishing an Income You Can't Outlive

Cash, dough, greenbacks, moollah, dinero—whatever the moniker, the amount of money we have will define what we can and can't do in retirement. Retirement is all about money and our ability to manage it so that we can use it during our retirement years and leave an estate for our loved ones if we choose to do so. Perhaps the most important point of this chapter is to convince you that **you must establish an income that you cannot outlive.** With life expectancy increasing, you run the very real risk of outliving your income.

In many respects, the art of asset accumulation is far less challenging than the art of asset distribution. The reason is that during our earning years, we have more time available to manage emergencies or a shift in our goals. Time is the commodity that will drive many of our decisions in pre- and postretirement planning, and we have less and less time available to us as we grow older. The other reason postretirement asset distribution is more challenging is that in retirement, we still have all of the issues of continuing to manage our assets in addition to the burden of managing the distribution of those assets to create or supplement other retirement income sources. When you retire from your main source of income, your job or business goes away.

Let's continue to look at this challenge from our mountain climbing perspective. At the start of the climb, you sense you have more time. You can typically enjoy the beauty of the surroundings and the majesty of the task before you. You may also have many choices for getting to higher steps on the mountain. But the higher you go, the more limited your choice of routes becomes; the terrain is more dangerous and the air becomes thinner and thinner. A mistake higher up on the mountain magnifies the risk. Similarly, a mistake in your postretirement strategy magnifies your risk of not being able to provide sufficient income to meet your goal. This is a critical chapter for you as we try to quantify the income needs, the income sources, and the risks that impact income during retirement.

Setting Your Objectives

Before experienced climbers make an assault on a mountain peak, they must address countless checklists, both mental and physical. They must allow sufficient time for the climb and ensure that the weather conditions will provide an adequate window of opportunity for the assault on the summit and the retreat down the mountain. The myriad logistics that must be taken care of include food, water, tents, permits, and oxygen. The failure to adequately prepare and provide for these needs could be catastrophic to the climbers and could cost them their lives in extreme circumstances.

In May 1996, nine climbers died on the face of Mt. Everest in the worst climbing accident in the history of the sport. Their deaths were the result of many factors, some physical and some mental. A surprise storm swept in quickly and furiously, but the storm alone was not responsible for the lost lives. Hundreds of climbers were attempting to summit Everest that day, and their numbers created a tremendous bottleneck just below the summit at a mark called the Hillary Step, some 28,750 feet above sea level but iron- ically only hundreds of feet from Everest's summit.

For many climbers and even their experienced guides, the drive to summit Everest outweighed the risks associated with being in the "death zone" above 25,000 feet where the air is rare and a human cannot survive for long without the aid of oxygen. With so many people trying to funnel through the Hillary Step, the delays left large numbers of climbers on the mountain later than they expected, resulting in the deaths of two profes- sional guides and seven climbers. In this case, a combination of impaired judgment and bad weather resulted in a loss of life.

The lesson to be learned here and applied to your pre- and postretire- ment preparation is that you must plan for as many contingencies as pos- sible, and you have to be honest with yourself and your loved ones with regard to your ability to accomplish these goals. Don't be afraid to seek help from a professional if you don't have the time and resources to man- age these goals yourself. Financial failure is rarely the result of market conditions and almost always the lack of adequate preparation.

There is clearly a crystal ball element to the process of setting objec- tives for retirement income. Regardless of your age group, it takes a certain amount of dedication and focus to look out into the future and predict your needs. When we look at the reason that people procrastinate in their retire- ment planning, we see that the complexity associated with this task is key.

Imagine the conversation in your own home as you try to balance everything on your plate that represents a current need and then ask your- self how likely you are to consider planning for an event that may not take place for 10 or 20 years. Unfortunately, most of us act on the need to plan for our retirement when some event prompts us to do so. It can be a pleas- ant event like an annual bonus or a child's birthday, or it can be a sad event such as the passing of a loved one or a public tragedy that brings a renewed focus to our own lives. Regardless of what draws you to the need, you must engage in the process of planning, a task that will begin here as a thought process and continue in Chapter 5 to provide you with planning tools to make the climb happen.

Utilization of Assets

One of the first decisions that you will make is which assets you want to use for retirement and which assets, if any, you want to give away or leave for the next generation. Obviously, the more you want to reserve for gifting or for passing to the next generation, the more you have to accumulate during your income years. And just because you identify an asset that you want to use as a gift at some point or pass to your children, you can still benefit from that asset during your retirement.

Let's say, for example, that Dennis and Mary Glover have a $30,000 Treasury bond that is yielding 6 percent interest. They may choose to keep the $1,800 a year in interest payments and leave the bond to Greg and Connie or the grandchildren. By the time you're done with this book, you'll be able to look at each asset you have, assess its characteristics, and choose how to apply it to your retirement income strategy.

Types of Income

As you reach the age of retirement, however you define it, you must look at the income sources that will provide you with the necessary cash flow to meet your expenses. In general, most people will have no more than four sources of postretirement income, including some combination of: Social Security, pension and qualified plan benefits, income from investments, and income from postretirement employment. Let's look at each of these to better understand their role in providing you with income continuity as you move from collecting a paycheck to enjoying your retirement living.

Figure 3–1 provides some sense of how people currently generate their postretirement income and how I believe the numbers will shift over the next 20 years to reflect a shift in the responsibility from the government to the taxpayer. Since this is more an art than a science, the numbers do not represent a single source, but rather a variety of sources collected from both the private and public sectors.

A recent poll sponsored by the National Retirement Planning Coalition (*www.retireonyourterms.org*) suggests that most consumers believe that approximately 25 percent of their postretirement income will come from Social Security. In reality, that number today is somewhat higher at approximately 38 percent, but is likely to go down in subsequent years as the government places the burden of retirement income more directly on the shoulders of the individual.

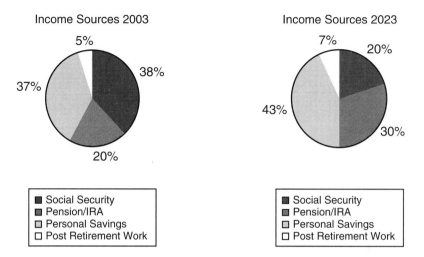

Figure 3–1   Americans' Postretirement Income Sources, 2003 and 2023

As you can see by comparing the two pie charts, over the next 20 years, income from your own pension and qualified plans will need to increase by 50 percent to compensate for an 18 percent reduction in income from Social Security. Personal savings will need to increase as well, but the increase in pension and qualified plan income represents expected tax law changes that should provide opportunities for individuals to increase contributions to supplemental retirement plans on their own behalf. The following sections discuss the income sources in detail.

Social Security

There are countless books on Social Security, its sordid past, and everyone's opinion of its future. Although your knowledge of the history of the system will not likely aid you in understanding its value in your retirement, I will provide a brief overview of the salient points for some historical perspective. Then, I will focus on the benefits as they pertain to you today and share some thoughts on the future of the system.

INFORMATION

Web Site Information

You'll find lots of good information at *www.socialsecurity.gov.*

History   To understand the true history of Social Security, you have to travel back in time to a period far earlier than the 1930s. Although President Franklin Delano Roosevelt championed the concept embodied in the services offered by the Social Security Administration, Social Security has been around for thousands of years. At the time of the Chinese Empire, around 500 BC, Confucius wrote that the empire routinely provided for the needy, the disabled, and the elderly. Other great societies have had their own ways of taking care of their people, well before 1935 when the Social Security Act was signed into law in this country. We have an acknowledged history of providing aid to those in need, including those in retirement.

More Information

INFORMATION   You can get a copy of your estimated Social Security benefits by calling 800-772-1213 or by going to *www.socialsecurity.gov/mystatement.*

The first efforts to provide for the needs of elderly Americans dates back to Thomas Paine in the late 1700s, and the topic was actually a campaign issue for Teddy Roosevelt in his reelection bid of 1912. However, it wasn't until the country suffered the travails of the Great Depression highlighted by 25 percent unemployment and a 70 percent drop in the stock market that the government endeavored to provide benefits for older Americans through the passage of the Social Security Act.

Since its creation in 1935, the Social Security Administration has gone through some agonizing financial difficulties. Most of these were the result of gross miscalculations in the population growth in the United States. The system simply cannot support the needs of future retirees. A study conducted in 1994 showed more Generation Xers believed they will see a UFO before they will see a Social Security check. The reason is that Social Security is a pay-as-you-go system. That means the Federal Insurance Contributions Act (FICA) taxes most of us pay today on our earnings go to pay the benefits of those who currently are retired. As the Baby Boomers reach retirement age, the retirement fund as currently configured will collapse under the financial strain required to pay the benefits.

Be Careful

Even the Social Security Administration recognizes the financial difficulty facing the system. Here is the disclaimer on the estimated benefits form you can have sent to you. "Your estimated benefits are based on current law. Congress has made changes to the law in the past and can do so at any time. The law governing benefit amounts may change because, by 2042, the payroll taxes collected will be enough to pay only about 73 percent of scheduled benefits."

The practical reality is that our elected officials will not let the system collapse entirely, but neither are they likely to solve the problem altogether. This will lead to more temporary fixes of the system as exemplified by presidents Carter and Reagan. During their presidencies, both worked hard to reform the system, but neither changed the fundamental model of the system responsible for today's problems. Under the presidency of George W. Bush, and most recently through proposed legislation sponsored by Congressmen Rob Portman and Ben Cardin, there has been an effort to reduce Americans' reliance on the system by providing people with enhanced retirement plans that continue to shift both the burden and the opportunity to the taxpayer. Only time will tell what role Social Security will play in your retirement, but don't expect it to be anything other than what it was meant to be, which is supplemental income.

Cost   As of 2004, you pay 6.2 percent of your salary, up to $87,900, into the system each year. That 6.2 percent is matched by your employer (or you pay an additional 6.2 percent if you're self-employed). In addition, you pay 1.45 percent of your entire salary into Medicare benefits, which are also matched. These numbers are indexed by the government and will increase over time.

Benefits   Social Security provides three separate and distinct benefits: retirement income, disability income, and survivor income. The amount of the benefit is dependent on a number of factors, including: how much money you put into the system, how long you put it into the system, and when you start receiving the benefits. I may be stating the obvious, but the more money you put in, the longer you put it in, and the later you begin taking the benefits, the greater your benefit is, subject to maximum limitations. Let's briefly look at each benefit.

Common Mistake

Most people assume that a surviving spouse gets the deceased spouse's Social Security benefit. The survivor is entitled to the benefit, but at a rate that is roughly half of the regular benefit.

♦ **Retirement.** Retirement benefits are calculated based on the average of the 35 highest years of earned wages. If you worked fewer than 35 years, you're penalized by the system, which imputes zeroes in years not worked, resulting in a lower benefit. The maximum benefit for an individual retiring in 2003 would range from $1,404 per month for those retiring early at age 62 to $2,045 per month for those retiring at age 70. The average retiree will receive roughly $900 per month for the year 2003 and the average couple, roughly $1,500. For Dennis Glover, who plans to retire in eight years at age 66, his inflation-adjusted Social Security payments would be $1,694 per month, or $20,328 per year. Table 3–1 shows the age at which you can receive full Social Security Benefits.

Table 3–1   Eligibility for Full Social Security Benefits

Year of Birth	Full Retirement Age
1937 or earlier	65
1938	65 and 2 months
1939	65 and 4 months
1940	65 and 6 months
1941	65 and 8 months
1942	65 and 10 months
1943-1954	66
1955	66 and 2 months
1956	66 and 4 months

Table 3–1   Eligibility for Full Social Security Benefits *(Continued)*

Year of Birth	Full Retirement Age
1957	66 and 6 months
1958	66 and 8 months
1959	66 and 10 months
1960 and later	67

Be Careful

In 1983, President Ronald Reagan signed into law the taxation of Social Security benefits under scenarios in which modified adjusted gross income exceeds $25,000 for an individual or $32,000 for a married couple. Up to 85 percent of Social Security benefits may be taxable.

◆ **Disability.** Social Security provides for disability payments to those covered in the plan who have not yet retired but don't count on Social Security disability payments to provide much in the way of assistance. To meet the Social Security Administration's definition of "disabled," someone must have been disabled for over one year and unable to perform in any occupation.

◆ **Survivor.** Survivor benefits can be paid to the surviving spouse at full retirement age or at a reduced benefit at age 60. Children under the age of 18 are also eligible for benefits, as are dependent parents over the age of 62. As with the regular benefits, the amount of the survivor, child, and dependent benefits are based on the earnings of the person who died. The more he or she paid into Social Security, the higher the benefits will be. The amount a survivor receives is a percentage of the deceased's basic Social Security benefit, up to 100 percent for a full-retirement-age surviving spouse.

Social Security and Divorce   No one likes to think about getting a divorce, but unfortunately, half of those marrying today will end up divorced. (I've often wondered if that statistic took into account Zsa Zsa Gabor, Liza Minnelli, and Elizabeth Taylor, but that's another story.) In a divorce, particularly with relationships that have lasted over 10 years, spouses may be entitled to Social Security and pension benefits.

An ex-spouse is entitled to Social Security survivor benefits under some circumstances. To qualify, the marriage must have lasted at least 10 years and the ex-spouse must be over the age of 60 to claim benefits. The 10-year rule is an important one; as you may recall, when the marriage of Hollywood superstars Nicole Kidman and Tom Cruise broke up, Cruise filed just before the couple's 10-year anniversary.

Ways to Maximize Your Social Security Benefits   As I said earlier, the amount you receive from Social Security varies based on how much you put into the system and when you start taking benefits. You have limited control over what you put into the system because it's dictated by the FICA taxes that serve to allocate a portion of your earnings into the system. You do, however, have control over when you and your spouse take money from the system.

Normal retirement age for purposes of Social Security ranges from 65 to age 67, depending upon year of birth. If we use Dennis Glover as our example, we can see how the benefit differs at the various retirement ages with Dennis beginning Social Security Benefits at age 62, at age 67 and at age 70. As you can see in Figure 3–2, at each step, Dennis gets a progressively larger benefit, increasing it by over 50 percent by waiting.

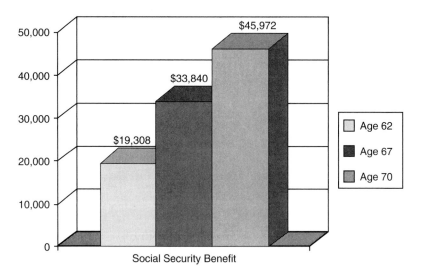

Figure 3–2   Social Security Benefit for Dennis Glover

In addition to getting a much larger benefit by postponing the start of retirement, Dennis could maximize spousal benefits. Let's just assume Mary Glover had also worked prior to retirement. Dennis and Mary are entitled to the greater of the individual benefits or the spousal benefit.

The Future of the System   The future of the Social Security system is an unknown. The reality is that approximately 3.3 people are currently contributing to the program for each person receiving benefits. This ratio results in an annual surplus that is created by the contributions and the excess interest earned on contributions. Currently, the Social Security trust funds have a surplus of $1.2 billion. By 2040, the ratio of contributors to benefactors will be reduced from 3.3:1 to 2:1, and the Social Security trust funds will be out of money. The Social Security Administration is predicting that benefits after 2040 will have to be reduced by 37 percent to match the contributions being made at that time if, between now and then, nothing is done to increase taxes or reduce benefits. Further cuts are expected later in the century.

Regardless of the political party controlling the executive and legislative branches of our government, the Social Security system will remain in place and will continue to provide our retired workforce with a fair benefit. It is likely the system will see some form of privatization between now and 2010 when 8 million Baby Boomers are retiring. Just as corporations have moved away from a reliance on defined benefit pension plans, the government will most likely look at providing additional tax incentives to individuals to supplement their Social Security benefits.

Pensions and Qualified Plans

Approximately one-fifth (20 percent) of postretirement income today comes from qualified plan assets. Within 20 years, that number will increase to just under one-third (30 percent) of postretirement income. These are broadly defined as assets on which you have not yet paid taxes, though there is one exception in the Roth IRA. The Roth IRA allows you to deposit after-tax income that produces tax-free benefits at retirement. Since Chapter 4 is devoted entirely to retirement plans, this section focuses solely on the distributions from qualified plans that should be used in structuring your retirement income.

Be Careful

Depending on how the government is currently taxing long-term capital gains, making after-tax contributions to your 401(k) may not be a wise decision. When gains on these contributions are distributed, they are treated as ordinary income, which may be taxed at a rate as high as 35 percent. If you invested this money outside the plan in a long-term investment, you might receive long-term capital gains tax treatment, which could be as low as 5 percent.

In Chapter 4, you'll learn that there are basically two types of qualified plans, defined benefit plans and defined contribution plans. This is an important distinction to make because with defined benefit plans, you'll receive a stated benefit, and with defined contribution plans, you'll have to determine when and how much income to withdraw from the plan based on how well the plan assets have performed.

Since the assets in defined contribution plans are generally invested at your direction but managed by a third-party fiduciary, market fluctuations may impact the amount that you may choose to ultimately take as income. In defined benefit plans, the plan must ensure that adequate assets are present to meet the financial obligations as required by the Pension Benefit Guarantee Corporation (PBGC). You'll get more detail on this in Chapter 4, but a little history lesson that may affect your income is worth a short departure.

Web Site Information

INFORMATION   To get more information on the Pension Benefit Guarantee Corporation, go to *www.pbgc.gov.*

Because defined benefit plans meet a defined benefit, they are a little more complex in structure. The plan must have an actuary perform an annual review and certify the plan under the guidelines and auspices of the PBGC. Underfunded plans must rectify their shortfall or run the risk that the PBGC will declare the plan bankrupt. The PBGC stands behind the assets of companies whose plans are declared bankrupt through premiums paid to the PBGC by employers who offer these plans. There is, however, a maximum benefit that the PBGC will pay.

Starting in the late 1980s, a number of corporations searching for capital in difficult times found that their defined benefit plans were dramatically overfunded. With a defined benefit plan, future benefits are calculated based on a formula that includes the expected number of years an employee will work, the percentage of the salary to which the employee is entitled at retirement, and the number of years in retirement for which the benefit will need to be paid. Then a very conservative interest rate is used as an assumption for asset growth and to calculate the contributions that must be made annually to meet the future benefits. The money then is invested, earnings are reinvested, benefits are paid out, and the cycle goes on—that is, until someone realizes that the real rate of return on the investment has far exceeded the interest assumption, leaving a significant war chest for future benefits.

Most companies invest retirement assets in a manner that provides some liquidity for short-term benefit needs with the bulk of the money invested longer term and typically in the equity markets. Over time, the equity returns outstrip the more conservative expected return on the invested assets, and there is an excess of capital required to meet the benefit needs for the present and, in theory, the future. And when corporations need money and money is tight, this excess capital sticks out like the tip of Mt. Everest on a clear day in Nepal.

With so many overfunded plans and a tough market and economy in the late 1980s, corporations started looking at a product called terminal funded annuities. With this product, a company would turn to an insurance company to guarantee the plan benefits for a lump sum of money that was typically much less than the amount in the current plan.

Let's look at a fictitious example with the Rampart Corporation. Rampart has $20 million in its defined benefit pension plan and has determined that by buying a terminal funded annuity, it can save $5 million. Rampart goes to Dynamo Insurance, and for $15 million, Dynamo guarantees the retirement benefits for the employees of the plan. Rampart is happy, having just picked up $5 million for capital expenses, Dynamo is happy because it has $15 million from which it can guarantee the retirement benefits and make a profit, and in theory, the plan participants are happy because their retirement benefits are guaranteed. Rampart then sets up a new qualified plan, most likely a 401(k) defined contribution plan, to supplement the retirement for existing employees and to provide for the retirement of new employees.

Following the 1980s, there was a craze among corporations to terminate the defined benefit plan, guarantee the benefits, and pocket the cash. Most used an insurance company to guarantee the benefits, but sometimes the company would simply have an actuary certify the plan's sufficiency, pull the excess assets out, and terminate the plan to lower its costs. As time went by and the markets and the economy continued to suffer, some of the companies that had terminated their plans found them to now be underfunded and were, in some cases, forced into bankruptcy by the PBGC.

Another scare occurred in 1993 when the Insurance Department in the State of California seized control of First Executive Corporation and its life insurance companies. First Executive Life was one of the preeminent providers of these terminal funded annuities, and those whose pensions were guaranteed by First Executive suffered many sleepless nights. Ultimately, those contracts were purchased by another insurance company, and thankfully, no retirees lost their pension benefits, though certain retirees did voluntarily elect to receive a lower amount and moved their money to different investments.

Be Careful

If you have a pension plan that pays you a percentage of your wages during your employment, check to see if your employer has an integration clause in the plan that allows it to deduct the value of any Social Security payment from your pension benefit.

Income from Investments

If you're a Baby Boomer, by the time you retire, the largest percentage of your retirement income will have to come from your own investments along with any inheritance you were able to invest on your behalf. That, and of course your lottery winnings, slot machine winnings, and all the money you will have won on the ponies over the years! This is why it is so important to start the saving process early and be dedicated to putting something away every year. Let's look at it another way: For every $1,000 of income at retirement, your personal investments will make up $430 of that total, exclusive of IRAs and 401(k)s.

INFORMATION

Web Site Information

The American Savings Education Council has some great information on saving for retirement. Try its "ballpark calculator" at *www.asec.org* to see how you're doing in saving for retirement.

Work in Retirement

Currently, 5 percent of the income generated by retirees is from part-time employment or self-employment. Although I have predicted this number to go up to 7 percent, I may be conservative in that estimate. The Baby Boomers who are retiring in 15 or 20 years are far more technology savvy than most seniors are today. Their skills may translate into any number of technology-related small businesses that can help to supplement postretirement income.

The Internet offers tremendous opportunities for seniors to help in any number of areas. Let's say you're a retired tire salesperson and you have a couple of hours a day you'd like to be available to consumers interested in buying tires and needing the knowledge you can provide. You get a job working for Tires.com in its prepurchase online help chat room. Tires.com pays you by the hour, or by the sale, and consequently, you generate some money for golf or a luxurious facial. There are countless examples of opportunities for seniors, and people who want to remain active and keep both their minds and their bodies toned. If you have something to contribute, do it. And if you choose to make money at it, so much the better.

Many corporations allow their retiring employees to continue to work on a part-time basis for a limited number of hours per year. General Electric allows its retired employees to work 1,000 hours per year in a program called Golden Opportunity. My father, who is 80 years young, retired from the retail business over 20 years ago. He works part time helping a commercial real estate company manage its properties, and in doing so, he generates 20 percent of his retirement income from part-time work. For the record, he also generates 25 percent from Social Security, 10 percent from a company pension plan, and the balance from his IRA.

Common Mistake

Don't make the mistake of keeping all your retirement eggs in one basket.

Creating Retirement Income

One of the most important planning decisions you'll make is how to best generate income for your retirement. Different sources of income have different characteristics and potentially different tax consequences. It's very important to be wise in establishing and maintaining your postretirement cash flow. Here are the various types of income and their representative taxation:

◆ **Qualified plan investments like pensions, 401(k)s, and non-Roth IRAs.** These distributions are generally fully taxable when withdrawn because no tax has been paid on contributions made to the plan. One exception is the Roth IRA, which is not tax deductible when a contribution is made, but all income from the Roth IRA is distributed tax free. Another exception to the common theme of pension benefits being taxed as ordinary income is any after-tax contributions made to your 401(k). If you make these contributions, they are taxed as ordinary income in the year they are deposited, so when you begin to take income, your contributions are returned tax free. However, you are taxed on any growth credited to those after-tax contributions as ordinary income.

◆ **Nonqualified plan investments.** On the opposite side, you have assets that have been invested on an after-tax basis. As these are depleted they are tax free, and the interest, dividend, or capital gains on these assets is taxed accordingly.

◆ **Nonqualified annuity payments.** Payments made to you by an insurance company under an immediate annuity or payments from a deferred annuity contract that has been annuitized are part return of principal and part return of interest on the investment. You'll learn more about annuities in Chapter 9.

Strategies for Managing Income

There are a number of strategies for managing your postretirement income. One idea, which I discussed earlier in this chapter, is to postpone taking Social Security until you reach age 70. A five-year delay is worth about 35 percent more in monthly benefits. You may want to consider buying a five-year immediate annuity to replace the income you are electing to defer from Social Security.

Common Mistake

The IRS has a very specific way of defining age 70, and your failure to understand its definition can cost you plenty.

If at all possible, make sure that you avoid penalties on withdrawals from your retirement plans. These penalties may include government, plan, or product penalties. The penalties range from 10 percent to 50 percent, plus interest due, and they can be applied to your plan by the IRS cumulatively and retroactively. A simple mistake made 10 years ago can cascade into a mountain of penalties and taxes.

Systematic Withdrawals

Perhaps the most common way that people create retirement income is through the use of systematic withdrawals from their investment programs. You simply choose how much you want to withdraw, and the mutual fund company, bank, or insurance company complies with your request. Most systematic withdrawals are programmed. This means that the request is automated to make your withdrawals easy and consistent.

Be Careful

Systematic withdrawal is a very popular tool to create income at retirement, but it does not guarantee income over your life expectancy. Be careful to utilize this technique in combination with other strategies that provide lifetime income.

The challenge becomes creating your systematic withdrawal program. To start, decide if your withdrawal program will be designed to liquidate that investment over some period of time, usually life expectancy, or to distribute income or earnings, leaving the core investment intact. You can also have the best of both worlds, choosing perhaps to leave 50 percent of the core assets intact.

If you choose to leave the core investment intact, you can simply have the earnings or interest sent to you on a monthly or quarterly basis. If you want to have a level distribution that doesn't change each month, you'll have to make some assumptions on the return on the investment and adjust your withdrawals up or down based on actual performance. You have to be careful when doing this, particularly in bear markets because you may eat away at your principal to the point where you'll exhaust your assets prematurely.

On the other hand, you may want to simulate payments over life expectancy, using the assets. In that case, you have to determine what life expectancy you want to use and the rate of growth you want to assume on the asset. The rest is just math as we calculate the amount you can distribute. Of course, there is no guarantee your life expectancy estimate will be accurate, and you also don't know in advance if the assumption you use for the rate of return will be accurate.

For illustration purposes, let's look at how these two systematic withdrawal scenarios work out. We'll assume an account with $500,000, an assumed interest rate of 4.3 percent for both examples, and we'll use the combined life expectancy of 26 years for a married couple who are both 65 years old. In the first scenario, we exhaust principal and interest over the 26-year period. In the second scenario, we keep the principal intact and generate only interest income for the 26 years.

If we choose to distribute all of our assets over the joint life expectancy, we generate $30,982 annually. This is $9,500 more than if we distribute principal only, but if we outlive our life expectancy, we'll be out of income. Using the interest only, we generate $21,500 and still have the original $500,000 in 26 years, as shown in Table 3–2.

Clearly, you can run as many "what if" scenarios as you like, and you'll need to do that to reach your own conclusion as to how you want to distribute your retirement assets. These are the challenges we face in planning and investing for retirement. You can never start the retirement countdown too early.

Insured Income

Insurance will be covered extensively in both Chapters 6 and 9, but we will address the use of insurance as a method of guaranteeing income here. In a broad sense, you can look at income insurance in the same manner that you would look at any other type of insurance that is as protection against a loss. In this case, the loss is really the replacement of income from our traditional job from which we are retiring.

Table 3–2   Required Minimum Distributions of a $500,000 Account over 26 Years (Assuming 4.3% Interest)

Distributed Over Life	Interest Only
$30,982	$21,500
$30,982	$21,500
$30,982	$21,500
$30,982	$21,500
$30,982	$21,500
$30,982	$21,500
$30,982	$21,500
$30,982	$21,500
$30,982	$21,500
$30,982	$21,500
$30,982	$21,500
$30,982	$21,500
$30,982	$21,500
$30,982	$21,500
$30,982	$21,500
$30,982	$21,500
$30,982	$21,500
$30,982	$21,500
$30,982	$21,500
$30,982	$21,500
$30,982	$21,500
$30,982	$21,500
$30,982	$21,500
$30,982	$21,500
$30,982	$21,500
$30,982	$21,500

As the first of 77 million Baby Boomers approach retirement age, the insurance industry is preparing for the opportunity to provide insured income to this enormous market. Insurance companies have provided guaranteed annuity income to consumers since 1772, but historically, these guaranteed income streams have been expensive and have not offered the consumer liquidity. In other words, once an income stream had begun, the consumer was committed to that income stream for a specific period of time or, more commonly, for the rest of his or her life. In recent years, the industry has reinvented itself to be in a position to support the market with more innovative products designed to meet the income needs of retirees.

Key Point

Annuities are discussed throughout the book as investments that can be used to accumulate assets for retirement and as vehicles for guaranteeing income after retirement. As with any other investment type on the market today, there are good and bad annuities and there are proper and improper ways to use an annuity. Rest assured that I will point out the differences and provide a balanced perspective on their use, as I will all other investments that are available to you. Unfortunately, people's motives are not always pure, and you could be provided with a one-sided slant on a given investment.

There are a number of strategic advantages to generating insured income. First, if you select a fixed interest immediate annuity, the income is assured and insured by the insurance company. Although this guarantee is only as good as the underlying insurance company, the industry is highly regulated on both State and Federal levels and has an incredible track record in protecting clients' assets.

What I refer to as income insurance is created by the purchase of an immediate annuity or through the annuitization of an existing annuity contract. In either of these cases, you are converting a sum of money into an income stream that can be guaranteed for almost any period of time, but typically for the rest of your life. In addition, you can have assign half, two-thirds, or 100 percent of that income continue to your spouse and have it guaranteed for the rest of his or her life.

Savings Tip

When you purchase income insurance with an asset you have already paid taxes on, you receive an exclusion ratio that provides tax-advantaged income. A portion of your payment is taxable interest, but a large portion is likely to be a tax-free return of principal.

Income annuities come in two basic flavors and then combinations of those two flavors: fixed rate immediate annuity and variable. The easier one to understand is the fixed rate immediate annuity. In this type of contract, you can trade the insurance company a sum of money for a guaranteed income stream. For example, let's say that you and your spouse want to purchase $8,000 of monthly income for the rest of your life with continued payments of $4,000 per month allocated to your spouse when you're gone. You also want to make sure that these payments continue for at least 15 years so that your beneficiaries still have an asset should you and your spouse both die within the first 15 years. To determine the cost of providing that income, the insurance company has to look at how long you and your spouse are likely to live and then match a secure investment to that time frame so that your income is guaranteed.

Keep in mind that the insurance company is typically buying that asset at the prevailing interest rates, so in low interest rate environments, your money will not go as far as when interest rates are higher. But your income is guaranteed and you can count on it. There are also fixed immediate annuities that have "cost of living" adjustments that will increase your payments at some fixed rate or according to some index. These types of increases do come at a cost and are generally tied to the Consumer Price Index, not any type of equity or bond market index. As I mentioned earlier, if you purchase the income insurance with assets that you have already paid taxes on, the income you receive is tax advantaged.

The other flavor of income insurance is not fixed, but variable. While this adds an element of risk to your income insurance, it also offers true inflation protection. With variable annuitization, the process is a bit more complex to explain, but the benefits are worth the effort on both our parts. As with the fixed income stream, you can first choose the amount of initial income that you want to provide.

Let's make the same assumptions that we made on the fixed side of $8,000 a month, reducing to $4,000 a month for the surviving spouse.

Unlike with the fixed income stream, you will typically be asked by the insurance company to pick an assumed interest rate (AIR) on which to calculate your initial benefit. But this is where the similarity ends. With variable annuitization, you select one or more subaccounts in which to invest your money. These subaccounts are investment funds, much like mutual funds. The variety of subaccounts is very similar to that you find in the mutual fund arena, with thousands of subaccount choices available in the universe of variable annuity products.

Let's assume that you choose an S&P 500 index subaccount for your variable insured income stream, and you pick an assumed interest of 3.5 percent. The insurance company calculates your initial payment by using the assumed interest rate and your expected mortality, and it is then expressed to you in terms of units that are converted into income at the value of the underlying S&P 500 subaccount. Don't worry, I'll walk you through this concept, but you see how complex some of these issues affecting your retirement can be. If the S&P 500 subaccount is trading at $10.00 per share and you have $8,000 a month in income based on the AIR you have chosen, you can purchase 800 shares of the S&P 500 subaccount to provide your income. As long as the fund grows at 3.5 percent, your monthly checks will remain the same. But as you would expect, the S&P 500 has historically returned a much higher growth rate, and if the S&P 500 grows at 6 percent for the next year, your payments will increase by the difference between 3.5 percent and 6 percent, or 2.5 percent. Conversely, your income may go down if the S&P returns less than 3.5 percent per year. But in theory, and in reality over the past 40 years, this strategy has worked exceptionally well for thousands of teachers and nurses who have owned and annuitized tax-sheltered annuities in their retirement plans.

Minimum Distributions from Qualified Plans

When you reach age 70.5, the IRS requires that you begin taking distributions from your qualified plans, including 401(k) plans, IRAs, TSAs, and 457 plans. You need to take this requirement into account when planning your income strategy. Here is a straightforward description of what the IRS requires:

> No later then April 1 of the year following the year in which you turn 70.5, you must begin to take distributions from your qualified plans and you must distribute those

assets over your remaining life expectancy or sooner. Your failure to take a required minimum distribution (RMD) is rewarded with the largest penalty assessed by the IRS absent fraud… 50 percent!

As always with our beloved government, there are countless rules and exceptions to those rules. The rules that govern these distributions are over 40 pages in length. I intend to spare you the gory details and focus on the main points of consideration as they apply to establishing and maintaining your retirement income.

 ### Key Point

If you own a Roth IRA, you're not affected by the minimum distribution laws, but your non-spouse beneficiaries are. A non-spouse beneficiary must begin taking distributions no later that December 31 of the year following the death of the IRA owner. These distributions can be taken in a lump sum or in period payments, but payments cannot be less than the amount inherited divided by the life expectancy of the beneficiary and recalculated each year.

Let's use Dennis Glover as an example of how the IRS determines your age for purposes of the required minimum distribution. Dennis was born on June 27, 1946. In 2016, Dennis will turn 70, and during that year, he will also turn 70.5 because his birthday is before June 30. Dennis must begin distributions in 2016, or not later than April 1, 2017. Now, let's look at the impact if Dennis had been born on July 3, 1946. He would still turn 70 in 2016, but because he doesn't turn 70.5 until 2017, he can postpone taking his required minimum distributions until that year or April 1, 2018, at the latest.

As long as you understand the following basic premise constructed by the IRS, you'll avoid the penalty. The premise is that you've been saving without paying taxes, so at age 70.5, it's time to start using the money and paying taxes. During the calendar year that you turn 70.5, it is imperative that you make an election as to how you want your minimum distribution calculated. The calculation is very straightforward; you simply take the balance of your IRA or qualified plan as of December 31 of the year you turn 70.5 and divide that number by your life expectancy, which at age 70 is 27.4 years. Each subsequent year, you reduce the life expectancy by recalculating the previous year's life expectancy[1]. Going back to Dennis, let's look at his RMDs for 15 years from age 70 to age 85 in Table 3–3.

Table 3–3   Dennis Glover's RMD, Ages 70–85

Age	Life Expectancy	IRA Balance	RMD
70	27.4	$178,000	$6,496
71	26.5	$181,794	$6,860
72	25.6	$185,430	$7,243
73	24.7	$188,878	$7,647
74	23.8	$192,105	$8,072
75	22.9	$195,075	$8,519
76	22	$197,750	$8,989
77	21.2	$200,087	$9,438
78	20.3	$202,088	$9,955
79	19.5	$203,661	$10,444
80	18.7	$204,809	$10,952
81	17.9	$205,488	$11,480
82	17.1	$205,649	$12,026
83	16.3	$205,240	$12,591
84	15.5	$204,208	$13,175
85	14.8	$202,495	$13,682

These rules are complicated by numerous exceptions that wreak havoc with your retirement planning because the penalty for missing or underestimating an RMD is 50 percent. To make matters more unsettling is that this excise tax is applied cumulatively and retroactively to all missed or understated RMDs. To make this point a bit more realistic, in 1991, I worked with a stockbroker whose client had inherited an IRA from his father. His father had never taken any distributions and had died at age 81. The excise tax penalty was over $400,000.

---

1. Uniform, Single and Joint Life Expectancy tables are at the back of the book

Be Careful

The date by which you have to begin minimum distributions is April 1 of the year following the year in which you turn 70.5. Many people wait until the year following the year in which they turn 70.5 to take these distributions, but often confuse April 1 with April 15. On a $10,000 distribution, that mistake could cost you $5,000 plus taxes on that $5,000.

You can complicate your life even more if you roll over your IRA in the year a minimum distribution is due. In that case, the IRS may consider the $5,000 that you didn't take as an excess contribution to your retirement plan, which is subject to a 6 percent penalty.

Common Mistakes Made

The following is a sampling of the types of mistakes that people commonly make when attempting to meet the requirements set forth for distributions from qualified plans:

- ◆ The spousal exception allows a plan participant whose spouse is more than 10 years younger to use a different life expectancy table providing more favorable RMDs. However, if the marriage is a second marriage for the plan participant, the spousal exception is not available.

- ◆ Many people confuse the RMD start date of April 1 of the year following the year they turn 70.5 with tax day, April 15. This is a cost error of 50 percent of the RMD.

- ◆ If you choose to wait until April of the year following the year in which you turn 70.5 to begin RMDs, you will actually have to take two distributions that year. The ability to defer the first distribution is a one-time, one-year-only special and only for 90 days from January 1 to April 1 of the year you begin distributions.

- ◆ You are not allowed to roll over an RMD in the year it is to be taken. As an example, if you were to move your money from one custodian to another custodian in a year when an RMD is due, you must withhold the RMD from the transfer. If you don't, you've just made an excess contribution to your IRA and you're subject to a 6 percent penalty tax.

◆ Let's say that you have three IRAs and a 401(k) from which you have to take RMDs. Many people think that you aggregate all plan assets and take the RMD from one of the sources. The regulations say that you can aggregate only your IRAs and take just the money from one IRA, but you cannot aggregate the 401(k) amount with the IRA.

This concludes our discussion of the required minimum distribution, not because we have exhausted the topic, but because we simply can't take any more time covering this area of the tax code. This topic can be very confusing, even to the best and brightest CPAs. There is still quite a bit to learn about these minimum distributions and how they impact retirement income, but to cover it in more depth here would hurt the very result that we are trying to achieve—to empower your retirement, not paralyze the process.

Income Allocation

With so many options available, we must establish the criteria that we will use for creating our retirement income. How much income will come from RMDs, how much from our personal savings? Should you buy an immediate annuity, and if so, what type? These are all decisions that you will have to make on your own. Since every one reading this book is different, there is no standard answer to give. It is my opinion that prudent individuals covers all of their bases and engages in what I call "income allocation."

With income allocation, you assign certain assets to specific income streams to ensure balance and flexibility. In general, we look at life expectancy, risk tolerance, and liquidity needs and create a recommendation for how much of our income should be insured and how much should be left to be taken through systematic withdrawals to reach the overall income goals. To help you better understand this concept, we going to will look at the ways you can structure your income plan at retirement in Chapter 12.

Life Expectancy and Your Retirement

When looking at your retirement, you need to factor in life expectancy. As you can see from our life expectancy table, a married couple who are both age 65 will live a joint life expectancy of over 87 years. If you retire at age 65, that's an average of 22 years of postretirement living. But remember that these are just averages. Any family of two has to deal with the genetics of combined generations. You and your spouse both have or had families that included parents and grandparents. As you know, these genetics forecast your life expectancy, as shown in Table 3–4.

Table 3–4   Forecasting Life Expectancy

	Life Expectancy		
Age	**Male**	**Female**	**Joint**[a]
35	75.77	80.21	84.19
45	76.69	80.79	85.66
55	78.24	81.8	86.19
65	80.75	83.6	87.28
75	84.62	86.53	89.34

[a] Joint Life assumes both same age.

You need to factor in not only the length of life, but the quality of life and the expense of living longer. It's more expensive to live from age 65 to age 75 for the average person than it is to live from age 45 to age 55. Increased expenses include doctor visits, prescription drugs, physical therapy, and potentially, in home health care or assisted living. All this must be factored into your income needs.

Risks to Consider During Your Retirement

As you consider the income that you require for retirement and the ongoing process of managing your assets postretirement, you may want to take into consideration the following risks that we have not discussed in this chapter and their impact on your retirement:

◆ **Market Risk.** This is the risk associated with the stock and bond market. Until a few years ago, many younger investors thought that the stock market was a one-way street leading to an early retirement. This makes sense for the younger investors because they had really never seen a bear in the woods the size of the one that hit Wall Street as the Internet bubble burst into many people's retirement funds.

◆ **Business Risk.** This is a significant risk today because investors and the government are requiring publicly held corporations to operate in an environment that is more open and honest to the investor. Accounting rule changes have also forced companies to be more open with investors as relates to accounting issues to reduce manipulation of the numbers that could paint the financial picture of a company different from its reality. Business risk can also be associated with an industry or sector that is not performing well.

◆ **Interest Rate Risk.** Many people buy bonds and bond funds. As interest rates rise, the value of your bond or bond fund will fall. Conversely, as interest rates go down, your investment is worth more.

◆ **Life Expectancy.** In this case, good news could be bad news. The good news is that you're living longer. The bad news is that life costs more money and you have to be prepared so that you don't outlive your income.

Savings Tip

After you retire, check with a local temp agency and register to do some part-time work.

◆ **Inflation.** The impact of inflation must be taken into account in your retirement planning. For example, goods and services that cost $100, 20 years ago would cost well over $200 today.

◆ **Health Care Issues and Costs.** From 2000 to 2003, health insurance costs increased approximately 20 percent per year. This is a huge risk to anticipate in your retirement. Not only are costs going up, but the benefits are sometimes being reduced, by both employers and the insurers. The move to get more and more drugs over-the-counter is a clear effort to reduce the cost of prescription drug coverage in insurance plans.

◆ **Legislative and Tax Changes.** One never knows exactly what to expect from our friends in Washington. Unfortunately, the only thing predictable about the political winds is that they are always blowing. And tax law changes are often temporary, with politicians capitalizing on short-term public opinion.

Summary

This is one of the most important chapters in the book and also one of the most complex. It is imperative that you understand the importance of establishing the proper postretirement income stream. For most Baby Boomers who retire at age 65 with a spouse of similar age, the likelihood is that you will have to provide for 20–30 years of postretirement income. Although now is the time to save for these goals, it is also critical that we understand what we will need when we are ready to retire. You don't want to be on the mountain, running out of oxygen and stuck at 28,000 feet.

Power Checklist

- ✔ Time is the commodity that will drive many of our decisions in pre- and postretirement planning, and we have less and less time available to us as we grow older.
- ✔ The ultimate goal of income planning is to provide a stream of income at retirement that continues for the balance of our life.
- ✔ Financial failure is rarely the result of market conditions and almost always stems from a lack of adequate preparation.
- ✔ The practical reality is that our elected officials will not let the Social Security system collapse entirely, but neither are they likely to solve the problem altogether.
- ✔ It is likely that the Social Security system will see some form of privatization between now and 2010, just before 8 million Baby Boomers begin to retire.
- ✔ You must be familiar with the rules governing required minimum distributions and their impact on your retirement income plan.
- ✔ Your retirement income plan should include consideration of insured income through an immediate annuity.
- ✔ In your retirement planning, you must be aware of the wide assortment of risks that you will face and have a strategy for handling them.

CHAPTER 4

No Plan Is an Island

It seems like such a long time ago when working for a company was, in many respects, for life. My father is 80, and he spent 30 years working for one company. I'll be 50 within a year, and I had five jobs before I was 35. Nevertheless, when my father was working, it was typical for corporations to provide workers with a pension benefit that could provide 50–100 percent of their final year's salary as a retirement benefit for the rest of their life. On the surface, that sounds fine and certainly is a good start, but with inflation chipping away at your income like an ice pick on a glacier, your buying power on a fixed pension has the potential to be eroded quickly. As I mentioned in the previous chapter, my father's pension is now covering only 10 percent of his retirement income needs whereas 20 years ago it was covering close to 50 percent of his income needs. Even in Japan, where the "work-for-life" culture has been the strongest, people can't count on retiring with the company they may have worked at for dozens of years.

Qualified Plans

Let me set the stage for this chapter and put it into the proper perspective. At present, almost everyone has the opportunity to contribute to what are broadly termed "qualified plans." If you make a buck, you can put it into an individual retirement account (IRA). However, not everyone participates in all types of qualified plans, so this chapter will have more appeal to some and less to others. It will also be a more targeted chapter, so you may want to skim some of the information. For example, if you have a 401(k) and an IRA, you'll get more information from this chapter than would a government employee who has only what is called a 457 plan.

However, government employees will also take note that they will have a larger burden in funding their retirement than will someone who has a pension plan, a profit sharing plan, and an IRA. So get what you can get from this material and sock it away for the next chapter where we start to do some "objective based financial planning." Remember that the laws pertaining to qualified plans can change at a rate that competes with bunny reproduction, as can the limits of contribution and the requirements for distribution. If you're not someone who spends much time on a computer, you may want to at least get comfortable with surfing the Web because it's by far the best way to stay current on important issues facing your retirement.

As we learn about qualified retirement plans, we have a frightening statistic to consider. According to the Employee Benefits Research Institute (EBRI), less than 50 percent of businesses with under 100 employees have retirement plans, and even more frightening is that only one in five of those employees who are eligible for these plans actually contribute.

That means that 90 percent of those working for small businesses do not contribute to a qualified retirement plan.

It may be helpful for me to clarify the differences between qualified and nonqualified plans. A qualified plan is "tax qualified," meaning that it meets stringent rules established by our government to protect the rights of the worker. This is done through rules and tests, which ensure that the plan is widely available to employees and that no discrimination takes place. When a plan is tax qualified, contributions made by the employer are tax deductible, as are contributions made by the employee. Your plan grows on a tax-deferred basis, but distributions are taxed as ordinary income.

Nonqualified plan are ones that don't meet the tests to become qualified and are therefore not tax deductible to the company or the employee. They are typically used when an employer wants to differentiate the retirement plans or other benefits it offers to its key executives.

Confusion may result when we add retirement plans that are not technically qualified plans such as IRAs, Tax Sheltered Annuities (TSAs), and 457 plans. Each of these plans provides individuals with the right to save pre-tax earnings for retirement and have them grow on a tax-deferred basis. Although the government does not technically consider these qualified plans, they enjoy the same benefits and are generally treated in the same manner when distributed, so for our discussions, they will be lumped in with that group.

As we take a closer look at each one of these options, keep in mind that these are placeholders for investments, not investments themselves. IRAs and 401(k)s are not investments; they are accounts into which you funnel your pre-tax contributions and they are then in turn invested per your instruction. The government is allowing you to enjoy tax-deferred accumulation through these accounts as you build your retirement nest egg.

Now that you understand the difference between qualified and nonqualified plans, you need to know that qualified plans fall into one of two groups: defined benefit plans or defined contribution plans. Some companies offer both, but that number is dwindling quickly because of the high cost of administering defined benefit plans and the inherent flexibility offered by defined contribution plans. Some qualified plans are more popular for small companies while others are better for larger companies. Some work better with small income gaps between employees, and some are used where there are large discrepancies.

As in our previous example, defined benefit plans offer you a predetermined benefit, such as 50 percent of your last year's salary or some average of your salary over a specific period of time. Here's a rundown of the types of qualified plans you may be participating in and enjoying benefits from as well as some basic information that you can use as a current point in reference.

Defined Benefit Pension Plans

A defined benefit plan is the granddaddy of retirement plans. Unfortunately, in the years to come, these plans will likely become the retirement equivalent of a dinosaur. In a defined benefit plan, as noted earlier, an employee's years of loyal service are rewarded with the continuation of income postretirement based on a predetermined formula defined by the company. These formulas vary from company to company, so if you're covered by a defined benefit plan, be certain to ask your human resources department to provide you with the information you need to review your benefits.

INFORMATION

Web Site Information

It's likely that your company has information on your pension or retirement benefits online. The information is typically on a corporate intranet that is available only to employees and usually requires a username and password to gain entry. Check with your human resources department to see if your company has such a site.

Regardless of the specific formula that your company may use, it is likely to be a function of the following factors:

◆ **Average annual base pay.** This is based on the last three years, five years, or 10 years of your annual salary, as determined by the company. The shorter the average period that is used, the greater the likely impact of this element on the formula because you are likely earning more each year. As you can see in Table 4–1, the average of the last 10 years is $94,334, whereas the average for the last three years is $110,897.

Table 4–1   Average Annual Base Pay for 10, 5, and 3 Years

Year	Salary		
1	$75,000	Last Ten Years	$0
2	$78,750		
3	$82,688		
4	$86,822		
5	$91,163		
6	$95,721	Last Five Years	$0
7	$100,507		
8	$105,533	Last Three Years	$110,897
9	$110,809		
10	$116,350		

◆ **Years of service.** Most companies will credit you with all the years of your service, but many will deduct years for any break in service. Still others may cap the number of years of service because this number is used to multiply your average base pay.

◆ **Multiplier.** The multiplier is applied to calculate the maximum percentage of your average annual base pay. It usually ranges from 0.01 to 0.02. To understand its impact, let's assume your company has a cap of 30 years of service for calculating pension benefits and it uses a 0.02 factor as the multiplier. We simply multiply 30 times 0.02, and in this instance, the maximum you could receive would be 60 percent of your average annual base pay.

◆ **Early retirement factor.** Many companies will allow you to take early retirement, but they will offset your benefit by this factor. Let's say that your normal retirement benefit would be 50 percent of your average pay for the past five years. A two-thirds factor would mean that you're entitled to two-thirds of the benefit that you would have received at the normal retirement age.

Key Point

Not all retirement plans are alike; in fact, the differences can sometimes be worth thousands of dollars a year to you. During your working years, be certain to evaluate a prospective company's retirement plans and compare them with those of other prospective employers.

That's the essence of defined benefit plans. On the whole, I think that these plans offer a fair deal to both the employer and the employee because they are loyalty-based retirement benefits. The longer you work for a company and the more that the company recognizes your contribution through merit increases to your salary, the more likely you are to enjoy a symbiotic win-win relationship.

Be Careful

If you're a participant in a corporate-sponsored defined benefit plan, make certain that you understand the particulars of the plan. Many plans have been frozen or significantly modified to limit the benefit paid to the retired employee.

Defined benefit plans are a lot like the movie *Pleasantville*. *Pleasantville* is a movie about life in the 1950s being changed (some would argue corrupted) by life in the 1990s. Two teenagers in the 1990s are watching a black and white sitcom from the 1950s that portrays life as infinitely less complicated with friendlier people with bigger hearts. Through the wonder of fantasy and the gift of technology, the two teenagers are curiously transported through the TV to Pleasantville in all its black and white glory. The rest of the movie tells the story of these kids as they impact life in the 1950s, and each time they affect a character through their interaction, the character turns from black and white to color.

There are a number of parallels between defined benefit plans and Pleasantville, but my point is that in the 1950s, defined benefit plans were uncorrupted just like Pleasantville. Then things changed. For the last 20 years, there has been a notable shift to defined contribution plans. Corporations saw an opportunity to reduce costs and to shift the investment and retirement burden from the employer to the employee. This shift was greeted by some as progressive and by others as regressive. I'm not certain that there is a right or wrong, just as in Pleasantville, but the cause of the change is defined through the following story that I want to tell you, with my added perspective, of course.

Common Mistakes

Most people accept what their company tells them as "the truth." The problem is that until we stop making mistakes, we will have some work to do to make sure that our retirement plan debit and credits are correct. Systems are only as good as the people programming them. Trust and verify.

This is ultimately a story about greed, but it is also a story about balance (sorry, no romance). In 1875, American Express introduced what most believed to be the first defined benefit pension plan for its workers. For the next century, companies offered their own versions of a defined benefit plan without any real federal oversight other than the IRS, which allowed pension contributions to be deductible to the employer. In 1963, Studebaker closed down its South Bend, Indiana, plant and 4,000 people lost their jobs and their pensions. As expected, the shock waves extended to Washington, D.C., where the late Senator Jacob Javits sought to reform corporate pensions and began work on legislation that in 1974 would be passed into a law known as the Employee Retirement Income Security Act (ERISA).

When formed, ERISA had one purpose: to protect the retirement savings of employees who are participants in private pension plans. That charter has since been modified to include employee health and welfare benefits. ERISA is the direct result of the government's legislating balance where it had become absent in corporate America. The almighty dollar has led more than one corporate CEO to turn his or her head away from employees and the government for the sake of better earnings.

But as I said, this *is* a story about greed and, more important, about communication. Without government intervention, corporations were changing their retirement plans on a whim and taking advantage of their employees because they could, and it made financial sense from a business perspective. Firing loyal and well-performing employees after 9 years and 11 months to prevent them from vesting in their pensions is just one example of how businesses were taking care of their own bottom line without regard to how they were getting there.

I've always said that bad things happen when we are out of balance, and there are countless examples in which whole industries have failed to police themselves, thus becoming subject to government intervention. In the early years of the twenty-first century in America, corporate scandals have become commonplace and present a glaring sign that things are out of balance. Remember the old adage, "Pigs get fat, hogs get slaughtered"? I'll be bringing us back to that concept later in the book. For now, store it in your memory.

INFORMATION

Web Site Information

Several sites offer rich information on defined benefits plans. Try *www.pensions-r-us.org* and *www.cashpensions.org.*

Cash Balance Defined Benefit Plans

There is a variation of the traditional defined benefit plan called a *cash balance defined benefit plan.* This hybrid plan contains elements of both a defined benefit plan and a 401(k) plan. Instead of a guaranteed benefit, each year the company sets aside a dollar amount attributed to your retirement account and applies either a fixed or a variable rate of interest to the deposit. The value of this account then becomes your retirement plan after you vest, which is in five years. Once you are vested, the account is portable if you leave the company and is more attractive to younger employees who may not stay with one company for the 10 years that would be required to vest in a traditional defined benefit plan. According to the General Accounting Office (GAO), approximately 20 percent of Fortune 1000 companies now sponsor a version of this plan.

Be Careful

Often, companies require integration with Social Security benefits to limit their cost of providing retirement benefits. In doing so, they may cap your pension benefit so that, in conjunction with your Social Security payment, it doesn't exceed the salary you were making before retirement.

These plans are very controversial today because they are viewed by many employees as a poor replacement for a pension. Critics argue that because employees have no say or control in how these assets are managed, they are at greater risk, and older employees complain that their expected pension benefits have been dramatically reduced in favor of this less expensive plan. Clearly, what has also caught the attention of employees is the zeal with which some corporate HR and finance executives have openly touted cash balance plans as a method of "slashing pension benefits." Finally, there are "wearaway provisions" that currently allow employers who are converting from defined benefit plans to cash balance plans to withhold contributions into new accounts for older employees for years. Doing so saves the company money but penalizes the loyal employee.

Cash benefit plans will likely be around for a long time to come. What is unknown is the level of information that will have to be provided to employees and the terms under which employers will be allowed to modify benefits of employees through the conversion. In 2003, House Representatives Bernie Sanders (I-VT) and George Miller (D-CA) introduced a bill to require companies to give employees 40 years and older the right to stay in a defined benefit plan if their employer switches to a cash balance plan. At the time of publication, this bill was still under consideration by the House. Stay tuned for more on this controversial topic.

Key Point

Many companies modified their defined benefit plans to defined contribution plans to reduce their costs and shift the investment risk away from the employer and onto the employee.

Defined Contribution Plans

Most of the businesses in our country are defined as small businesses. These companies represent 99 percent of all employers and over half the workforce in America. Yet many of these businesses cannot afford to provide defined benefit pension plans. For those companies, a variety of plans can be made available to employees at a very low cost. These plans all provide employees with the right to reduce their income by the amount that they invest in their retirement plan. By far, the most popular plan used today is the 401(k), with over 480,000 active plans covering 47 million people and representing over $1.8 trillion in assets. That's where we'll start our discussion on defined contribution plans.

401(k) Plans

401(k) plans have been around since the passage of The Revenue Act of 1978. In the eight years following its creation, Congress and the IRS fine-tuned the product to be essentially what we have today. Unlike a defined benefit plan, which pays a specified benefit, 401(k) plans are defined contribution plan. This means that both you and your employer make contributions to the plan on your behalf, and you manage the manner in which your money is invested, subject to the options provided you by your employer. In today's world, employees usually have at least a dozen options choose from. These are discussed in Chapter 12.

Be Careful

401(k) plans have been under intense scrutiny since a scathing report was issued by the Department of Labor in 1998. The issue is hidden costs, and plan sponsors are now required to fully disclose all costs so that you can see the true value of your investment. Be sure to look at plan fees and 12b-1 fees assessed by mutual fund companies.

The fundamental difference between defined benefit and defined contribution plans is that the risk of meeting retirement objectives is shifted entirely away from the employer and directly onto the employee. Generally speaking, there are three reasons that corporations have migrated from defined benefit plans to defined contribution plans, and they are money, money, and money. My suspicion is most companies would say the three are cost, regulation, and liability. In the end, they all relate to the bottom line. In addition to the pure cost of the actual defined benefit, the more complex regulations cost money, and the additional liability for managing that money is also a significant cost, hence my belief that this shift to defined contribution plans is really all about money.

INFORMATION

Web Site Information

For more information on 401(k) plans, check out *www.401kforum.com.*

Regardless of these facts, over 40 million Americans are now enrolled in 401(k) programs, making their deposits and managing their assets. The 401(k) is likely the plan you have available to you, and there's a lot to know about these savings plans.

In 2003, you could contribute up to $12,000 to your 401(k) plan. That amount will increase by $1,000 each year through 2006 and will be indexed thereafter. On top of that, most employers match contributions at some level. In fact, approximately 97 percent of employers provide some match in their 401(k) plan. Although there is no "typical" matching, employers often match 100 percent of the employee contribution up to a fixed percentage, say 3 percent. The overall limit on annual amounts, including your employer contributions, is the lesser of 100 percent of income or $40,000.

Savings Tip

If you have a 401(k) available to you, invest in it. At a minimum, you should maximize your employer's contribution. If your employer matches 100 percent of your contributions, you'd be wise to put in at least 3 percent.

All contributions made by the employee are vested immediately, and the employer can choose to vest its contributions immediately or over a period from three to seven years. Also note that employers may not choose to match in cash deposits. They may match in company stock, a typically much cheaper currency for the company. This practice can also provide the employee an additional incentive to make sure the company thrives.

Be Careful

Be careful if you're a part-time employee because most plans allow corporations to exclude part-time workers, and some businesses take advantage of this policy, keeping only part time-workers "employed." If you're part time and not covered, you'll need to consider one of the IRAs discussed in this chapter.

Though it is not common, your employer may require a waiting period of up to one year before you're allowed you to participate in the plan. More typical is to have no wait or a short wait of three to six months. Also, you can borrow up to 50 percent to a maximum of $50,000 from your 401(k) if you have to. The interest that you pay is put back into your account, so you're really losing only the difference between what you pay yourself in interest and what you would have made using your current investment strategy. Be cautious though—you must pay this back within five years unless you use it to purchase a home, in which case you have 10 years.

As I mentioned earlier, a glaring difference between a defined benefit plan and a defined contribution plan is the responsibility of managing the money that is invested by both the employee and the employer. With a 401(k), you are at the controls of your retirement plane and you can take it almost anywhere you want. Your company will determine the investment options available to you, but the list is typically very extensive and will include a wide assortment of mutual funds and some type of guaranteed interest account. From there, you handle the mix of the assets in your plan and you live with the investment results.

Many corporations load their 401(k) plans up with company stock. At the time of the Enron scandal, which left tens of thousands of worker with worthless retirement plans, a number of Fortune 500 companies held inordinate (you could argue unconscionable) amounts of their stock in the plans. Included in those were Procter & Gamble, with just under 95 percent of its plan assets in company stock, and McDonald's, with just under 75 percent in the golden arches stock. You must be sure to diversify your contributions and let your voice be heard in your HR department if your company is loading up on corporate stock in your retirement plan. You should be able to sell your stock in the plan and reinvest the proceeds as you see fit.

403(b) Plans

A 403(b) plan is typically offered in lieu of a 401(k) plan to teachers and to employees of nonprofit organizations, also known as 501(c) (3) organizations. It is very similar to the 401(k), so this section focuses on only the important differences between the two plans.

Be Careful

The Economic Growth and Tax Relief Reconciliation Act of 2001 offers additional saving opportunities for retirement, but it also carries a "sunset" feature. In this case, unless the opportunities are extended by the Legislature, they revert back to their original limits in 2011.

Perhaps the biggest difference between 401(k) plans and 403(b) plans is the more limited investment options that are available in 403(b)s. Most school districts and nonprofits try to keep costs very low and typically offer fixed and variable annuities to their employees. In recent years, offerings have been expanded to include mutual funds, providing a brighter future for these retirement plans.

Any time you mention annuities and qualified plans, you will undoubtedly hear a chorus of people proclaiming that it makes no sense to ever buy an annuity in a qualified plan. I will also tell you that those who make that comment either don't understand what they are saying or have purposely chosen to emotionalize a generalization. The statement "You should never put an annuity into a qualified plan" is an extreme generalization, and as you know, extreme generalizations are rarely true. This case is no exception. A far more accurate—and true—statement would be "The additional expenses associated with certain variable annuity features may or may not ultimately be worth the cost."

In Chapter 9, we will have a lengthy discussion on annuities and insurance, so I'll keep this brief and to the point.

There are two types of annuities used to accumulate assets; one is called a fixed annuity, and the other is called a variable annuity. Within these two types are a number of flavors to choose from, but essentially, fixed annuities are guaranteed interest rate contracts insured by the company. In contrast, variable annuities are typically invested in the market at your direction and will fluctuate with market returns. They both have very different objectives and very different cost structures, with fixed annuities having no cost to purchase and no cost to administer. Variable annuities, on the other hand, have fees to cover benefits not found in the fixed annuity. These fees can range from a low of 0.40 percent to a high of 1.75 percent.

Now let's get back to the extreme generalization I mentioned about annuities. If the only advantage that an annuity offered were tax deferral, the critical statement would have merit. But annuities have a host of other benefits found only in contracts offered by insurance companies, and many people find value in those benefits. For example, all variable annuities provide beneficiaries with protection in the event of death. Some provide more and some provide less. Those that provide more charge more for that added protection. So the question that should be asked by the consumer is, "Are the benefits worth the cost of the benefits?" That discussion takes place in Chapter 9.

Be Careful

Watch out for expensive annuity products in 403(b) plans that are sometimes sold by salespeople far less interested in your wellbeing than in their paycheck. But don't paint all products and salespeople with the same brush because there are good low-cost annuity products available and there are people who care about what they sell.

One final note on the sale of 403(b) investments to teachers and nonprofit organizations as it relates to the nature of the sale of these investments: Historically, the cost of selling investments in the 403(b) market has been very high and the investments have reflected that cost. Arguably, some investments have been priced so high that you would have probably been better off paying your taxes and investing in an indexed fund.

The key factor in this cost is labor. Since it takes the same amount of time for a sales representative to sell a $500 annuity or mutual fund as it does to sell a $50,000 annuity or mutual fund, very few want to sell the $500 plan. To provide incentives to the salespeople, a disproportionate commission was paid on small contributions, and the investment used in these sales was much more costly than the investment used in the $50,000 sale. This problem has slowly evolved but still exists. Everyone wants to pursue the clients with a lot of money and very few want to work with smaller sales. The solution will be found in better education of both the consumer and the salesperson as well as in a more effective use of technology to deliver the information that is needed to educate this market.

Key Point

Thanks to the passage of the Economic Growth and Tax Relief Reconciliation Act of 2001, employees who are 50 and older can utilize a "catch-up" provision to accelerate contributions. The limits are set by the government and apply to 401(k) plans, 403(b) plans, SIMPLE IRAs, and IRAs.

There are a couple of other key points to make relative to the differences between 401(k) plans and 403 b) plans. In 403(b) plans, there is typically no employer match because the sponsoring organizations historically don't have the money to fund contribution on the employees' behalf. The reality of no employer match is that 403(b) plans do not enjoy the same participation as the 401(k) plans. One advantage that 403(b) plans have enjoyed is the catch-up provision, which allows an employee the ability to really sock away retirement money using a special "15-year rule." This rule allows participants to increase their contribution by $3,000, more than the 2004 limit of $13,000. To qualify, the participant has to have 15 years of service with the same employer and can not have averaged more than $5,000 in previous years. There is a $15,000 cap on the catch-up as well. And as the *coup de gras,* 403(b) participants can also layer in the latest catch-up provision included in the Economic Growth and Tax Relief Reconciliation Act of 2001. All told, in 2004, 403(b) participants who qualified for all the catch-up provisions could put away $18,000 toward their retirement instead of the normal $13,000.

Savings Tip

Some participants in 403(b) plans may have the ability to participate in a 457 plan as well. This is a great opportunity for saving because you can double up on your pre-tax savings.

457 Plans

457 plans are similar to 403(b) and 401(k) plans and are directed primarily at government employees and nonprofit organizations. I should warn you that these are the least attractive retirement plans you will see because their assets can be subject to creditors leaving you in the lurch. Technically, they are not even in the same category as 401(k) and 403(b) plans because they are considered deferred compensation plans. If you work for a nonprofit organization or any other privately owned business that can sponsor a 457 plan, your plan assets are a part of the business and subject to creditors. If you're a government employee, the government stands behind you 457 plan assets.

The government has done a lot to improve these plans over the past several years. It has increased the contribution limits to be consistent with 401(k) and 403(b) plans and made them portable by allowing them to be rolled over into an IRA. It has not, however, changed the fact that getting money out of 457 plans is far from easy—you have to retire, reach 70.5, or have a financial hardship. The bottom line is that 457 plans are not as flexible and not as reliable as other alternatives.

Federal Pension Plans

Federal government employees participate in one of two plans offered by the government: the Civil Service Retirement System and the Federal Employees Retirement System. Regardless of the type of plan, these are very complex systems, different from anything we have covered thus far in this chapter. In essence, federal employees are covered by a defined benefit plan, containing elements of a defined contribution plan called a Thrift Savings Plan. For federal employees hired after the mid 1980s, they also participate in the Social Security program but have lower defined benefit amounts than those hired prior to the mid-1980s.

Profit Sharing or Stock Bonus Plans

Profit sharing plans, while not significant in today's retirement plan picture, have been around for well over 200 years, dating back to companies like Sears, Eastman Kodak, and Procter & Gamble. The Depression nearly wiped out these plans, which saw a resurgence in the 1950s and 1960s. Profit sharing plans have elements of defined contribution plans whereby your employer shares profits with you within the qualified plan. Those contributions are made exclusively by your employer, while you make no contribution, and the contributions are completely discretionary. They are typically coupled with a 401(k) plan so that employees can add to their retirement savings.

Employee Stock Ownership Plans

Employee stock ownership plans (ESOPs) fall into that fringe category of little-used retirement plans. In an ESOP, your employer deposits shares of the company stock that provide a deduction to the company and establish your stake in the company. The problem with these plans is that you have no control over your shares until you have been with the company for about 10 years *and* are over age 55. Additionally, the tax treatment of these plans is very complex and requires the services of competent tax counsel.

Simplified Employee Pension-IRAs

Simplified Employee Pension-IRAs (SEP-IRAs) are designed for small businesses and are typically utilized by those with fewer than 10 employees. The nice feature about a SEP-IRA is that employers do not have to contribute each year and can make up for years when they don't contribute by overcontributing in subsequent years, subject to an annual maximum of 15 percent. Also, there is no vesting in SEP-IRAs, unlike 401(k) and other plans. Since SEP-IRAs started before the passage of the Small Business Job Protection Act of 1996, employees could contribute up to 25 percent of income to an annual maximum of $40,000 in 2003, indexed for future years. Indexing is a method of adjusting the maximum contribution to keep pace with inflation. Any SEP-IRA plan that started after the Act was passed will allow only employer contributions.

Be Careful

Self-employed business owners using a SEP-IRA have the same limit of 25 percent of income up to $40,000, but this must be calculated on net earnings and must include a deduction for half of the self-employment tax.

Savings Incentive Match Plans for Employees

The Savings Incentive Match Plan for Employees (SIMPLE) became a reality in 1996 with the passage of the Small Business Job Protection Act and is available to businesses with fewer than 100 employees. With a SIMPLE plan offered by their employer, employees can contribute up to $8,000 per year into what is essentially a scaled-down 401(k) plan. The contribution maximum is $9,000 in 2004, $10,000 in 2005, and indexed thereafter for inflation in $500 increments. Your employer is required to match contributions dollar for dollar up to 3 percent or provide a 2 percent contribution for all employees. Unlike 401(k) plans that have vesting schedules for employer contributions, SIMPLE plans immediately vest all employee and employer contributions, making this plan very portable for employees.

Wake-Up Call

Over 90 percent of those who work for a small business with fewer than 100 employees do not contribute to any formal retirement plan. Reaching your retirement goal without a formal saving plan is a fool's errand.

SIMPLE plans have their unique quirks though, including strict rules on tax-free transfers and harsh early withdrawal charges. Normally, if you withdraw money from a qualified retirement plan, you pay the income tax on the amount withdrawn plus a 10 percent penalty if you're under age 59.5. In a SIMPLE plan, that penalty jumps to 25 percent in the first two years.

Keogh Plans

House Resolution 10 was passed in 1963, creating a new type of retirement plan for self-employed individuals. Named after its sponsor, New York Congressman Eugene Keogh, these plans created the first real opportunity for self-employed individuals to establish their own retirement plan. All of these plans have their nuances, and the Keogh plan has its fair share as well.

To be eligible for a Keogh plan, you must either file a Schedule C with your income taxes, have a subchapter S corporation, have an LLC, or be a partner in a business that files a Schedule K. As you can see, Keoghs are complex, which is why you don't see too many of them around today.

Making them even more complex is the fact that there are three ways you can set up a Keogh, and each of those carries its own unique set of regulations. You can have a profit sharing Keogh, a defined contribution Keogh, or a defined benefit Keogh.

The maximum amount you can contribute to a Keogh depends on whether it is a defined contribution Keogh or a defined benefit Keogh. In 2003, the annual benefit for a defined benefit Keogh plan participant could not exceed the lesser of 100 percent of the participant's average compensation for his or her highest three consecutive years or $160,000. For a defined contribution Keogh plan, annual contributions and other additions in 2003 (except for earnings) could not exceed the lesser of 100 percent of the compensation actually paid to the participant or $40,000.

Individual Retirement Account Plans

We have dealt primarily with employer-sponsored defined benefit or defined contribution plans thus far. Now we move into the world of individual retirement accounts (IRAs). IRAs have been part of our retirement fabric since their creation in 1974. IRAs fill the gap where no other retirement plans are available or where you have not maximized your other retirement plan contribution and qualify for an IRA as well. And since IRAs are designed to meet the needs of those without access to other plans, you'll find that these plans do not offer high contribution limits and are generally not available to high-wage earners as the deductibility of deposits gets phased out at the higher-income levels.

 Common Mistakes

When people need money, they may have to tap their retirement plan assets, and when they do so, they can avoid the pre-59.5 penalty by taking systematic withdrawals. Unfortunately, many people have made the mistake of misreading the IRS code on these distributions which require that distribution continue for five years or until age 59.5, whichever is later. If you violate this regulation, the IRS will come after you for all taxes and penalties retroactively and cumulatively. Exceptions can include first-time home loans, medical expense reimbursement, and education expenses.

Traditional IRAs

The traditional IRA allowed an individual to put away $3,000 per year in 2003, $3,500 for those 50 years or older. As you see in Table 4–2, those limits increase until they reach $5,000 in 2008. You can see that the IRA maximums are much lower for a traditional IRAs than for other qualified plans. You should also keep mind that IRAs qualify for the catch-up provision as noted in our discussion of TSAs above.

Money deposited in traditional IRAs is tax deductible and grows on a tax deferred basis until you begin taking withdrawals at retirement. Withdrawals made prior to age 59.5 are subject to a 10 percent penalty as well as the tax on the money withdrawn. There are exceptions to that rule, but you must take substantially equal payments based on your life expectancy and take those payments for at least five years or until age 59.5, whichever is later.

Savings Tip

Get your kids started in an IRA when they are young. A good habit would be to motivate your kids to put 20 percent of what they earn into a Roth IRA. Agree to a 50 percent match by putting some money back into their pockets to help them get started.

Key Point

Using a stretch IRA is a helpful way for you or your beneficiaries to receive income over your lifetime with the ability to accelerate withdrawals as needed. A stretch IRA is an IRA that you have received as the result of being a beneficiary of an IRA. Let's say that your father passed away several years ago, leaving his IRA to your mother. When your mom passes away, she names you as her beneficiary, and instead of paying taxes immediately, you can have the payments made over your life expectancy per the IRS Single Life Table.

Table 4–2   Maximum IRA Contributions, 2002–2008+

Tax Year	Under Age 50	Age 50 or Older
2002	$3,000	$3,500
2003	$3,000	$3,500
2004	$3,000	$3,500
2005	$4,000	$4,500
2006	$4,000	$5,000
2007	$4,000	$5,000
2008 and after	$5,000	$6,000

You may qualify to make tax deductible contributions to an IRA if you are not eligible to contribute to a qualified retirement plan at work. In most cases, if you are working full time and your employer offers a plan such as a 401(k), you are considered eligible to invest in the 401(k). While that choice is yours to make, if you qualify to contribute to a plan at work, you have to meet an additional set of requirements that are income related to be able to make deductible contributions to an IRA. In general, the IRA phases out your right to deduct contributions to your IRA if you make more than $65,000 in adjusted gross income. Adjusted gross income is all income less a number of items including: contributions to qualified retirement plans, alimony, moving expenses, student loan interest, rental real estate losses, and half of any self-employment taxes paid.

Savings Tip

You can now contribute the maximum amount for a nonworking spouse into an IRA. Historically, you were able to add only $500 for a nonworking spouse. This is a great way to double the amount you put into your IRA.

Roth IRAs

The Roth IRA, named for William V. Roth, the retired Republican senator from Delaware, became a reality with the passage of the Tax Payer Relief

Act of 1997. The passage of this bill and the launch of the Roth IRA stimulated a huge IRA renaissance. Not much had been happening in the IRA market since Congress took away the deductibility of IRAs for many people in 1986. Within one year, IRA contributions dropped by two-thirds and have been slow to grow since then. Along comes the Roth IRA, allowing you to deposit after-tax dollars into the plan and then enjoy tax-free accumulation and tax-free distributions. It's no wonder that in five short years, over 16 million people opened or began converting to the Roth IRA.

By far the biggest advantage of the Roth IRA is its ability to utilize tax deferred growth and compound interest to allow you to accumulate a tidy sum of money for your retirement. As good as the Roth IRA is, you'll have to save more than the maximum allowed in these plans if you want to live comfortably in retirement. Let's look at an example to illustrate the point.

Assuming that you are 45 years old and that you will deposit $3,000 into a Roth IRA each year for the next 20 years, earning an average of 10 percent per year, your account value will be $189,000 when you retire at age 65.

Now, imagine that you set up a second fund, this time one whose annual growth is taxable at a combined rate of 38 percent for federal and state taxes. You also deposited $3,000 a year earned the same 10 percent. In 20 years, you would have $120,000, or roughly $70,000 less than with the Roth IRA.

The Roth IRA does have its unique manner for handling withdrawals that are deemed preretirement. For starters, the contributions that you put into Roth IRAs are after-tax dollars, so you can recapture those at any time without a penalty. Regarding the earnings, any withdrawal during the first five years will be met with taxes and a 10 percent penalty. Withdrawals made after the five-year period and after age 59.5 carry no penalty and you'll pay nothing in taxes. Keep in mind that *both* the five-year and age 59.5 rules must be met unless you're disabled or are a first-time home owner withdrawing no more than $10,000. If you violate either the five-year rule or the age 59.5 rule, you'll pay taxes and a 10 percent penalty on any earning distributed. The good news is that unlike with the traditional IRA, you are never forced to take your money from the Roth. You can leave it in for as long as you like, and you can pass the proceeds to your heirs tax free. (Heirs may have to deal with estate taxes depending on the size of the estate passing the asset.)

To Roth or Not to Roth

Whether or not to open a Roth IRA is an easy question for almost everyone to answer. The Roth IRA beats the traditional IRA hands down. The double advantage of accruing earnings on a tax-free basis and withdrawing them on a tax-free basis will win almost every time.

The only credible comparison would be if you deducted your traditional IRA contribution, taking the tax savings and investing those savings to supplement the traditional IRA. In that scenario, you can come close to the Roth IRA, but you will rarely beat it.

Converting to a Roth IRA

You have the option of converting your existing IRA into a Roth IRA if you meet certain criteria set forth by the IRS. The advantage of making the conversion is that although you pay taxes on the amount rolled over, you won't pay taxes on the money distributed at retirement. And there is no IRS requirement that you take distributions from the Roth IRA at age 70.5.

In determining whether it is in your best interests to roll over an IRA into a Roth IRA, your first consideration should be your age. Fundamentally, the younger you are and the less you have in your traditional IRA, the better the argument for converting to a Roth IRA—if you qualify to convert the IRA at all. Married couples filing jointly with adjusted gross income in excess of $100,000 need not apply. Married couples filing separately need not apply, regardless of adjusted gross income. You'll find a Roth IRA converter on the *www.retirementcountdown.com* Web site.

Divorce and Plan Assets

A divorced spouse has certain rights to qualified plan assets, and a court will often issue a qualified domestic relations order (QUADRO) to specify spousal benefits. This is important from a tax perspective to the spouse who is entitled to these benefits. Most people who have just gotten divorced don't want to leave the money commingled with their ex-spouse's. The options are to do an IRA rollover, take a lump-sum distribution, or take periodic payments based on life expectancy for five years or until age 59.5 (if the spouse is under age 59.5), whichever is longer. If the spouse receiving the benefit wishes to take those systematic withdrawals instead of the IRA rollover, arrangements for the payments must be made. Once the IRA is rolled over, this is no longer an option.

How Much Should You Put into Qualified Plans?

Now that we have a solid understanding of the different types of qualified plans that may become available to us, the next question is, how do we decide an amount to put into these plans? The general answer to that question is as much as you possibly can without risking a cash flow short-age for living expenses or emergencies. That is easy to say but difficult to execute. One thing that you clearly do not want to do is invest in a quali-fied plan and then take the money out prior to your retirement.

Some experts suggest that you shouldn't maximize your tax-deferred contributions, pointing to the difference between income taxed as ordi-nary gains and income taxed as long-term capital gains. With qualified retirement plans and traditional IRAs, the earnings on your investments are taxed as ordinary income compared with investments in products made on an after-tax basis that are typically taxed at much lower capital gains rates.

What this argument suggests is that if you invest your money after taxes in a tax efficient vehicle such as indexed funds or you buy and hold a portfolio of stocks over a long-term period, you pay less in taxes because long-term capital gains are currently taxed at a maximum rate of 15 percent. To make this argument work, you have to assume very high income tax brackets at retirement compared with the low capital gains rates of today.

Be careful when considering this advice because you don't know what tax rates will be when you retire. The lower the margin between ordinary income taxes and capital gains taxes, the more attractive it is to save through your qualified plan or IRA. Tax-deferred qualified plans and IRAs offer you an opportunity to establish a systematic savings program you might not otherwise take advantage of.

Be Careful

If you're a union worker, your union may have negotiated retire-ment plan contributions separately. In this case, you may or may not be eligible for company-sponsored plans.

In assessing your options, you need to have a very good understand-ing of the plan or plans available to you. If the plan is a defined benefit plan, you have little to do in terms of making decisions other than to ensure that you understand the value of that benefit when you consider changing jobs. I am certainly not saying that you should stay in a job that you are unhappy with just because of the company retirement plan. Instead, I am suggesting that anytime you make a serious decision, you should weigh the benefits against the alternative. If you have other plans available to you, ask these questions to make sure you have enough information to make an educated decision:

- Does your employer match your contribution, and if so, using what formula?

- Is there a vesting schedule for the employer match, and if so, what is it?

- Do you manage the investment choices or does the employer?

- How wide is the assortment of investment products that are offered?

- How much of the plan assets are in company stock, and how often are you allowed to sell your stock and rebalance your portfolio?

- What are the annual costs of the plan that are paid by you or passed down to you?

These are just some of the questions that you need to answer so that you can carefully consider how much money you want to put into the plan. If the plan is reasonably priced, has a good employer match, and does not rely heavily on company stock, you most likely want to contribute at least the maximum to get your employer match. You should also think about contributing all the way up to the maximum amount allowable as long as doing so leaves you with adequate resources to live.

How Should You Invest Your Qualified Plan Money?

Once you have made your decision and committed to saving through a qualified retirement plan or an individual retirement plan, your next task is to choose the investments that go into the plan. If you're investing through a company-sponsored plan, your investment choices will be limited to those offered through the plan. If you're investing in an individual plan like an IRA, you control where the investments are made, subject to some limitations that are truly there to protect your interests.

Any dollar you invest needs to be coordinated with other dollars and invested based on a number of parameters. The fact that a dollar is a tax-deferred dollar does make a difference, but it is just one of many factors to take into consideration. When you look at any asset that will not be utilized for a long period of time, you should allow yourself to take greater investment risk. In Chapters 7–11, you will learn all about the various investment products that are available to you, and in Chapter 12, you'll learn how to put them into a cohesive plan.

With regard specifically to qualified plans and traditional IRAs, a few tips can make your investments even more tax efficient. For example, a qualified plan or IRA is not a good home for money market funds, nor is it a prime candidate for bond funds until you are close to retirement. Money markets are best suited to providing for emergency cash or maybe a place to hide if you really think the equity and real estate markets are overvalued. Bond investments are typically used to create income, unless you feel that interest rates are uncharacteristically high and you are expecting to make money not only on the income generated but also on capital gains from selling the bonds for capital gains.

Finally, I would suggest that you look at all your investments and use the qualified plan to house more of your aggressive investments or investments that have a very high propensity to generate short-term capital gains because you'll be able shelter those in the qualified plan or IRA. For example, some equity mutual funds turn over their portfolio of stocks four times in a given year. That means that they sell the underlying stocks on average over four times in one year, and most of their returns are taxed at ordinary income rates. Having these in your plan can be very tax efficient.

Summary

You need to know that each of these plans has its own distinguishing features. I personally believe our legislators have made retirement plans far too difficult to compare and understand. It shouldn't be this difficult for average Americans to understand their qualified plan options. Because your qualified plan assets are a significant part of your retirement income, you must take great care to ensure that you maximize the benefits that these plans offer in a way that is in keeping with your overall financial plan. Remember, this category is responsible for generating roughly one-third of your postretirement income.

Power Checklist

> ✔ Remember that qualified plans hold investments, but they are not investments in and of themselves. A pot will hold water, and a fire

will heat the water. Your qualified plan is the pot, and your investments are the water.

✔ Defined benefit plans offer you a continued paycheck after you retire, based on your average salary over a specified period of time.

✔ Ninety percent of people working for small businesses do not contribute to a qualified retirement plan.

✔ ERISA, which is enforced through the Department of Labor, protects the interests of employees with retirement plans and is the direct result of the government's legislating balance where it had become absent in corporate America.

✔ 401(k) plans are extremely popular, with over 480,000 active plans covering 47 million people and representing over $1.8 trillion in assets.

✔ Many corporations load their 401(k) plans up with company stock, so be careful!

✔ The following statement is an extreme generalization: "You should never put an annuity into a qualified plan." Extreme generalizations are rarely true statements.

✔ Roth IRAs are great for those who qualify to have them.

CHAPTER 5

Goal-Oriented Retirement Planning: Energy for Your Retirement

Over the course of the last four chapters, I have laid out the framework for the work to be done in this chapter. The work that we will do here is the key to making your retirement plan achievable. It starts with an understanding of the challenges you face in achieving your retirement goals, and it ends with the establishment of a plan to reach those goals. In the Introduction, I offered up the five steps that you see below as a guide to managing your achievement of any goal that you choose to set.

The Key to Success in Anything You Do

Define the task and articulate it
Set reasonable goals and expectations
Create a framework for achievement
Manage and modify
Execute, *do it,* don't quit.

With financial planning in general and retirement planning specifically, it is imperative that the planning process begin as early as possible. As I mentioned earlier, you can't make up for time lost in the savings process. Time and rate of growth are the two biggest components to a successful retirement strategy. Most people focus far too much on the investment side and far too little on establishing a plan and maintaining that plan. The following story illustrates what you are trying to avoid.

In 1983, I was living in Southern California and training stockbrokers, insurance agents, and financial planners on how to position retirement products with their customers. As part of my job, I would do at least three public seminars a week and countless face-to-face meetings with planners and their clients.

On this particular occasion, I was with a stockbroker from Riverside, California, calling on two of his clients who lived nearby in an upscale mobile home park. (I know what vision you conjure up when you think of a mobile home, but this was a very nice living unit owned by two of the nicest people you ever wanted to meet.) The wife was a retired school-teacher and the husband was still working as a welder for a medium-sized company. They had two grown children who were both working and married, and they were the proud grandparents of two granddaughters and a grandson. The wife had done a fairly good job of saving in her 403(b) plan with the school district, but she didn't have any employer match and she didn't contribute anywhere near the maximum amount that she could have. Her husband, on the other hand, didn't even have a qualified plan at work, and as a couple, they had next to no savings.

Wake-Up Call

"The ultimate measure of a man is not where he stands in moments of comfort and convenience, but where he stands at times of challenge and controversy." —Dr. Martin Luther King, Jr.

I suspect you know where this is leading. Let me get there quickly so that I can make the point. They wanted to know how far her 403(b) and their limited savings would get them in addition to Social Security. Their hope was to replace at least 75 percent of their combined income for their retirement. They weren't even close. They would be lucky to eke out just over 40 percent of their preretirement income. This isn't a happy story, and it wasn't any fun trying to explain to them what their options were at this stage in their lives. They just weren't prepared to retire.

There is a bit of happy ending to the story. When faced with financial adversity, they made the decision to do something about it. The husband realized he would need to continue working full time for at least five years past age 65, and the wife, an avid hobby seamstress, decided to go to work part time repairing clothing for a local department store. Their decisions got them to about 60 percent of their goal, and they modified their spending to bring expenses in line with their retirement income.

Wake-Up Call

"When all is said and done, there is more said than done."
—Anonymous

So why did this wonderful couple fall short in their efforts to retire on their terms? And why do people fail to meet their goals in general? In this case, they simply had not planned at all. They had assumed that reaching their goal was something they had time to deal with later. I will tell you they are not alone in their thinking. In Table 5–1, I have listed five reasons I think drive people to missing their goals and the typical result that occurs.

Table 5–1   Five Reasons People Miss Their Goals

Reason for Possible Failure	Resulting Action
They don't have any goals.	They give up before they start.
They have unreasonable expectations.	They get frustrated and quit.
The task or goal is bigger than they thought.	They get frustrated and quit.
They lack external support from friends and family.	They have an even harder time.
They are conditioned to accept a result other than the achievement of their goal.	They give up.

Let's put the final touches on this topic by putting failure into perspective. Anthony Robbins, a renowned author, psychologist, and captivating motivational speaker, doesn't like the word "failure." As a matter of fact, in his book, *Unlimited Power,* Robbins puts failure into perspective by changing the lens we use to assess things and simply calls failure one of two possible results to any action. He maintains that you get positive and negative results to actions, and those of us who persevere choose to take negative results or experiences, learn from them, and repeat them less frequently. The more we experience negative results, the more we can improve by learning from those experiences.

Wake-Up Call

"Failure is the line of least persistence." —Zig Ziglar
"A goal properly set is halfway reached." —Zig Ziglar"

Michael Jordan, arguably the best to ever play the game of basketball and one of the game's most prolific scorers, failed 50 percent of the time he shot the ball. Cal Ripken, the Baltimore Orioles great and consistent third baseman, failed to get a hit 73 percent of the time he was at bat. Yet we all know these two athletes were far from failures. The lesson here is to put failure into perspective and use the experiences you get to modify your behavior going forward.

Create a Culture for Success

Success doesn't come naturally to all people, nor is success something that is innately in your blood. The fact of the matter is that you can learn to be successful and it can be as simple as making it a priority in your life. It has often been said that success is the result of preparation meeting opportunity. Preparation is the result of planning, practicing, and learning. The artist who drew my cartoons for this book, a wonderful man named Frank Hill, opined that he doesn't know anyone who has gotten worse by practicing. On the other hand, opportunity is a numbers game; if you keep your goal in play and utilize every possible opportunity to achieve it, you greatly increase your chances of success.

But success is more than that. Success is a culture, and you have to create and foster the culture of success in your life. Part of that is your responsibility and part is the responsibility of your support group of family and friends. It is up to you to do everything in your power to achieve your goals and to minimize whatever is subversive to your goal.

 Key Point

If you want to achieve a goal, you need to have the deck stacked in your favor. That means that you must leave nothing untried for accomplishing your purpose. Make sure your friends and family understand your goal, and seek their moral support as well.

Let's take a simple goal of being on time to meetings or to social events. Very few people like to be late, and quite frankly, those who do, have other items on their personal agenda. But being late doesn't just happen; it happens because you have lost control of time and failed to regain that control soon enough to accomplish your goal. Maybe you didn't ask for support from your friends and family or you put another priority ahead of being on time. The point is that you can control your environment whether it's the discipline of being on time or the discipline of putting $100 a month into a retirement savings program to meet the financial objective you have set as a retirement goal.

Know When to Give Yourself a Break: The Philosophy of Success

Here's my final point before moving into the retirement goal-setting element of this chapter: Managing goals and working on personal issues that affect our ability to achieve those goals is *hard work*. Along the way, you will tend to be tough on yourself—a natural byproduct of pushing to be successful. Be careful to manage the intensity of the toughness because it can work against you. People who are successful and who are great achievers have an exterior and an interior, just like the rest of us.

When Michael Jordan had a bad game, you could see the anger and disgust on his face. But I suspect the tape playing in his head was more balanced than the look on his face. That inner tape was probably being critical, supportive, and focused. He was likely mad at himself for not executing the way he knew he could and for not meeting a standard he had set through years of practice and game experience. But he also was likely to have put it into perspective and recognized that not every game would be the best game of his career. He probably reflected on his experience and his accomplishments and told himself not to be too hard on himself based on this one game or one experience. That's simply how successful people balance pushing themselves and supporting themselves. If the message is always negative, it is next to impossible to succeed. So the next time you get angry with yourself, put the experience into perspective, learn from it, and don't beat yourself up over it too much. After all, it was just another experience that brought positive change to your life.

Take a Current Snapshot

As you now get into the process I call goal-oriented retirement planning (GORP), you will have to do some work. I'm sure that when you picked up this book, you didn't expect that I would do all the work. This is the first chance for you to begin to get organized and start the planning process. What you'll need to do is take stock of your current financial picture by collecting information on all of your assets, liabilities, and objectives.

Tables 5–2—5–4 can serve as a rough guide to collecting the information that you need for this part of the book. Don't pay too much attention to the cost and time horizon of the "objectives" of the puzzle since we'll walk through that together. In the meantime, put down the book, collect the information, and we'll continue when you're ready.

Table 5–2   Sample Assets Assessment

Type of Asset	Current Value	Time Horizon
Home	$750,000	Long term
Mutual fund	$37,600	Long term
CD	$30,000	Short term

Table 5–3   Sample Liabilities Assessment

Type of Liability	Amount of Liability	Term
Home mortgage	$580,000	26 years
Car loan	$12,600	26 months
Second mortgage	$41,000	52 months

Table 5–4   Sample Objectives Assessment

Objective	Cost of Objective	Time Horizon
College education	$145,000	4 years
Salary replacement	$1,785,000	21 years
New car	$45,000	36 months

Now that you've collected the data we need to begin the process, let's review a harsh reality we need to face head on. Each of us will likely fall into one of four categories as it relates to achieving our retirement goals:

◆ **Those with no reasonable chance to retire without compromise.** I'm starting with this group because it is clearly the largest in our society today. These are harsh words to read, but unfortunately, some people simply have no chance of achieving their goal. For most of us, this is not someone else's problem—it's ours. The reasons are various, but the reality is no less painful. To understand the extent to which your goals might be compromised, you first need to have a goal. Second, you need to see what it will take to reach that goal, and finally, you must determine how realistic the goal is in light of the cost. If you find you cannot realistically achieve your goal, you have to quickly decide what compromises you are willing to make. Remember, we can adjust only two things in this formula: assets and liabilities. If you don't have sufficient assets to meet your liabilities, you must earn more, do better with your invested assets, or spend less. GORP is designed to help you with the framework to manage this process yourself or to elevate your level of understanding so that if you seek professional counsel, you are much better prepared to protect your best interests.

◆ **Those with some chance to retire without compromise.** If you fall into this category, you have a chance to meet your retirement goals, but you have to "mind the store." Retirement on your terms is not a certainty, and small misses in your accumulation of assets for retirement or miscalculation of expenses in retirement could easily force you to face compromises in your plan. You really need to be mindful of the tradeoffs between current spending and the impact that spending may have on reaching your goals. Monitoring is the key to success once you have properly aligned your goals.

◆ **Those who will likely retire without compromise.** This is a group of individuals who will likely be able to retire on their terms if they avoid major miscalculations or disasters. Many people in this group feel that because they have significant assets and a good income, they really don't need to plan for specific objectives. This is a dangerous but time-convenient philosophy. Even if you fall into this group, you should have a game plan for your retirement that you monitor on a scheduled basis.

◆ **Those who can't miss retiring without compromise.** The members of this fortunate group probably aren't reading this book or any book on retirement. They have so much money that even if they make a big mistake, it will have little impact on their retirement. For the rest of us, we need the help of a system to give us the best chance of retiring with compromise.

Taking Small Steps Through GORP

GORP is a way to break retirement planning down into small steps that are easy to establish, monitor, modify, and achieve. Rather than looking at financial or retirement planning as a monolithic task, GORP allows you to take a snapshot of the elements that go into your plan and lets you isolate and focus on single goals or events. Finally, GORP allows you to map assets to goals so that you match the characteristics of a given asset to the characteristics of a given goal.

The foundation of GORP is to create and foster the proper environment for planning. If we were attempting an assault on a mountain, particularly one with an elevation in excess of 15,000 feet, we would not simply drive our car to the starting point, throw on a backpack and start moving our legs uphill. Aside from the tactical preparation involving logistic arrangements such as food, clothing, equipment, and shelter, we would have physical preparation. That physical preparation involves the acclimation of your body to altitude to help avoid illnesses, like high-altitude pulmonary edema, which can result in death. To do that, climbers will sometimes spend months on the mountain going from one camp to the next and coming back down again to acclimate to the altitude.

Using GORP, you treat goals and assets separately. Once you have created your initial set of goals, you can apply assets to those goals to determine if you have sufficient assets to meet your needs. If you don't have sufficient assets, look at how much you need to save in addition to your current assets to reach your goal.

Establishing Your Goals

To illustrate the concept of GORP, let's look at our fictional family. Here are the family details:

- ◆ Dennis Glover—58 years old
- ◆ Mary Glover—56 years old
- ◆ Greg Glover—35 years old
- ◆ Connie Sharp Glover—35 years old
- ◆ Katie Glover—14 years old
- ◆ Tommy Glover—11 years old

The Glover family gives us the opportunity to look at a multigenerational family. Dennis and Mary Glover, the parents of Greg, have been married for 37 years. Their son Greg and his wife Connie, who are in their mid-30s, have been married for 15 years and have two kids, Katie and Tommy. Connie's parents have passed away, but the kids are fortunate to have Greg's parents around to provide lots of love and presents. Greg and Connie are concerned about saving for their retirement and are concerned about Greg's parents as well because they have been struggling to make ends meet.

They have decided that they need help in achieving their retirement goals. As a matter of fact, they recently realized that they really don't have any goals at all. Like so many of their friends, they have saved some money in their qualified plans and have been able to sock away the occasional bonus before it evaporates into clothes, food, or a vacation. But as they now look out into the future, they realize that before they know it, retirement will be right around the corner.

Common Mistake

We often take on more than we can handle. Take smaller steps and the task will seem less intimidating.

The first step for the Glovers using GORP is to define their goals without regard for how they will be achieved. The list of goals can be as long or as short as needed. What is important is that each goal has its own unique characteristics that have to ultimately be matched to one or more assets.

Let's take college education as an example. The Glovers are expecting both Katie and Tommy to go to college. To create a goal for college education, the Glovers have to analyze their need and determine the cost. They will need to take the following into account to create their goal:

◆ Cost of college in today's dollars, then adjusted forward for inflation.

◆ Numbers of years in college for each child, taking into account any possible post-graduate work.

◆ Any offsets such as scholarships or money the children will have to come up with to support their own education.

◆ Any special characteristics of the goal. In this example, the college cost will not be drawn down all at one time; rather, it will be paid out over a number of years. Also, since this goal is to fund college education, the Glovers may want to consider setting up a 529 plan (discussed later in this chapter) that allows them to put money away for the kids' college education without having to pay taxes on the money as it accumulates and as it's distributed (as long as the distribution is for college education).

In the case of the Glovers, they will have one child beginning college in four years and the other beginning college in seven years. We now have to make some assumptions for the Glovers to complete their goal. We'll assume that Katie and Tommy both want do post-graduate work, but Greg and Connie have made it clear to the kids that they need to help with the cost of post-graduate studies. If the children go to public colleges, the cost will be $145,000, and if they go to private colleges, it will cost $309,000. These estimates are based on college prices increasing at 5 percent a year. This rate of increase reflects the cost of college education at a growth rate higher than the rate of inflation, which historically has been the case.

Table 5–5 provides another look at the children's education assuming Katie (light gray) attends a public school and Tommy (dark gray) attends a private school. The black colored area shows the annual costs to the Glovers so that they see the annual cash flow drain associated with this scenario. As you can see, the total college cost under this scenario is $233,111, with the greatest cash outlay in 2011 when the two kids are in school simultaneously.

Table 5–5   The Glovers' College Plan

	Katie	**Tommy**	**Public**	**Private**	**Annual Cost**
2004	11	14	$12,831	$27,353	
2005	12	15	$13,473	$28,721	
2006	13	16	$14,146	$30,157	
2007	14	17	$14,853	$31,665	
2008	15	18	$15,596	$33,248	$15,596
2009	16	19	$16,376	$34,910	$16,376
2010	17	20	$17,195	$36,656	$17,195

Table 5–5   The Glovers' College Plan *(Continued)*

	Katie	Tommy	Public	Private	Annual Cost
2011	18	21	$18,055	$38,488	$56,543
2012	19	22	$18,957	$40,413	$40,413
2013	20	23	$19,905	$42,433	$42,433
2014	21	24	$20,900	$44,555	$44,555
2015	22	25	$21,945	$46,783	
Totals			**$67,221**	**$165,890**	**$233,111**

529 Plans

The Glovers may also want to look into 529 plans to save for college education expenses on a tax-free basis. When Congress passed the Small Business Job Protection Act of 1996, a provision was included to make it easier for families to save for college. Named after a section of the Internal Revenue Code, the Qualified Tuition Program (QTP), or 529 plan, formally recognized the need for families to save for college by authorizing terrific features like tax-deferred accumulation and favorable tax treatment of qualified withdrawals. These plans are broadly available for college savings programs and prepaid tuition programs.

Most 529 plans have the following significant tax advantages in common:

◆ **Tax-deferred accumulation.** Investment earnings in a 529 college savings plan accumulate federal income tax-deferred until the money is withdrawn, meaning that your savings are able to grow faster than comparable taxable accounts. State income tax treatment may vary.

◆ **Federal tax-free earnings.** Investment earnings will be distributed federal income tax-free when used for qualified higher education expenses.

◆ **Reduction in estate taxes.** Contributions are considered gifts and are typically excluded from the account owner's estate.

◆ **Accelerated gift tax treatment.** 529 plans qualify for a special gift tax exclusion. You can elect to contribute up to $55,000 per beneficiary free of gift taxes or $110,000 if you are married filing jointly in one lump sum, to as many beneficiaries as you desire.

Once you make this maximum gift, however, you cannot make any other gifts to that beneficiary for five years. Alternatively, you may make annual contributions of up to $11,000 per beneficiary (or $22,000 if married filing jointly) and qualify for the gift tax exclusion. Contributions in excess of $55,000 will reduce your unified gift tax credit.

Most 529 plans have the following control over assets and beneficiaries:

◆ **Broad control and use of assets.** 529 college savings plans allow the account owner to maintain control over the assets for the life of the account. Plan assets can be used to pay for qualified higher education expenses such as tuition, fees, room and board, books, and supplies at any accredited post-secondary institution in the United States, whether the program is for two years or four years.

◆ **Flexible beneficiary designation.** You can change beneficiaries to another "family member" of the original beneficiary at any time without penalty. You can name anyone as a beneficiary—a child, an adult, or even yourself.

◆ **Penalty-free withdrawals.** Funds can be withdrawn without penalty if the beneficiary receives a scholarship for an amount up to the scholarship amount or in the event of the death or disability of the beneficiary. Ordinary income taxes would be owed on any investment earnings included in gross income.

Next Steps

The Glovers have now completed their first goal and can bookmark the cost of that goal in their planning. The next step is for the Glovers to repeat this process for every goal that they can currently identify. The general formula for establishing those goals should be the same:

1. Define the cost in today's dollars.

2. Inflate the cost based on the number of years between today and the expected date the goal needs to be achieved.

3. Define the characteristics of each goal so that when we match the assets to the goals, we can be consistent.

Adding Goals and Prioritizing

Now it's time for you to begin to lay out your own goals for retirement planning. Table 5–6 lists some broad categories for you to consider, with some specific goals as subcategories. By breaking these out into as many goals as possible, we achieve two things:

- We make the overall process easier to understand because it's easier to tackle a bunch of smaller goals than one large goal.

- We can prioritize the goals in the event that we cannot reach all of them. This is going to be very important considering our earlier discussion about being realistic in our goal setting.

Table 5–6   Sample Goals for GORP

Category	Goals
Home	First home, vacation home, retirement residence
Transportation	Car, boat, RV
Education	College for self, child, or grandchild; student loan repayment; golf lessons; piano lessons
Estate	Funding inheritance
Personal	Credit card repayment, country club membership
Retirement	Income replacement, life expectancy emergency fund, Social Security maximizer
Medical	Braces, nursing home (self or parent), Medicare/Medicaid
Business	Start your own
Home Improvement	Remodel, addition, patio, pool

Matching Assets to Goals

Once you have completed your initial goal setting, you should be left with aggregate goals that reflect the total future cost to fund your retirement plan. Now that you have the cost side of the equation laid out, we need to take stock (pun intended) of both your assets and your cash flow to see how they match up to your goals as well as determine where you need to save more or modify your goals.

Be Careful

Liquidity and marketability are two similar yet different characteristics for describing the state of an asset. As an example, real estate is very marketable but generally not very liquid. Money markets, on the other hand, are both liquid and marketable.

Each asset you own has a series of characteristics that will ultimately determine how you apply that asset to one or more of your goals. We discuss these characteristics in greater detail in Chapter 12 where we cover managing your investments. However, some basic level of understanding is required at this point to allow you to assign assets to goals. Table 5–7 shows a variety of investments and then looks at several characteristics of those investments.

The first characteristic is the expected term of the investment. Some investments are better suited to long-term goals and others to short-term goals. As you can see from the table, stocks can be either short- or long-term investments, but for the most part, you don't want to be on the short side with stocks too often because you are increasing your risk and are not being very tax efficient. Great short-term investments are money markets, bank certificates of deposit (CDs), savings accounts, and Treasury bills. Long-term investments include real estate, stocks, bonds, and related mutual funds.

Wake-Up Call

The longer you wait to start saving for retirement, the harder it gets. Compound interest works in your favor when you save early and works against you when you save late.

The next characteristic is liquidity, the amount of time it takes to get your money. Liquidity is very important to us when we need money.

Some investments, such as money markets are highly liquid, whereas other investments, such as real estate, are not considered by experts to be very liquid at all. Some investments are liquid at a cost. If you own a two-year CD and want to cash out before the maturity date, you can forfeit up to six months' interest and in some cases even lose principal.

The final characteristic that we will consider here is the investment's sensitivity to inflation. Inflation erodes our buying power and can also erode the value of certain investments. For example, bonds and bond funds do not perform well during inflationary times since interest rates are rising. At the opposite end are investments like gold and real estate that tend to do well in inflationary times, or perhaps more aptly stated, they perform better relative to other investments during inflationary periods. I should add I don't consider gold to be a good investment tool, and you can read more on that subject in Chapter 10.

Table 5–7   Investment Characteristics

Type of Asset	Term	Liquidity	Inflation Sensitive
Stocks	Mid-long	High	Moderate
Bonds	Mid-long	High	High
Stock mutual funds	Mid-long	High	Moderate
Bond mutual funds	Mid-long	High	High
Real estate investment trusts	Mid-long	High	Low
Gold	Long	Low	Low
Money market	Short	High	Low
CD	Short	High	Low
Art	Long	Low	Low
Real estate	Mid-long	Low	Low

Savings Tip

Banks offer short-term products called certificates of deposit (CDs) that are insured by the Federal Deposit Insurance Corporation (FDIC) up to the maximums and enjoy higher rates of return than regular savings or money market accounts.

Matching the characteristics of your assets to the characteristics of your goals is critical to the success of GORP. The essence of GORP is to not only make it easier for you to organize and articulate your goals, but also to more efficiently manage the investments required to achieve those goals.

GORP forces you to be disciplined in your approach to investing by creating the path to systematic investing and by forcing you to invest in only that which is consistent with your goals. All too often we invest for the wrong reasons. We get a stock tip, we read an article, or maybe we just throw a bonus from work into a mutual fund. But what we don't do is think about what that investment means to our big-picture retirement plan. How does that stock or mutual fund tie in specifically to a stated goal?

Let's take our goal of funding college education for the Glover kids and see how GORP maps assets to goals (see Table 5–8). We know the Glovers have decided on the goal of sending Katie and Tommy to college. We also know the anticipated cost is $233,111 over a seven-year period starting in 2008. Consider the snapshot of the Glovers' assets and their value today and growth over the next 20 years using some assumed rates of growth. The rate of growth is not what is important here, so don't get caught up in the specifics. We'll have plenty of time to discuss assumed rates of growth later in the book.

The shaded area represents the only practical sources of funding for this goal based on matching objectives. The easy ones to eliminate are Greg's 401(k) and Connie's IRA because these are assets that will be assigned to providing retirement income. The primary house could actually be a funding source, but it comes at a price because pulling equity from the house will create a larger mortgage and increase expenses. The logical alternatives are the money market, the CD, the stocks, and the mutual fund. Using GORP, we need to choose one or more of these as sources for our goal. The best match would be either the money market account or the CD because they are highly liquid assets.

Managing the Shortfall

The problem the Glovers will have is one many other families will face as well: They simply don't have enough money to meet their needs without losing balance in their overall retirement plan. Under their current investment strategy, the college education alone will wipe out their liquid assets, leaving them with their retirement plans and their home as their key assets. As I said earlier, one of the key benefits of GORP is that it isolates the real problem the minute you start to match assets to goals. The

Table 5-8 Matching the Glovers' Goal-Based Objectives

	Primary House	Greg's 401(k)	Connie's IRA	Money Market	CD	Stocks	Equity MF
2004	800,000	82,000	57,000	60,000	25,000	18,000	32,000
2005	824,000	86,920	60,420	61,200	25,750	19,260	33,600
2006	848,720	92,135	64,045	62,424	26,523	20,608	35,280
2007	874,182	97,663	67,888	63,672	27,318	22,051	37,044
2008	900,407	103,523	71,961	64,946	28,138	23,594	38,896
2009	927,419	109,734	76,279	66,245	28,982	25,246	40,841
2010	955,242	116,319	80,856	67,570	29,851	27,013	42,883
2011	983,899	123,298	85,707	68,921	30,747	28,904	45,027
2012	1,013,416	130,696	90,849	70,300	31,669	30,927	47,279
2013	1,043,819	138,537	96,300	71,706	32,619	33,092	49,643
2014	1,075,133	146,850	102,078	73,140	33,598	35,409	52,125

Table 5-8 Matching the Glovers' Goal-Based Objectives (*Continued*)

	Primary House	Greg's 401(k)	Connie's IRA	Money Market	CD	Stocks	Equity MF
2015	1,107,387	155,660	108,203	74,602	34,606	37,887	54,731
2016	1,140,609	165,000	114,695	76,095	35,644	40,539	57,467
2017	1,174,827	174,900	121,577	77,616	36,713	43,377	60,341
2018	1,210,072	185,394	128,872	79,169	37,815	46,414	63,358
2019	1,246,374	196,518	136,604	80,752	38,949	49,663	66,526
2020	1,283,765	208,309	144,800	82,367	40,118	53,139	69,852
2021	1,322,278	220,807	153,488	84,014	41,321	56,859	73,345
2022	1,361,946	234,056	162,697	85,695	42,561	60,839	77,012
2023	1,402,805	248,099	172,459	87,409	43,838	65,097	80,862
2024	1,444,889	262,985	182,807	89,157	45,153	69,654	84,906

Glovers have to decide how they will solve the problem. They can get part of the way there with their current investments, but they will need to save more to comfortably achieve their goal. Another option would be for Greg and Connie to explain to the kids that they simply can't afford to fund a private school education and they both have to go to public schools.

Common Mistakes

Are you carrying credit card debt? If you are, you are inevitably paying far too much in interest that cannot be deducted on your taxes.

Any time you are faced with a shortfall, you must determine what compromises you are willing to make to achieve the goal. These aren't always easy decisions, but by creating smaller goals, you can manage smaller problems should there be a disconnect between the goal and your assets.

I wish there were an easy answer for everyone when it comes to managing the shortfall. Too often, we shrug our shoulders assuming that the problem will go away through inheritance or a lottery ticket. Sometimes we assume that someone else, perhaps our spouse or a financial planner, will solve the problem. Unfortunately, that's not the most prudent approach to financial planning. This is the hard stuff—no easy answers, just compromise. My best advice to you is to sit down and discuss the shortfall with your spouse and professionals you trust. Often, you can correct the shortfall by repositioning existing assets and by being more prudent about saving money.

Let's move on, but not before helping the Glovers with their goal. If the Glovers want to leave the goal intact, they will need to save an additional $1,000 each month for the next four years. This will allow them to fund the kids' education without totally depleting their current savings of $155,000. You get this number by adding up the four possible investments that can be utilized for this goal. The $155,000 is not enough by itself to pay for the education, though by saving $1,000 a month, the Glovers can afford to pay for the education and still have $15,000 to assign to another goal.

Another option the Glovers have is to reduce the amount needed for the goal by going back to the kids and limiting their choices to only public schools. By doing that, they reduce the cost to $145,000. If they make that change alone, they can achieve their goal and have $40,000 to assign to another goal. As you can see, this is all about options that you have and options that you need to create a solid retirement solution.

Modifying and Achieving Your Goals

Once you have completed the initial phases of defining goals and applying assets, you need to set up a schedule to review your progress. You also need to make certain you modify your goals as needed. For example, if Katie Glover were to receive a scholarship to go to college with all expenses paid, Katie's parents could modify their goal, which would allow them to reassign the asset they attached to that education goal. It's always good to set up regular meetings to discuss these goals, and I would suggest you do so at least quarterly.

Planning Your Retirement Goals

It is well beyond the scope of this book to take each retirement planning goal and build out the objectives and the costs. That is personal work that you'll have to do. You will find more specific examples of how to use GORP in Chapter 15. My purpose is to help you walk through the most important goal that you will have: funding your postretirement needs. The balance of this chapter focuses on defining your goals for retirement.

Budgeting for Your Objectives

Most of us do not use a budget. Budgeting for a lot of people is the financial version of getting on the scale, and the reasons for avoiding both are essentially the same: We don't want to know the truth about our finances just as we don't want to know the truth about our weight. It's actually pretty interesting. We kind of know how much money we spend, just as we can use our clothes as a gauge if we need to lose some weight. We do it by feel.

INFORMATION

Web Site Information

There are a number of budgeting software programs, but the leader is clearly Quicken at *www.quicken.com.*

Unfortunately, we can't play it loose when talking about our retirement. Your work here and now is to commit to building and living by a budget. I can tell you you'll be glad that you did once you have it set up. If you already have a budget, good for you—you'll be able to move on to modifying your budget for postretirement planning. If you haven't built a budget, all you have to do is fill in the blanks. In the Appendix, I have provided a sample budget, and you can also see one on the *www.retirement-countdown.com* Web site. However you get it done, you need to know where your money is coming from and where it is going before moving on to the next step in the process.

Key Point

Budgeting for some people is the financial version of getting on the scale.

Retirement as a Goal

The biggest and arguably the most important goal that you will have in your financial plan is your retirement. I recommend that you consider the complete retirement picture as a goal, but if you find that it helps to break it up by establishing smaller goals, that works just as well.

To set up your retirement goal, you need to determine all of the elements of your retirement to help in defining the costs. The reason that you need to have your preretirement budget established is that the work you have done will provide the foundation for the modifications that we need to make in retirement. For example, while you are working, your employer will typically pay for the cost of health care. But when you retire, this is a cost that you will have to bear.

Savings Tip

You may want to look at guaranteeing a part of your retirement income by purchasing an immediate annuity. These contracts can be structured to pay out a specific amount of money for the rest of your life. Consider this option only as part of a balanced retirement income strategy.

We need to go back through the budget and update the expense side of the equation for your postretirement life. To help you put the expense side into perspective as you plan, the following sections provide information on the areas for which your expense budget will likely go up and down during retirement.

Expenses That Tend to Increase During Retirement

With changes in lifestyle after you retire, you could be spending more money related to health, recreation, your home, and your hobbies.

Medical   As previously mentioned, your medical costs will increase postretirement, and you'll need to budget for this expense accordingly. After you retire, you will likely be covered by Medicare. Medicare coverage is defined more thoroughly in Chapter 6, but generally speaking, Medicare provides hospital benefits at no cost and medical benefits at a cost of approximately $800 per year. Unfortunately, Medicare has very limited benefits, and many people choose to supplement Medicare with private insurance generically called MediGap, while others layer in long-term care insurance for catastrophic illnesses that require very expensive care. You'll need to quantify these costs in your state, but for bookmarking a budget number, you should assume $10,000 to cover your bases if you want complete coverage.

Be careful not to underestimate the cost of healthcare. Over the three-year period of 2001–2003, healthcare costs rose by an estimated 20 percent each year. In addition, longer life expectancies have resulting in postretirement headaches for many people when it comes to medical expenses.

Recreation, Travel, and Entertainment   Most retirees grossly underestimate the additional costs associated with recreation, travel, and entertainment. When you retire, you do more, not less. You'll eat out more, you'll travel more, and you'll buy the kids and grandkids more presents. These additional costs must be factored into your budget. The best way to do that is to look at what you've spent in previous years and increase that number by 20 percent for the first five years you are in retirement. If you haven't budgeted in the past, you need to sit down and think about the average number of times you eat out, the average number of vacations, and so on, and then you need to increase that number by 20 percent.

Home Improvements   While you're working, there is little time to do anything other than basic maintenance around the house. After you retire, you are likely to face many critical decisions. One that often comes up is what do you plan to do with your home? Many people will sell their homes and move into a smaller home, a condo, or an apartment. But those who choose to remain in their residence, often redecorate and make the home more of a retirement residence. Any additional cost associated with those improvements will drive up the initial cost of retirement.

Hobbies   When people retire, they have the time to devote to their hobbies. This could result in added cost to the budget depending on the particular hobby.

Expenses That Tend to Decrease During Retirement

On the other side of the equation, you may save some budget dollars in a number of areas. These include work-related costs such as dry cleaning, lunches, transportation, and clothing. In addition, discounts given to senior citizens (and in many cases, reduced taxes) all add up to saved dollars.

The Bottom Line on Postretirement Cost

In the end, you need to understand how much more or less you will spend in retirement so that you have an accurate number to use when setting your goal. I wish I could share some statistics with you that support my contention that postretirement spending is greater than preretirement spending for at least the first five years. Although that statistic is not readily available, I have spoken with a number of people anecdotally who have confirmed this assumption.

To give a visual sense of what I'm suggesting, look at Figure 5–1. What you see is a curve that represents spending five years before retirement and then 20 years following retirement. I have increased the cost of expenses by 3 percent each year starting at $100,000 per year to cover inflation. I have also increased postretirement spending by 15 percent for the first five years and then stepped down expenses by 5 percent twice during the next 15 years. This is not perfect science, but it does provide you with a visual concept of this discussion point.

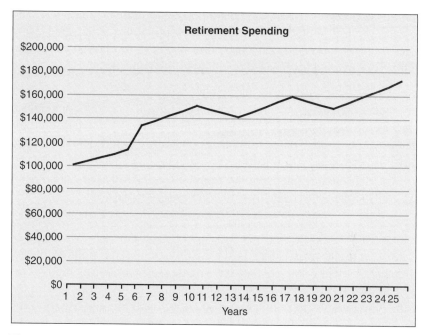

Figure 5–1   Retirement Spending

Life Expectancy and Your Retirement

With all of the medical and health advances over the past several decades, life expectancy has increased dramatically. What that means for many of us is that we will be living up to a third of our lives after we retire. Perhaps even more dramatic is the realization that for every year you work, you will have to earn enough to support one half of a year of retirement.

Be Careful

Life expectancy is a key ingredient in planning for retirement. If you underestimate your life expectancy, you could run out of money when you can least afford to.

If you are in good heath at age 65, the likelihood is that you will live until you are in your mid-to late 80s. You can't afford to underestimate your life expectancy when establishing your retirement goal. You can, however, modify your life expectancy as you can any other goal using GORP, but the consequences can be dire if you're too late to be able to modify your income level based on a longer life expectancy.

INFORMATION

Web Site Information

There are a number of life expectancy calculators online, but an interesting one is on the Northwestern Mutual Web site at *http:// www.nmfn.com/tn/learnctr--lifeevents--longevity.*

Another issue to consider is the quality of life we want to live in retirement. A lot of folks feel they have made sacrifices during their working years that they don't want to make after they retire. A minister in the Pacific Northwest once said, "We've added years to life, not life to years. Life is not measured by the number of breaths we take, but by the moments that take our breath away."

Do You Want to Have Leftovers?

One of the more sensitive areas for us to cover is inheritance and the way that impacts GORP. If it is important to you to leave assets to children, grandchildren, religious organizations, or others, you need to plan that as one of your goals. You also have to decide if you want to deplete your assets as your life expectancy reduces over the years or if you want your assets to remain stable over your retirement whereby you live off the interest alone. It is very expensive to live off interest, and most people won't be able to afford this option.

It is wise, however, to create a life expectancy emergency fund. Here's how that would work: You and spouse determine that your combined life expectancy is 27 years. But what if you live beyond 27 years? The goal of the life expectancy emergency fund is to ensure that if you live beyond your life expectancy, you have income to meet your needs. You can do this by having sufficient assets to produce the necessary income, or you can buy an income annuity that guarantees a certain amount of money for the rest of your life. Either way, you need to identify it as a goal and properly fund the goal.

Charitable Giving and Charitable Trusts

You may find yourself wanting to establish a goal of either giving or leaving money to a charity. There are a number of ways to do this, starting with an outright gift. Obviously, any gift that you give has to be accounted for in your retirement planning because it's an asset that can no longer be applied to a goal. Of course, the good news is that your charitable donations have the double benefit of aiding the organization and you. The charity gets the cash, stock, or other asset, and you receive a tax deduction.

If your assets are relatively unlimited, you will likely be setting up a foundation from which your donations can be managed and doled out with as much discipline and discretion as you like. If you have moderate assets and you itemize your taxes, you might consider a donor-advisor fund. This is a fund managed by a professional money manager on behalf of a foundation or a financial institution. Most major fund families like Fidelity and Vanguard sponsor donor-advisor funds. With a donor-advisor fund, you can make the irrevocable donation to the foundation or financial institution and choose when you want assets to be distributed to the charities of your choice. The minimum donation is typically from $5,000 to $25,000, and the fee for managing the donor-advisor fund is usually 1 percent of assets. In addition to the charitable trust management, you have the mutual fund fee associated with the choices that you make for having the money invested prior to distribution to the charity.

The tax benefits are a nice advantage as well. You can deduct up to 50 percent of your adjusted gross income in any given year. So, for a couple or an individual in the 35 percent tax bracket, a $10,000 donation generates a $3,500 tax savings. You can donate stock instead of or in addition to cash subject to the 50 percent rule. The nice thing about donating stock is that your tax deduction is based on the value of the stock at the time of the donation, not at the value at which you purchased the stock.

Let's say that you own 1,000 shares of GE stock at $30 per share. When you make the donation to the donor-advisor fund, the stock price has appreciated to $40 per share. You get credit for a $40,000 donation and you don't have to pay capital gains tax on the $10,000. Obviously, you would never want to donate a stock on which you have a loss because you would also lose the capital loss tax advantage.

You can also give the gift that keeps on giving by setting up a charitable remainder trust. The concept is similar to that for the donor-advisor fund, but in this case, the donation is made to a trust, which typically sells your donated asset but generates income back to you for use during the remainder of your life, hence the title "remainder trust."

Charitable trusts are most commonly used by those with estates that are significant and by donors who want to move assets out of the estate but generate an income on the donated asset until they die. This is accomplished through either a charitable remainder annuity trust (CRAT) or a charitable remainder unitrust (CRUT). With a CRAT, you receive a fixed dollar amount per year, and with a CRUT, you get a fixed percentage of the asset. The assets used to set up these trusts are almost always highly appreciated assets. They may be real, like art or real estate, or they may be a stock or bond. These are also likely to be assets that are not generating an income, a common goal of the donor setting up a remainder trust. When you donate an asset like real estate or art, a charity can sell the asset without taxes and provide income to the donor.

The final trust option that we'll look at is called the charitable lead trust (CLT). A CLT works just the opposite of the CRT. It is not the donation made to the charity but the income from the asset for a specific period of time, say 20 years, that is the asset. At the end of the period, the asset reverts to whomever you name as the remainder beneficiary. The asset is then distributed to the beneficiaries per the owner's wishes.

Gifting

If you plan to give assets as gifts, this also needs to be a goal that is funded or recognized as an expense that will impact your ability to save. Obviously, you can't gift an asset and still apply it to an objective. You and your spouse are currently allowed to gift up to $11,000 per year each ($22,000), up to a lifetime maximum of $1,000,000. You should always check to make certain that you have the latest gift tax credit information because it changes periodically.

Creating Your Income Replacement Goal

Once we have isolated the amount of income we need to live on and have gotten comfortable with our life expectancy, we can set our sights on creating a goal. The goal is stated as income replacement, and the formula looks something like this:

Total budgeted expenses −
expected Social Security and pension benefits ×
life expectancy =
lump-sum or periodical payments required

You can solve for the one-time cost to provide this goal, but you'll most likely want to solve for the annual cost of funding this goal. You can also solve for funding this goal over a specific number of years.

Let's assume that our total budgeted expenses are $100,000 per year and we expect a total of $15,500 from Social Security and pension benefits. This leaves us with $84,500 to fund each year for 22 years, assuming that we use age 87 as our life expectancy. To calculate the amount we need to have available to meet our goal, we also need to input the amount of money we currently have available to meet this goal. If we have $250,000 in available assets today, we would need to find another $1,000,000 to meet our goal or be willing to contribute $34,000 per year for the next 20 years. If we were starting without any savings, the numbers would be even more dramatic. We would need $1.5 million or be willing to save $50,000 a year for 20 years.

Don't worry—you won't have to do the math for these calculations because a variety of calculators are available for you to use on your own or with a financial planner. Alternatively, visit *www.retirementcountdown.com* and use the GORP tools.

Summary

All chapters of this book are important for you to understand, but this is the most critical. This is the foundation that teaches us to break these big goals down into smaller goals, to get our arms around them, and to keep us from procrastinating. It also underscores the need for us to plan, plan, and plan. Waiting is the worst thing you can do if you have any doubts about your ability to meet your retirement goals.

I also want to put another point into perspective as we close this chapter. As a writer and someone who has lived in the financial services industry for 25 years, I sometimes struggle with finding a balance between providing too much information and not providing enough. This chapter exemplifies that struggle. If given the luxury of limitless pages to write and without concern for losing your attention, I could write a book on this chapter's content alone. But the practical reality is that I have limited time and space to accomplish my mission, which is getting you started on the road to defining and reaching your retirement goals.

Wake-Up Call

A key reason that people do nothing is that they believe that if they don't take action, they can't fail. This is very flawed logic; for most people, doing nothing about their retirement will result in failure rather than the achievement of their goals.

As I said earlier and will undoubtedly say again, you have to do a lot of this work. And if you don't have the time to invest, do some soul searching and muster up the effort to bring in some help.

Power Checklist

- ✔ With financial planning in general, and retirement planning specifically, it is imperative that the planning process begin as early as possible. You can't make up for time lost in the savings process.

- ✔ When faced with financial adversity, make the decision to do something about it.

- ✔ Put failure into perspective by changing the lens you use to view the results. There are two possible results to any action, and we learn from both.

- ✔ It has often been said that success is the result of preparation meeting opportunity.

- ✔ If you find that you cannot realistically achieve your goal, you have to quickly decide what compromises you are willing to make.

- ✔ Goal-oriented retirement planning (GORP) is a way to break financial planning down into small steps that are easy to monitor, modify, and achieve.

- ✔ Matching the characteristics of your assets to the characteristics of your goals is critical to the success of GORP.

✔ GORP forces you to be disciplined in your approach to investing by creating the path to systematic investing and by forcing you to invest in only what is consistent with your stated goals.

✔ One of the key benefits of GORP is that it isolates the real problem the minute you start to match assets to goals.

✔ You have to decide if you want to exhaust your assets over the balance of your life expectancy or keep your assets intact and just use the earnings to meet your needs.

✔ Planning takes time, lots of it. Make the time or get someone to help.

✔ You may want to look at charitable donations. If you don't have millions to donate, look at donor-advisor funds. If you have millions, look at setting up your own foundation and look into charitable remainder trusts and charitable lead trusts.

✔ If you plan to gift assets, you also need to fund that goal or recognize it as an expense that will impact your ability to save.

PART II

UNDERSTANDING RISK AND YOUR PRODUCT CHOICES

CHAPTER 6

Understanding and Managing Risk

Does a trapeze artist work without a net? Does a mountain climber ascend without being tied off? Does a surgeon operate without sterilized equipment? Does a person invest without regard for risk? The answer to all these questions should be a resounding *no!* Unfortunately, we often leap before we look, and the consequences can be less than optimal.

Wake-Up Call

Risk management is pervasive in all aspects of our lives, but we sometimes overlook the tools or tasks used to ensure that we reach our retirement goals. Saving now and spending later is one way of managing the risk of retiring without sufficient assets.

Risk management is the application of products, services, and techniques to reduce or eliminate the element of risk from a given situation. Another way to look at risk management is to look at obstacles that may keep you from achieving your goals. Those obstacles pose a risk to you, and anything you can do to mitigate that risk helps you achieve your goal. This chapter covers the types of risk associated with financial planning and some options available to you to reduce that risk.

Many Ways to Manage Risk

When you ask people what they think risk management means, they'll generally tell you insurance. That's not a bad answer because much of our risk is contracted out to a third party like an insurance company. But true risk management touches all parts of life.

If following September 11, 2001, you went out and purchased items for your home that provided additional security, you engaged in risk management. We do it all the time and don't think twice about it. We fasten our seat belts, we install childproof cabinet locks, and we have our teeth cleaned. Much of what we take for granted in our daily lives is actually a form of risk management. What we need to do now is assess risk and the management of that risk as it applies to our retirement savings.

First let's look broadly at the common risks that we face in financial and retirement planning:

- You'll live too long.

- You'll die too soon.

- Your marriage won't last.

- The market will go down and you'll lose.

- The market will go up and you'll lose.

- The company whose stock or bond you buy will go out of business.

- You will no longer be able to work because of a disability.

- Your spouse will die and you won't be able to handle the remaining responsibilities.

- You don't have sufficient assets to meet your retirement goals.

- You won't be able to fund schooling for your kids.

These are all common risks we face in day-to-day life, and how we choose to face them will ultimately determine our ability to minimize these risks. There are other broad risks that each of the common risks above may fit into, but to further our education, let's consider the broader risks and how they can be managed.

Types of Risk

A variety of risks fundamentally apply to financial services in general and retirement products specifically. There are also additional risks that would not typically be associated with investments or financial planning that you may want to add to the list. By the end of this chapter, you'll not only be able to add a given risk but will also be in a better position to think through ways to mitigate that risk.

For example, let's say that you and your spouse have dramatically different thoughts on investment risk. Taking this a bit further, assume you're willing to take moderate to high risk levels on a portion of your investment to achieve the potentially greater reward, but your spouse is not willing to take any risk and wants to invest only in products with no risk of principal. The risk here can be defined as the risk of not achieving your retirement goal. If your spouse will not compromise, you have to mitigate the risk of not achieving your goal by increasing your savings or modifying the goal.

Savings Tip

Keep in mind that securities vary in risk. Picking different investments with different rates of return will help ensure that large gains offset losses in other areas.

Systematic Investment Risk

Systematic investment risk represents risks that are... predictable. Unsystematic investment risks are those that are out of our direct control, such as events like 9/11 or Hurricane Hugo. These unsystematic risks will impact our investments, but there isn't anything we can do from an investment standpoint to avoid them. Systematic investment risk represents known risks that, while we have little control over them, we can reduce or eliminate. The following sections discuss the systematic investment risks that you should be familiar with.

Market Risk

Sometimes known as volatility, market risk is typically the first risk that people try to quantify. Market risk is what leads us to the taking Pepto Bismol on days when the market is down and giving high fives when the market is up. Volatility is movement up or down during a given period of time. The more the stock or bond moves in shorter periods of time, the greater the volatility.

Volatility is actually a reactive tool and the result of a behavior, not the behavior itself. For example, the news about a company will drive its stock price up or down. Volatility is simply the quantification of the result of that news and the resulting effect on the stock. There is more on this topic later in the book when we talk about the beta coefficient, a close kin to volatility.

Credit and Business Risk

Credit and business risk is the risk that a company will be unable to pay the contractual interest or principal on its debt obligations or that the company actually goes out of business. Take United Airlines as an example. When it declared Chapter 11 bankruptcy in 2003, it immediately began its reorganization. As a result, United's stock was delisted (taken off the major New York Stock Exchange) and its bond prices, which had already gone in the tank, dropped even further.

More Information

Each of the major stock exchanges requires that listed companies maintain specified standards. When a company declares Chapter 11 and files to reorganize, it is common for the exchange on which the stock is listed to delist the stock. This does not necessarily mean that you can't trade the stock. The stock will most likely continue to trade over the counter but not on a listed exchange. See Chapter 7 for more details.

Rating agencies such as Standard & Poor's and Moody's rate corporate bonds from a high of AAA to a low of C (see Table 6–1). The lower the rating, the greater the risk and the more the company will have to pay to attract bond investors.

Table 6–1   Rating Corporate Bonds

Bond Ratings	S&P	Moody's
Highest quality	AAA	Aaa
High quality	AA	Aa
Upper medium quality	A	A
Medium grade	BBB	Baa
Somewhat speculative	BB	Ba
Low grade, speculative	B	B
Low grade, default possible	CCC	Caa
Low grade, partial recovery possible	CC	Ca
Default, recovery unlikely	C	C

Credit risk is of particular concern to investors who hold bonds in their portfolios. The lowest risk bonds are government bonds, especially those issued by the federal government; corporate bonds typically have the most credit risk but also have the higher interest rates. The lowest five grades from either Standard & Poor's or Moody's are not considered investment grade, meaning that they are termed "junk bonds."

Foreign Investment Risk

Foreign investment risk refers to the risk that a foreign company or a foreign government won't be able to honor its financial commitments. When a country defaults on its obligations, it can also harm the value or performance of the companies that are based in that country. Foreign investment risk applies to stocks, bonds, mutual funds, options, and futures that are issued by other countries or companies other than those in the United States. This type of risk is realized by many investors in emerging markets or countries that have a severe deficit.

Consider the reliance of U.S. companies on foreign markets and measure that risk. If Pepsi were generating 80 percent of its revenues from foreign countries or companies, Pepsi stock would likely be more negatively impacted by international affairs than would the stock of a competitor that generates only 20 percent of its revenues overseas.

Currency Risk (Foreign Exchange Risk)

Currency, or foreign exchange, risk is different from the foreign investment risk in that this is the risk that the currency of a given country fluctuates significantly against the dollar and impacts the companies you have invested in as well as the stock prices themselves. Currency risk applies to all financial instruments that are in a currency other than your U.S. dollars. Foreign stocks are usually traded as American Depository Receipts (ADRs) to make it easier for U.S. investors. But if the underlying value of a foreign currency fluctuates significantly against the dollar, your investment may be in for a ride up or down as a result of that fluctuation.

Currency risk can also work to the benefit of a company and hence its stock value. In the case of Eastman Kodak, for instance, if the yen is strong against the dollar, it provides a competitive advantage for Kodak over its biggest Japanese competitor, Fuji. Because of a weaker dollar, Kodak film is likely to be less expensive to a Japanese consumer than Fuji is.

Interest Rate Risk

Rising and falling interest rates have a direct impact on bonds and a less direct impact on stocks. The effect is more dramatic on bonds because the yield (payment) on bonds is interest-rate sensitive. The effect on stocks is not as direct, but higher interest rates mean higher costs to companies that need to use debt to finance their businesses, and those costs will be borne either by the consumer through higher prices or by the business through lower margins.

Table 6–2 is a good example of interest-rate risk. Let's say you buy a bond that has a 5 percent coupon and a 23-year maturity. The table shows how the value is affected by interest rate (yields) changes. As you can see, a 3 percent increase in interest rates results in a 33.80% loss in value, whereas a 3 percent decrease in interest rates results in a gain of 67.20 percent in value.

You must also be aware of a risk related to interest rate risk and that's reinvestment risk. If you own income-producing investments, you'll have to make an assumption as to what interest rate you'll earn on any reinvestment of income received. To the extent your assumptions are too high, you may not achieve your goal because the reinvestment of income is included in our goal setting.

INFORMATION

More Information

You'll learn more about bonds in the next chapter, but a bond has a price, a maturity, and a coupon. The price is what you pay for it, the maturity is when the bond is due to be paid back, and the coupon is the interest that is paid to you each month, quarter, or year. As the coupon rate or yield on new bonds is established, it can affect the value of the bond that you own.

Inflation Risk

Inflation risk is the risk that any investment will not keep up with inflation. To mitigate inflation risk, people often turn to real estate and gold. Another alternative would be indexed CDs or indexed annuities.

Table 6–3 and Figure 6–1 illustrate how the S&P 500 and the Dow Industrial Average have tracked against inflation. You can view the visual graph or look at the data on a year-by-year basis. You'll note that the S&P underperformed inflation 30 percent of the last 10 years and the Dow underperformed inflation by 40 percent over the past 10 years. Figure 6–1 uses numbers from July 1, 1993, through June 30, 2003.

Diversification Risk

Diversification risk is the "all-your-eggs-in-one-basket" risk. Diversification of your portfolio creates balance and reduces the volatility of the portfolio.

Table 6–2   Bond Price Value 5% Coupon

			Bond Price Value 5% Coupon			
Yield	8%	7%	6%	5%	4%	3%	2%
Value	$662	$752	$862	$1,000	$1,173	$1,392	$1,672
Difference	–33.80%	–24.80%	–13.80%	0	17.30%	39.20%	67.20%

Table 6–3   Tracking Inflation, 1994–2003

	1994	1995	1996	1997	1998	1999	2000	2001	2002	2003
Inflation (%)	2.61	2.81	2.93	2.34	1.55	2.19	3.38	2.83	1.59	2.32
S&P (%)	2.26	22.65	13.86	49.12	17.43	18.56	9.47	–16.73	–24.74	7.75
Difference (points)	–0.35	19.84	10.93	46.78	15.88	16.37	6.09	–19.56	–26.33	5.43
Inflation (%)	2.61	2.81	2.93	2.34	1.55	2.19	3.38	2.83	1.59	2.32
Dow (%)	4.00	25.00	26.00	35.00	17.00	22.00	–6.00	1.00	–13.00	–1.00
Difference (points)	1.39	22.19	23.07	32.66	15.45	19.81	–9.38	–1.83	–14.59	–3.32

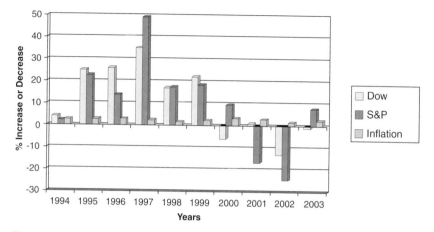

Figure 6–1   The Dow, S&P, and Inflation, July 1, 1993, Through June 30, 2003

I had a good friend in Chicago who in 1978 jumped into the disco craze like a lot of other people. He was a shirt wholesaler who represented several lines and sold them to a variety of stores. Then disco hit, and he had a hot manufacturer that wanted him to focus on its products exclusively. My friend did just that, and within six months, Sears was a huge buyer of his company's shirts, generating well over 80 percent of his business. He bought a luxury condominium at Lake Point Towers on Lake Michigan with gorgeous views of the lake and the windy city. Although John Travolta was dancing to the Bee Gees' classic, *Staying Alive,* disco didn't. My friend lost the Sears account and the craze faded, leaving him a victim of diversification risk.

More Information

INFORMATION   For more information on diversification, go to *www.morning-star.com* or *www.Ibbotson.com.*

When you look at diversification risk, it's the last risk, or "lens" as I refer to it, that you want to apply. This is only common sense because we need to compare one investment with the other to look at diversification.

Diversifying your portfolio may not be the sexiest of investment topics. Still, most investment professionals agree that although it does not guarantee against a loss, diversification is the most important component to helping you reach your long-range financial goals while minimizing your risk. But remember that no matter how much diversification you do, it can never reduce your risk to zero.

Understanding the Beta

Beta (or beta coefficient) is a means of measuring the volatility of a security or portfolio of securities in comparison with the market as a whole. This is very important in understanding and managing investment risk. Beta is the result of a fairly complex analysis, but the result is that a beta of 1 indicates that the security's price will move with the market. A beta greater than 1 indicates that the security's price will be more volatile than the market, and a beta less than 1 means that it will be less volatile than the market.

By way of an example, utilities stocks and bank stocks may have a beta of less than 1, whereas high-tech Nasdaq-based stocks typically have a beta greater than 1 because they offer the possibility of a higher rate of return but are also more risky. You can think of beta as the tendency of a security's returns to respond to swings in the market. For example, if a stock's beta is 1.2, it's theoretically 20 percent more volatile than the market. It stands to reason that if you expect the markets to perform well, you'll get the greatest gain from securities with a high beta, and if you expect the markets to do poorly, you'll have less risk with lower beta stocks.

Managing Investment Risk

Each of the broad risks has to be taken into consideration as you build your portfolio of assets. Ideally, your portfolio should be spread among many different investment vehicles such as cash, stocks, bonds, mutual funds, and perhaps even some real estate. Let's look at how we typically classify any investment that you make in your portfolio (see Figure 6–2).

The pyramid in Figure 6–2 is a standard in the financial services industry. The shape symbolizes lower risk at the base of the and higher risk at the top. Unfortunately, the pyramid is designed to look at only "principal risk," the risk that your principal is in jeopardy. It's not that looking at principal risk is a bad thing, but we get so caught up in it that we don't look at the other risks associated with an investment. Sometimes the risk can't be defined by the product, but rather by the underlying investment.

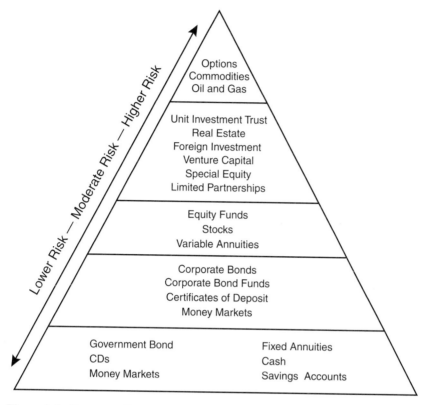

Figure 6–2   Investment Pyramid

Take the case of the mutual fund or the variable annuity. Both of these investment tools have a huge assortment of underlying portfolios of stocks, bonds, and sometimes real estate that make up the funds in mutual fund parlance and subaccounts in variable annuity parlance. This is an important distinction because the principal risk associated with a given mutual fund or subaccount could range from low to high, depending on the objectives set or in the prospectus for each of the subaccounts.

The Third Dimension of Investing: Changing Lenses

We have to look at risk from a three-dimensional point of view on any possible investment. In order to understand this, you need to first grasp the concept of each dimension or factor. The first dimension (see Figure 6–3), the horizontal axis of the illustration, shows time. Regardless of what we do, time marches on. This is not a dimension that we can control directly or indirectly. The second dimension, the vertical axis, represents value. Value is the result of the impact of the third dimension over any period of time marked along the horizontal axis. What I'm suggesting is that the third dimension is a series of factors that determine the rate of growth on your investments. These factors can be simple or complex and create varying degrees of risk. Imagine each factor as a layer of risk that impacts value over time. If you could peel back a layer, you could see the role that specific factor plays in determining the performance of an investment.

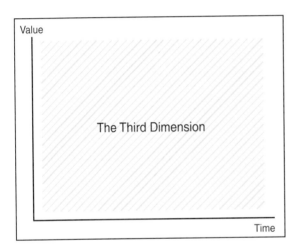

Figure 6–3   The Dimensions of Investment

You will find that some factors are general, such as the overall economy, some are specific to an industry or a sector within an industry, and some are specific to the company itself. The best way to quantify this risk posed by these factors is to lay out the various types of risk and then assess each investment, putting on the individual lens of the risk we want to evaluate.

For example, if you were considering an investment in Cathay Pacific Airlines (listed on the Hong Kong exchange as 0293.HK), what risks would you be looking at today? You will most likely be concerned about the business risk associated with the airline industry, the foreign investment risk posed by a rapidly changing government, and the currency risk associated with the Hong Kong dollar versus the U.S. dollar. You have to think about these, be comfortable with them, and determine how much money you want to invest in this stock. You might want to consider a mutual fund that specializes in the transportation industry if you feel strongly about the industry, or you may want to consider a specialty fund that focuses on China or the Pacific Rim.

After you apply these various risk lenses, it's time to apply the diversification lens. I wish that I could tell you that this is an easy thing to do, but without the aid of a computer or Web-based tools, the manual process is challenging in both time and intellect. There are, however, programs that can help you. One such program offered by Morningstar is called X-ray. X-ray allows you to build a portfolio of cash, stock, bonds, and mutual funds and analyzes the portfolio to provide detailed information on diversification of your investments. Another terrific Morningstar tool is the Stock Interception program that actually analyzes your mutual funds and tells you how much securities duplication there is in the funds that you own.

Let's say that you own a Fidelity balanced growth fund and a T. Rowe Price equity fund. You may not realize that these funds could be investing in one or more of the same securities. This program looks at the most recent holdings of the mutual funds and informs you of any duplication and the significance of the duplication.

Diversification means different things to different people. I was in a meeting with a broker and his client at which the client expressed his own view of diversification. He said something like this, "I diversify. I have accounts with Merrill Lynch, PaineWebber, and E.F. Hutton." He truly believed that he was diversified because he had multiple brokerage accounts. He might have gotten lucky, but that is not true diversification! With the stock market volatility driving dramatic shifts in the market every week, there needs to be a safety net for individual investors. Diversification is the answer.

Monte Carlo Simulation

One way to make certain that you have the proper distribution of assets and you are using reasonable assumptions for growth is to use a Monte Carlo simulator. This is a computer-modeled analytical tool that evaluates risk using a random series of returns. Its name comes from the infamous casinos of Monte Carlo where games of chance have spawned a tool that can help reduce risk. The Monte Carlo simulator is used to paint a more realistic picture of how long-term investment cycles impact long-term investments. Most projections use an assumed investment, an assumed period of time, and an assumed rate of return.

As an example, we invest using an assumed investment of $25,000, an assumed period of 20 years, and an assumed interest rate of 6 percent. Monte Carlo simulators keep the investment ($25,000) and the number of years constant (20), but they vary the investment return to show the impact of good and bad years. This is a much better long-term indicator than a straight 6 percent a year for calculating future value. The assumption is that in a dice game, you don't roll a four each and every time—sometimes you roll a five, sometimes a one. The same should apply in investing, and you should be able to see the impact of various scenarios to be able to effectively manage risk. You'll read more on Monte Carlo simulators in Chapter 12.

Health/Mortality Risk

You have two risks with health and mortality: the hope of living longer than your life expectancy and the possible fate of not living to your life expectancy. If you haven't properly planned for the consequences, both are problematic. Table 6–4 illustrates a variety of life expectancies for men and women. As you can see by the grouping, if you're a male between the ages of 35 and 75, you're likely to live into your mid-80s. If you're female in that age range, you're likely to live into your late 80s. As you plan your goals, you need to pick a target mortality for both, which is 81.4 years for people age 65. In other words, if you and your spouse are 65 today, your combined life expectancy is 81.4 years. But as the table illustrates, the longer you live, the more your life expectancy changes. If you're both alive at 75, your new joint life expectancy is 84.7 years.

Table 6–4   Male, Female, and Joint Life Expectancy

	Life Expectancy		
Age	**Male**	**Female**	**Joint[a]**
35	75.77	80.21	84.19
45	76.69	80.79	85.66
55	78.24	81.8	86.19
65	80.75	83.6	87.28
75	84.62	86.53	89.34

[a] Joint Life assumes both same age.

Web Sites with Life Expectancy Calculators

http://72t.net/MD_LifeEx.aspx
www.retirementcountdown.com
www.beeson.org/Livingto100/quiz.htm

The Role of Insurance

Insurance can play a role in several areas because it pertains to risk management for financial, retirement, and estate planning. The application of specific insurance products includes the following:

- ◆ Life insurance to satisfy estate liquidity needs and to provide sufficient income replacement for the premature loss of a loved one

- ◆ Disability insurance to provide salary replacement insurance to allow you to continue to fund retirement

- ◆ Income replacement insurance to provide an ongoing income stream after you retire no matter how long you live

- ◆ Health, long-term care, and MediGap insurance to minimize the depletion of assets after your retire

Be Careful!

It generally pays to shop around for your insurance coverage, and is it rarely wise to have all your insurance needs met by one insurance company. Convenient, yes—efficient, probably not.

Life Insurance

Chapter 9 covers life insurance more extensively, so for now I'll focus on quantifying the risk of dying prematurely. If you were to purchase life insurance based on true risk exposure, you would end up increasing and decreasing the face amount according to your changing needs. Unfortunately, that's not very practical or cost effective. Virtually any insurance policy you would want to buy should be underwritten so that you can get the most competitive rates. The life insurance policies that you see advertised with the slogan "no physical required" are designed and priced for people who have a reason for not wanting to be examined. In that respect, insurance companies are not too different from banks in that when you need the services the most, they are either unavailable or cost prohibitive. For the vast majority of us, the underwriting process will yield a lower cost than policies that are not underwritten.

Common Mistake

Many people don't read and don't understand all the fine print in an insurance policy. You really need to take the time to read and understand any contract that you sign. I realize these are boring and laborious, but you need to be certain to read the exceptions to coverage and understand both your rights and the company's rights.

You can find insurance coverage that allows you to increase the face amount of the policy by being underwritten for an amount of insurance greater than what you initially require. These usually add what the industry calls riders to the policy. These riders state the terms under which you can increase the coverage. For example, let's say that you require only $100,000 of life insurance today, but you want to be able to increase that amount to $150,000 should you need the additional coverage in the future. The insurance company will underwrite your policy as if you were going to elect the higher coverage, and it will approve you based on that assumption. Your cost, however, will reflect the lower face amount of $100,000 until you decide to increase the face amount.

You choose how much coverage you need by looking at your future expenses and replacing as much of the expense as possible. In other words, if you or your spouse were to die today, what amount of money would you need to provide for the welfare of the family? If you don't have a spouse or partner, and you don't have children, you aren't likely to have much of a need for life insurance unless you need to protect a large estate from the erosion of estate taxes.

If you are married with children, the risk must be assessed on both partners because both are likely involved in managing different elements of life. One may be responsible for earning income while the other is responsible for raising a family and running a household. Keep in mind that when assessing needs, you need not replace all the income for an entire lifetime. You have to make realistic assumptions. If the goal is to provide your surviving partner with sufficient income to manage the household without working, let that assumption define the amount. If your partner will likely go back to work or find other means of funding expenses, the amount might be lower.

Disability Insurance

Most employees do not purchase their employers' supplemental disability income insurance and very few self-employed business owners insure for this risk. When you look at the statistics on how many people become disabled, you see that can be a very costly mistake. Between the ages of 35 and 65, seven out of 10 people will become disabled for three months or longer. In addition, one out of seven employed people will be disabled for five years or more before age 65, with the average long-term loss due to disability being more than five years.

Many people think that Social Security or state programs are the answer, but rarely do these combine to provide sufficient income if you become disabled. It's extremely difficult to qualify for Social Security benefits and it takes a great deal of time before benefits begin. You must prove that are you incapable of performing not only your usual occupation but any occupation. If you qualify, the maximum payment for a 35-year-old earning $100,000.00 per year in 2004 is $1,974.00 per month. Remember that when you purchase and pay for disability insurance, the benefit you receive is not taxed as income.

Disability insurance is not inexpensive, and you have to read over the policy limits and understand the following:

◆ How long does the company pay the benefits? The most expensive policies are ones that pay benefits until age 65. Others pay for shorter specific periods of time such as 36 or 60 months.

◆ What is the definition of disabled? This will be a critical element to any policy that you purchase. The definitions will vary. You should consider a plan that defines disabled as being unable to continue in your present occupation, also known as "own occupation" coverage. This definition simply means that if you were a doctor and can no longer practice medicine, you are likely to be covered. You want to avoid policies that are "any occupation" because they will not pay benefits unless you are totally disabled.

◆ How long is the elimination period? An elimination period is similar to the deductible on your health insurance or auto policy. In this case, it will be the amount of time you will have to wait until benefits are paid. The longer the elimination period, the less expensive the coverage will be. Keep in mind that most large employers offer short-term disability as a standard benefit. Check to see how long your company will pay short-term disability and then have you personal policy pick up after that.

Income Replacement Insurance

Income insurance, also known as immediate annuities, is discussed extensively in Chapter 9. Annuities are the only way to literally insure a lifetime of postretirement income. The choices available include income guarantees for a specific number of years, income for life, or some combination of these two. At your direction, payments can be fixed and guaranteed by the insurance company, or they can be set initially and go up and down based on the manner in which you have chosen to have the underlying investments managed. Finally, you can also have the payments cover you and your spouse on the basis most consistent with your wishes.

For example, Dennis and Mary Glover want to have a $5,000-a-month payment guaranteed for the rest of their lives together and have that reduce to $3,500 for the balance of the lifetime of the surviving spouse. Furthermore, they want to make certain that payments continue for at least 20 years, meaning that if they both die before the 20-year period ends, Greg and Connie receive the balance of the payments. Assuming that they begin this income when Dennis retires at age 67, the cost of these guaranteed payments would be $943,000.

Health Insurance

According to a recent study done by Fidelity, the average 65-year-old couple that retires today and has no access to an employer-sponsored health plan needs about $175,000 to fund out-of-pocket medical expenses in retirement. Even those with employer-sponsored postretirement benefit plans have the means to pass along costs to their retired workers. As you prepare to GORP your way to a successful retirement, you must consider healthcare costs.

To determine your exposure to healthcare risks, you first have to identify your options. If you retire before age 65, you'll be too early to qualify for Medicare, so you'll have to either pay for individual medical coverage or be supported by your former employer if it has a postretirement health benefit. A study by the Employee Benefit Research Institute (EBRI) shows that a 55-year-old retiring today and still part of a group insurance program will need roughly $83,000 to cover typical insurance premiums plus out-of-pocket expenses for the 10 years it will take to qualify for Medicare. If you don't have access to a group policy, the amount needed for 10 years of individual coverage is even more staggering: up to $256,000 for someone with a chronic condition requiring prescription drugs.

Even post-Medicare, your budget is still in danger. If your employer doesn't provide you with supplemental insurance, you'll need to pay for drugs and other services that Medicare doesn't cover. According to the EBRI, a 65-year-old without employer coverage would need at least $116,000 for Medicare supplement and drug coverage through age 80.

Let's assume for a moment that Dennis needs to replace his health insurance coverage. At age 58, health makes a big difference in the price. For example, if we assume that Dennis doesn't smoke, is fit, and takes no medications, he can buy a comprehensive policy with a $20 physician copayment and $300 deductible for $300 a month. However, if Dennis is a little overweight and takes allergy medicine, the rate jumps to $375. If he also has a chronic condition, such as high blood pressure or cholesterol, his premiums will rise to $550. Finally, if he is undergoing cancer treatment, assuming he could even get coverage, the premium would be in excess of $1,000 a month.

With healthcare costs rising at a rate three times the rate of inflation, postretirement group healthcare cannot be an assumed guarantee. More and more companies faced with rising healthcare costs for retirees are passing the cost increases along, which means more money out of the retiree's pocket that wasn't expected. Don't assume that if you're covered under a postretirement health plan sponsored by your previous employer that you won't be saddled with some, if not most, of the cost.

Savings Tip

One benefit of enrolling in Medicare if you are working past the age of 65 is that it grants you and your dependents access to COBRA for 36 months, twice the normal time period. So if you work past 65, hold off on enrolling in Medicare, which starts the three-year clock ticking even though you still have group coverage.

The problem for many companies is that the costs of providing these benefits are growing faster than their underlying businesses, especially now as the Baby Boomer generation nears retirement. What complicates matter even more is that many large S&P 500 companies are not budgeting or accruing these expenses. When they become realized, you will see some perspiration at shareholder meetings and you'll find that your costs may start to creep up. A recent study by Credit Suisse First Boston revealed that 328 companies in the S&P 500 have set aside only $57 billion in assets to cover $365 billion in obligations.

In September 2003, telecommunications company Lucent announced that it was increasing deductibles and copayments for about 50,000 retired managers and dependents. The reason for this was that retiree healthcare costs had increased 85 percent while its retiree population jumped 22 percent. At the rate healthcare costs are increasing, Lucent said that it had to take action or face close to $1 billion—about 10 percent of its annual revenues—in annual retiree healthcare costs in the near future.

As you begin to frame out the costs for healthcare, asking the following questions may be helpful:

- How much of my doctor and hospital bills will be paid for?

- How much will I have to pay each month?

- How much will I have to pay (deductible) before the plan begins to pay?

- How much will I have to pay for office visits to the doctor?

- Does this plan pay for preventive healthcare? This includes routine medical checkups and shots, such as a flu shot, to prevent disease.

- Does this plan have rules for people who already have serious, chronic medical problems? Will these rules keep me from getting the care I need? If so, for how long?

- What services are covered by this health insurance? Will it pay for care at a hospital emergency room, or urgent care center? Does it cover routine surgery, hospital stays, doctor visits, nursing home stays, home healthcare, and medical equipment and supplies?

- Does this plan cover visits to the eye doctor and the dentist?

- Does this plan cover prescription drugs, and if so, at what cost?

- Does this plan pay for catastrophic medical costs, costs that are so high it would take most of my money to pay for them? Is there a limit to how much I must pay each year?

- What is the yearly or lifetime limit to how much the plan will pay for medical costs?

Long-Term Care Insurance

Long-term care (LTC) insurance is perhaps the single fastest growing area for life insurance companies. Long-term care is a step beyond traditional medical and nursing care. It includes all the assistance you could possibly need if you ever have a chronic illness or a disability that leaves you unable to care for yourself for a prolonged period of time. Individuals can receive long-term care at home, in an assisted living facility, or in a nursing home.

Long-term care provides assistance with daily living activities and typically includes bathing, dressing, transferring, eating, and continence.

Long-term care can also include some forms of short-term rehabilitation; for example, it can cover a three-month rehabilitation after a knee replacement. Although the use of this insurance is typically provided when we are older, you can also qualify if nursing care or home health-care is required after a serious illness or accident. Approximately one-third of LTC cases are people under 60.

The statistics support the need for most consumers to manage this risk. While most of us have car and fire insurance, the incidence of claims is actually very low. Approximately one in 1,200 homes actually catches on fire, and approximately one in 240 people makes car insurance claims. The same cannot be said for LTC. Roughly 60 percent of men and women over the age of 65 will need long-term care. By 2020, 12 million people will need care, and most of these people will receive care at home.

Dennis and Mary are well advised to consider buying a joint LTC policy. When buying LTC, you want to consider the amount of the daily benefit, the elimination period, and the length of the benefit. If we assume a $200 daily benefit, a 90-day elimination period (during which no benefit is paid), and lifetime payments, the premium would be $3,800 a year. The greater the daily benefit need, the higher the premium; the shorter the elimination period, the higher the premium; and the longer the benefit, the higher the premium. This gives you some guide for gauging increases and decreases in the premiums to meet your needs.

Medicaid, Medicare, Medicare+Choice, and MediGap Insurance

Let's start with the basics and quickly move through your options as you consider government-aided medical services. Medicaid is really healthcare coverage for those in or near poverty. You would not likely want to be in the financial condition required to qualify for Medicaid.

Medicare offers several types of health plans. If you live in an area that has more than one Medicare health plan, you can choose the plan that is right for you. Medicare is offered in its traditional form where it is administered by the federal government through select private insurers or through a newer program called Medicare+Choice.

Medicare is in two parts. Part A is hospital insurance and covers your costs on an inpatient basis at either a hospital or skilled nursing facility, including hospice. It also pays a limited amount for home care if it is specified in hospital discharge orders. If you contributed to the program via FICA tax withholdings during your career, you are not likely to have to pay premiums for Part A services.

However, you will have to cover some other costs. For an $812 deductible, Medicare covers 100 percent for each benefit period for the first 60 days of a hospital stay (semiprivate rooms only; TVs and telephones not included). For the next 30 days, it pays for all costs minus a $203-a-day copayment. You also get 60 nonrenewable lifetime reserve days, which can be added as needed onto the first 90 days of a hospital stay. Medicare A covers the cost of these days less a $406-a-day copayment. Each benefit period begins on the first day you enter the hospital and ends after you have gone 60 consecutive days without hospital care. Skilled nursing facility coverage lasts a maximum of 100 days during a benefit period. There is a $101.50-per-day copayment for days 21 to 100 in this period.

Part B services are your doctor-related services and outpatient hospital care. Medicare pays 80 percent of the approved cost of a given service, as defined by Medicare. Doctors who "accept assignment" agree that the approved cost will constitute payment in full. Those who don't can charge up to an additional 15 percent, and the beneficiary will be reimbursed only 80 percent of the approved cost by Medicare. Part B also covers 50 percent of most outpatient mental-health services; 80 percent of physical, occupational, and speech therapy; and 100 percent of most part-time skilled home healthcare.

The cost of Part B are monthly premiums of $54, an annual deductible of $100, your coinsurance (the uncovered 20 percent of the assigned cost), and any additional charges, if a doctor does not accept assignment, up to 15 percent. Premiums are usually deducted from your monthly Social Security payments. Beneficiaries who delay enrolling in Medicare B beyond their first chance to do so may wind up paying higher premiums.

Key Point

In late 2003, the Senate passed new legislation that approved a host of changes to Medicare. The most publicized new benefit is a Medicare-backed discount drug card at an estimated cost of $30 to the participant. This will be followed in 2006 by prescription drug coverage that could provide participants with up 75 percent coverage of their prescriptions.

As an alternative to Medicare, some private insurance companies offer what is essentially a Medicare C program also known as Medicare+Choice.

Medicare+Choice is a government-subsidized but a privately sold alternative to the original Medicare program. You can choose among managed-care plans like HMOs or fee-for-service plans. These plans are not available everywhere, so you need to check with your state because benefits vary.

You must be enrolled in Medicare A and B in order to sign up for a Medicare+Choice plan. If you try one of these plans and are not happy, you can always switch back to the Original Medicare Plan. Medicare+Choice plans must offer at least the same coverage as the Original Medicare Plan. Some plans offer prescription drug or additional hospital benefits. The HMO versions replace Original Medicare's 20 percent coinsurance with a lower copayment. Beneficiaries must continue to pay their monthly Medicare B premiums. Beyond that, the costs vary with the private insurance companies; the government does not determine what fees are acceptable. Overall out-of-pocket costs may wind up lower than with the Original Medicare Plan, even though additional premiums and, in the case of fee-for-service plans, deductibles may be required.

MediGap coverage is designed as a supplemental plan meant to fill in the "gaps" in Original Medicare coverage. MediGap insurance is sold by private insurance companies in plans that run from very comprehensive to less comprehensive. As with Medicare+Choice plans, these plans vary from state to state, so it's important to see what's available where you live. It is important to understand that MediGap plans are not subsidized by Medicare, and a MediGap plan is of little use to anyone who is enrolled in a Medicare+Choice plan.

MediGap policies help cover such Medicare costs as deductibles, copayments and coinsurance. The more comprehensive plans may also provide some coverage for prescription drugs, routine eye exams, or dental care. As with Medicare+Choice plans, only those already enrolled in Medicare A and B can purchase this insurance. Anyone over 65 should sign on during the six-month period immediately following his or her enrollment in Medicare B. Waiting may result in coverage being denied. The more benefits a MediGap plan provides, the higher the cost. On top of your $54 monthly premium for Part B of Medicare, expect to pay anywhere from $100 to $300 per month for MediGap coverage.

Risk of Doing Nothing

Without a plan of saving and investing to fight inflation, many people will not have sufficient funds to provide for their children's education and for a comfortable retirement. All too often, the most comfortable path to choose is the one that appears to offer the least resistance. Doing nothing is easy because it doesn't require us to take a risk. The problem is that we get lulled into a false sense of security and don't realize until it's too late. At that point, we are no longer in a position to do much about the problem. The longer you wait, the greater the risk you will have to take to meet your goals, and the greater the risk that you will fail to do so.

INFORMATION

More Information

There has been, and will always be, a relationship between the amount of risk you are willing to take and the reward that comes with that risk. This risk/reward equation will be an important consideration in later chapters.

Summary

It is impossible to eliminate all types of risks from an investment pyramid. Your individual "risk tolerance"—your "risk/reward temperament"—your concerns and feelings about inflation, safety, and so on, should be determined. You can then manage risks in a way that will help you become more comfortable with the degree of risk you decide to assume.

With risk management, you will have to determine how much you want to protect against and at what cost. This is the balancing that we do anytime we have to weigh a cost and a benefit. This is easy when we are faced with insurance for our personal property, but more difficult when we are facing our own mortality through health, life, and disability insurance. I suggest that you start by looking at the cost of providing reasonable coverage in these areas, and the next step is to decide if you will scale back overall on the coverage or drop entire lines of coverage in favor of full coverage in other areas.

For example, when you lay out the costs for life, disability, income replacement, and health insurance, you may choose to fund only certain risks and take the chance either that the other risks will not materialize or that you'll have sufficient financial resources to handle the uninsured risk. The financial and retirement planning process is not a short one, but it's also not that difficult if you approach it using GORP as we discussed in Chapter 5. What you do is break insurance out as a goal with the various elements as subordinate goals. Then you plug in the individual costs and look at your overall ability to fund that goal. You'll get much more information about insurance in Chapter 9 to better prepare you for your task. For now, think about what risks you're interested in insuring, and then you can calculate the costs and balance that with your other goals.

Power Checklist

> ✔ With risk management, we often leap before we look, and the consequences can be less than optimal.

> ✔ Look at risk management as an opportunity to eliminate obstacles that may keep you from achieving your goals.

> ✔ We practice risk management all the time; we fasten our seat belts, we install childproof cabinet locks, and we have our teeth cleaned.

> ✔ Much of what we take for granted in our daily lives is actually a form of risk management.

> ✔ The traditional investment pyramid is designed to look at only one form of risk, "principal risk," which is the risk that your principal is in jeopardy.

> ✔ You must quantify your postretirement insurance needs and make certain they can be adequately funded.

> ✔ Study the different postretirement government-sponsored health plans, including Medicare, Medicare+Choice, and MediGap coverage.

> ✔ Risk management is more than just managing investment risk. You must look at health and mortality risks, planning risks, and the risk of doing nothing.

CHAPTER 7

Equity Investments: Taking Stock in Your Retirement

IMPORTANT NOTE

The next five chapters cover a lot of ground on all types of investments. It's *really* important for you to understand that I can provide only a broad overview of these product areas.

The next five chapters position the products you'll most likely want to consider purchasing and utilizing in your quest to retire on your terms. It is critically important for you to keep these chapters in perspective as you begin to develop your goal-oriented retirement plan (GORP). I have rarely seen people miss their retirement goals primarily because of the performance of their investments. Don't get me wrong: The market goes up and down, and you can gain or lose a lot of value over a relatively short period of time. What I am saying is that the number of people who have failed because they invested their retirement money in poor investments is small compared with the number of people who have simply failed to save at all.

It goes back to a core belief that you have to start a systematic savings program now. And if you already have a savings program, you need to make certain that the plan matches your objectives. That is a process that will begin in Chapter 12 and continue well into the years that you are enjoying your retirement.

The countless books available on investing vary greatly in their approach from *Investing for Dummies* (4th Edition written by Eric Tyson, published by Hungry Minds, Inc. 1999) to *Active Portfolio Management: A Quantitative Approach for Producing Superior Returns and Selecting Returns and Controlling Risk,* 2nd Edition (by Richard C. Grinold, Ronald N. Kahn, published by McGraw-Hill, 2000). If you were looking for investment advice alone, you probably would not have purchased the book you're reading now. In other words, you didn't buy my book to become an expert in option straddle theory; rather, you bought it because you are concerned about your retirement. My goals in this section of the book are to provide you with a starting point for looking at the types of investments that are best suited to your personality and your background and then to help you put together a strategy for managing those investments.

More Information

A share of stock represents your ownership equity stake in a company. Your stock can be common stock or preferred stock. Preferred stock is usually available to only early investors who are taking significant risk with their money. The preferred stockholders will likely have additional rights like preferred dividends. Also remember that in the event of a bankruptcy, common stockholders are usually at the end of the line, behind bond holders and preferred stockholders, as well as others.

Over the past 25 years, it has truly amazed me to see all types of salespeople in virtually any industry proclaiming that their product was the "only product you'll ever need." It is sheer folly to assume that one product or one product category can meet all of your needs—particularly in the financial services industry. The salespeople I love to hate the most are those who misrepresent nonliquid investments, such as precious metals and collectibles, as a sound and sole basis for a financial plan. I will tell you right now the strategy is flawed for any number of reasons; but what concerns me most is that salespeople who market any product without regard for how that product meets your needs care only about themselves. As we head into an entire section of the book discussing products, your number one goal is to focus not only on the product, but how the product can be applied to your goals. My philosophy has always been to encourage people to invest broadly for diversification but not to ignore areas of personal interest.

My best friend is a devoted art collector, and when I say that I mean he *really* is an art collector. For him, it is not just a hobby, but a passion. He knows the exact value of a piece, and he also realizes if he wants to sell a piece, it's going to take time. For financial planning purposes, he makes art a finite percentage of his assets to ensure that he has balance in his investment portfolio. Any amount that he invests over his threshold is money that he has invested in his hobby of art collecting, not as part of his managed financial plan. This is a wise approach to financial planning and investing.

I think you need to nurse your passion in life to make investing more fun. Many people don't make saving a proactive exercise because it just isn't fun for them. I would suggest that you look at what makes you passionate, like your business or your hobbies, and see if there are investment opportunities that you can get excited about. I know a lot of doctors who invest in all types of medical companies from equipment manufacturers to biotechnology start-ups. They are supporting their professional passion and using their expertise to identify equity opportunities. Keep in mind that although you should nurse your passion, you have to be careful in applying it to your investment portfolio. There is more to picking an investment than just identifying product opportunities.

Let's say that I'm a radiologist and there's a new technology that revolutionizes the magnetic resonance imaging (MRI) industry. It may be tempting for me to jump on the penny stock of this new company that invented and patented the technology, but I need to look beyond the product to factors like the company's management and financials. These are areas that may or may not be in the field of expertise that I have chosen—in this case, radiology—but they are critical to the success of any business. Please understand that this argument is applicable for any profession, not just the medical profession.

More Information

INFORMATION

Penny stocks are publicly traded securities that sell for less than $1.00. These are high-risk investments in unproven companies, usually with a very short track record.

While you nurse your passion, you have to set reasonable dollar limits, and you may be wise to consider indirect investments like mutual funds specializing in a given area rather than try to pick individual stocks. Also, nursing your passion does not mean making investments that don't meet the overall criteria of your plan. In our discussion of GORP in Chapter 5, we separated our goals and investments. Each investment you consider has characteristics that must be matched to reach your goal. If any part of the match is wrong, you may not achieve your desired result. With all of that as background on the next several chapters, let's dive into the equity markets.

History of the Stock Market

People have been investing in the stock market since the 1790s, when the Philadelphia Stock Exchange started trading out of a coffee house several blocks away from the spot where the Declaration of Independence had been signed. Although the early trading was in government-issued notes, by 1792, trading had begun in what are now called publicly traded companies. It's an interesting story, which you can find by going to the Philadelphia Exchange Web site (*www.phlx.com/exchange/history.html*).

You have to imagine yourself back in 1791, when there were no cars, no electricity, and a bunch of political and financial men sitting in a tavern talking about the news coming down from New York City. At that time, news came into the country primarily from New York and traveled to Philadelphia via horseback. Unfortunately for Philadelphia merchants, the travelers included speculators and inside traders who were using the information to take advantage of the merchants. The Philadelphia brokers set up an ingenious way to get information to the merchants and brokers much faster.

Initially, they set up a series of points high atop hillsides along the route up through New Jersey and into New York. Then they placed people atop those hills with binoculars and lights and developed a system of light flashes to communicate news coming from New York so that they had the information before the scoundrels arrived on horseback. That system stayed in place until 1846 when the telegraph replaced their crude but effective system.

Shortly after the Philadelphia Exchange opened, the New York Stock Exchange (NYSE) followed suit and opened in 1792 at an outdoor site on Wall Street. In 1903, the Exchange moved into its current home at 18 Broad Street. The NYSE, commonly referred to as "The Big Board," had historically dwarfed all the other exchanges, with over 2,800 companies listed on the exchange.

More Information

INFORMATION   Market capitalization, or market cap, is the market value of a given stock. Total market cap is the cumulative total of all stocks listed on a given exchange or combination of exchanges.

However, over the past decade, the National Association of Securities Dealer Automated Quotations (NASDAQ) has gained tremendous prominence, with roughly 4,000 companies representing a total market capitalization of almost $4 trillion. Even with that growth, the NYSE remains the market cap leader, representing approximately 80 percent of the total market capitalization of companies in the United States. To calculate market capitalization, multiply the price of a company's shares by the number of outstanding shares. Total market capitalization is the sum total of the market capitalization of all the public companies. At the end of 2003, the total market cap for all listed stocks traded on U.S. exchanges was $14.5 trillion.

INFORMATION

More Information

The Key Stock Exchanges in the United States are:
New York Stock Exchange
NASDAQ (includes the American Stock Exchange)
Pacific Stock Exchange
Chicago Board of Options

Stock market exchanges provide for the orderly sale of securities through a system of members. The members are not the client companies, but rather a group of brokers who buy and sell the securities for their clients or themselves. A company that wishes to go public to raise money will apply to an exchange, and if it meets the exchange's qualifications, the stock becomes listed and the company can do an initial public offering (IPO). Often a company will simply move from one exchange to another without any need to raise capital. This could be for any number of reasons, but typically it will be because it wants to better align its business with an exchange or because it prefers one exchange's requirements to another's. As an example, a small technology company will likely be listed on the NASDAQ, but it may choose to switch to the NYSE when it reaches a certain size.

INFORMATION

More Information

Some stocks are traded "over-the-counter"(OTC). OTC stocks are company shares not listed on any exchange and, hence, traded only over the counter. In fact, the big OTC stocks are generally traded on the NASDAQ.

As consumers, we need to know that if we are interested in buying or selling a stock, there will be a ready market for that stock. We open an account with a brokerage company that will either make a market in the stock that we want to buy or sell or will go to another market maker to facilitate the sale. There is an old adage that I want to use here to make my point: "You don't need to know how the watch is built; you need to know if the watch tells time." Most people don't have the time or the desire to fully understand how many things work. My suspicion is that for this book, you'd prefer to know that there is a stable system for buying and selling publicly traded securities rather than get into how the system operates.

More Information

INFORMATION

Much has been made of the bulls and the bears and how they got their names. There is not a consensus on this one, so I'll go with the most plausible answer that I have found. Apparently, the genesis of these terms is tied to the upward pointing horns of the bull, signifying the launching of its prey (market goes up) while the connotation of the bear is the exposed claws ripping down (market goes down).

The Securities and Exchange Commission

For the first 140 years that stocks were traded, there was no real federal regulation in effect. That changed with the crash of the stock market in 1929 and the subsequent depression in the 1930s. Congress passed two laws, the Securities Act of 1933 and the Securities Exchange Act of 1934, to help protect consumers, and the Securities and Exchange Commission (SEC) was created in 1934 to supervise these two laws. Fundamentally, the SEC is charged with interpreting federal securities laws, amending existing rules, proposing new rules to address changing market conditions, and enforcing rules and laws. Since then, the SEC has lived through many cycles in the market, and in the early years of the 21st century, the SEC has been occupied with managing corporate wrongdoing, excessive exchanges of variable annuities, and mutual trading practices.

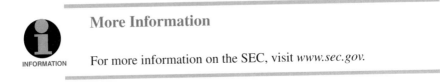

More Information

INFORMATION

For more information on the SEC, visit *www.sec.gov.*

Why Invest in the Stock Market?

As you ponder the different product choices available for your savings efforts, perhaps the most important element will be equity investments. Since 1927, the Standard and Poor's 500 has shown an average annual compounded return of 11.74 percent per year. To put that into perspective, a $1,000 investment in the S&P 500 75 years ago would now be worth over $4.1 million. I seriously doubt that I'll have to do too much work to convince you that equities need to be part of your financial future. For most people there is an allure to investing in the stock market that is a financial rite of passage. Table 7–1 summarizes the compound annual growth rate of a variety of investments as compiled and released by Ibbotson Associates.

Table 7–1   Compound Annual Growth Rates of Investments, 1925–2002

Investment Type	Annual Compound Growth (%)
Small company stock	12.1
Large company stock	10.2
Long-term government bonds	5.5
Treasury bills	3.8
Inflation	3.1

Ways to Invest in the Stock Market

There are two ways to invest in the stock market: through the purchase of individual stocks and through the purchase of shares in mutual funds, which are discussed in great detail in Chapter 11. The concepts associated with equity investing apply to both individual stocks and mutual funds, so let's start by looking at what you'll need to consider in choosing which path or which combination of these makes the most sense to help you achieve your goals.

Saving Tip

Mutual funds are professionally managed pools of securities. These funds offer diversification and professional money management, two key elements to reducing risk that we discussed last chapter. They also offer investors with limited cash to save with minimum investments as low as $25 per month.

How to Choose Your Equity Investments

As I mentioned, you really can't have a long-term goal funded without the use of equities. Unfortunately, there are about as many theories on how to invest in equities as there are equities themselves. Most of the strategic discussions take place in Chapter 12 after we have considered all of the investment options available to you, but this chapter covers the basics of investing in equities. In other words, don't worry too much about how we will apply equities to meet your goals because we cover that later in the book. Focus here on learning about the equity markets and consider the manner in which you want to select your equity investments.

Large-Cap, Mid-Cap, Small-Cap, and Micro-Cap Stocks

In the equity market, stocks fall into a number of categories so that we can group them together and evaluate their performance. One such grouping, or class, is based on the market capitalization that we recently discussed and uses the terms large-cap, mid-cap, small-cap, and micro-cap to align companies according to their size. Table 7–2 provides the general capitalizations in these classes, although you'll find quite a bit of variance from one source to the next.

Large-cap stocks are the stocks of companies whose names roll off your tongue with ease. They are companies that have stood the test of time and are not likely to go out of business. They tend to be market leaders, and their stocks traditionally are not as volatile as the mid-cap and small-cap stocks. Large caps are the most conservative of the equity investments, though their returns can beat mid-cap and small-cap stocks during difficult times in the market when people flock to safety. However, they are not immune to market disruption or the impact that a bad quarter can have on stock price.

Key Point

As you consider investing in individual stocks, you may want to consider buying only large-cap stocks for your personal portfolio and using index funds and other professionally managed mutual funds to bring in a focus on small- and mid-cap stocks.

Mid-cap stocks are not slouches by any stretch of the imagination, and they are stocks you are still most likely to recognize, like Starbucks, Aetna, and Staples. These are companies whose stocks tend to be more volatile than those their large-cap counterparts, and they don't show up in as many mutual funds as large- and small-cap companies because mid-caps are usually on the way up to a large-cap or on their way down to a small-cap.

Table 7–2   Varied Capitalizations

Class	Market Capitalization	Examples of Companies in this Group
Large-cap	Over $10 billion	Microsoft, General Electric, Coca-Cola, Wal-Mart
Mid-cap	Between $1.5 billion and $10 billion	Aetna, Starbucks, Moody's, Staples,
Small-cap	$300 million to $1.5 million	Pier 1, Sylvan Learning Centers, Fossil, Northwest Airlines
Micro-cap	Under $300 million	You probably won't know them

Small-cap stocks are typically not as small as you might think. For investment purposes, these stocks are the most volatile of the three major capitalization groups. They also need to be part of your investment strategy to meet long-term goals. To illustrate this point, consider that small-caps have outperformed large-caps since the 1920s, but when they were bad, they were really bad. That means you need to make sure you assign small-caps to your long-term goals because their risk profile does not support placement in intermediate-term portfolios.

There is a final cap group with valuations so small that they have earned the accurate name micro-caps. Even today's profitable companies started as micro-cap stocks. So, if you want to get in on the next Microsoft, you need to allocate a small amount to this category. Clearly, you should invest in these companies only through a mutual fund, unless you have excellent information sources that can make you feel comfortable with the stock. Unless you're an expert, you should leave micro-cap investing to the professionals.

Value, Growth, or Both

Another way to view companies, for the sake of your investments, is the manner in which they grow. If a company chooses to reinvest its earning into the business to maximize its growth, it is referred to as a growth company. On the other hand, if the company elects to pay out a dividend to shareholders and invest smaller amounts into growing the business, it is considered a value company. As a general rule, more conservative companies like banks, utilities, and insurance companies tend to be value stocks, while technology companies tend to be growth stocks.

Savings Tip

For diversification, consider buying the actual stock index. The Dow, the Standard & Poor's 500, and the NASDAQ are available for purchase as Exchange-Traded Funds. These are not mutual funds per se; they are fractional shares of the underlying stocks. The symbol for the Dow Jones Industrial Average is DIA, the symbol for the S&P 500 is SPY, and the symbol for the NASDAQ is QQQ.

When you buy individual stocks, you want to evaluate the type of company or stocks you are looking at. Value stocks tend to grow more slowly and often lag the market for periods of time. But it's critical to look at the income that a given stock pays out as part of your analysis because those dividends can add up at the end of the year when you're looking at performance. (At one end of the spectrum, Peter Lynch, the legendary money manager and renowned speaker from Fidelity, was primarily a growth stock investor. At the other end, perhaps the most well-known advocate for value investing is Nebraska billionaire Warren Buffett.)

As you can see, there are not as many rights ands wrongs as there are choices. It's all about paths, and the worst thing you can do is have no path at all. So, whether you like Peter Lynch's wisdom or Warren Buffet's wisdom, you'll likely do fine as long as you take action. There's no reason not to combine styles and create your own mix to your own specifications.

Another reason that people recently have been looking at value stocks is the dividends that they pay. In 2003, the tax on dividends was reduced to 15 percent from the previous treatment of ordinary income. Investors who buy Bank of America stock with a 4.0 percent cash dividend are putting 3.4 percent in their pocket after taxes, assuming the stock price remains stable. In a low-interest-rate environment where money market accounts are yielding .50 percent, taking some risk on a value equity stock may make some sense. As you look at mutual funds, you'll find that professional managers offer portfolios of growth stocks, value stocks, or a blend of the two.

Dividends

Dividends are the manner in which corporations distribute their earnings to their shareholders. Historically, dividends ran about 3 percent until around 1990, when they plummeted. Many experts today feel that low dividends are indicative of an overvalued market. What they are saying is that the dividend, which traditionally does not change very often, won't keep up with the rising stock price. To illustrate, let's look at a stock that trades today at $20 per share with a $1.00 dividend, or 5 percent. In a year, the stock has grown to $40 per share and the dividend has not changed from $1.00, but the dividend yield has now gone down to 2.5 percent.

Style Boxes

The Chicago-based global investment research company Morningstar has created and used what it calls "style boxes" to illustrate where a company of a mutual fund would be classified on a scale of small-cap to large-cap and value to growth. We'll refer back to this concept in Chapter 11 to understand how the style box can be used to check our portfolios and see where our investments line up in the style box. What you see in Figure 7–1 is a dot for the size of each company. There are two large-cap value stocks, one medium-cap value fund, and so on.

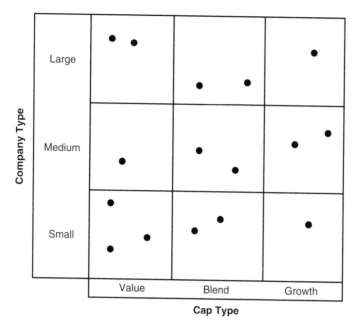

Figure 7–1   Sample Style Box

Considerations for Buying Individual Stocks

I won't mince words here. I think that you need to be very careful when investing in individual stocks. As investing relates to goal-oriented financial planning, you simply cannot match a single investment in a company stock to a goal. You won't meet the diversification test required to minimize the risk associated with that goal. You can, however, pick and manage a small group of individual stocks if doing so can get you motivated about saving and investing. But take care to keep the number of stocks small. Even professional money managers have strict limits on the number of companies they will invest in at any given time.

INFORMATION

More Information

There are a number of sources that you can use to get financial information on companies. One of the oldest sources is Value Line, which you can find at *www.valueline.com*. It offers a number of tools to help you understand the financials on over 1,700 publicly traded companies.

I will also add the following cautionary advice: Don't buy individual stocks unless you are willing to take the time necessary to manage them. That includes not only the up-front research on the purchase of the stock, but also the ongoing maintenance associated with owning it and selling it. I make it a practice to buy stocks only when I can manage the portfolio. I also buy stocks in only businesses I have thoroughly researched. Often, I'll go for extended periods when I own only mutual funds and stock indexes and no individual stocks.

Key Point

There are a number of ways to research companies' financials. Each company must file an annual report, called a 10-K, with updated information. You can usually view a 10-K for a given company by going to the company's Web site, or you can go to *http://edgar.sec.gov/*. Another great source for financial information is *http://finance.yahoo.com*.

With that as background, let's talk about the factors you'll need to understand and be aware of as you buy stocks. You'll note that some of the factors you'll need to assess are quantitative and some are qualitative. Qualitative measures tend to be much more difficult to assess because they aren't black and white. Quantitative tools measure anything that can be quantified, such as the price earnings ratio of a company or its 52-week high or low. You'll see how professional money managers pick and choose the stocks that go into their portfolios. Of course, you can always resort to throwing darts at the stock page, but I don't think you want to stake your retirement plan assets to a game of chance… and good aim.

Management Team

It goes without saying that a company's management team is vital to the success of the company. Consider the management team's background, look for experience and turnover, and try to find any details that give you a sense of the management's style. My own experience has shown me that each corporation has its own unique personality driven by the CEO and adopted by senior management. I don't believe for a minute that what happened to Enron was beyond the reach of the CEO—that's where policies and practices originate.

All corporations of size have posted mission statements and goals, but rare are the companies that truly live by those statements. Often these are but plaques on the wall and affirmations in annual reports. Unfortunately, you can have a good management team with a bad product. Regardless of how good the team is, you can't maximize value with a poor product or business model.

Financial Information

Financials for a company consist of the following:

◆ **Cash Flow.** You need to understand the company's cash flow to understand what options it has to grow the business. If the company is profitable, is it generating enough cash to ensure company growth, including product research, product development, sales, and marketing? You want to make certain that the company is well funded, and if it has debt, you need to know if the debt will truly accelerate earnings or create an unbearable cash flow burden on the company.

◆ **Earnings Per Share.** This is amount of earnings or losses per share. It is part of calculating the Price Earning Ratio.

◆ **Price earning ratio.** Price earning (PE) ratio is the relationship between a company's stock price and its earnings. If we own a stock that is trading at $50 per share and the company earns $5 per share, the PE is 10. The PE can tell us if the stock is overvalued or undervalued. A very high PE could mean that the stock is overpriced, but it could also mean the company and the market are expecting explosive growth and the stock price is just lagging the earnings. A very low PE could mean that the company has had trouble or is positioning to break out of a slump.

◆ **Sales/revenue growth.** Logically, you want to be investing in companies that are growing. Looking at historical information can provide you with the slope of revenues over the past several years. This sales growth, combined with the profit picture, can tell you a great deal about the growth of the business and the way management is handling expenses.

Other Data

You also want to keep an eye on other data points like the volume of shares traded on a daily basis. The 52-week high and low will give you some historical perspective on the stock's price. It is wise to think about other obvious questions, like why a particular stock is trading at its 52-week low when the market is up 15 percent and its peer companies are trading at their respective highs.

Buying on Margin

Most people buy stocks or bonds with cash they have saved or through the sale of some other investment. Typically, to buy a stock or bond, you must have cash equal to or greater than the amount required to purchase a given investment. If you don't have the cash but you have significant other securities in your account, most broker dealers will allow you to purchase your investment by borrowing the money, also known as using margin. Margin is a loan, pure and simple. You are essentially borrowing from the broker-dealer, using your securities as collateral and paying interest on the amount you borrow.

Most people use margin to create leverage with their investments. For example, let's say Greg and Connie Glover want to buy 100 shares of Sumatra Coffee Company stock at $10 per share. The cost of the stock is $1,000. Greg and Connie have $18,000 in securities that they own already and don't want to sell those securities or move money from another account to cover the purchase. Since they have $18,000 in securities being held by their broker-dealer, they can borrow up to the limit set by their broker dealer to purchase the Sumatra stock.

Margin buying is regulated by the Federal Reserve Board. Currently, you can borrow up to 50 percent of the value of your portfolio. In addition to the Federal Reserve Board rules, your broker-dealer sets a maintenance requirement. That's the percentage of equity you're required to hold in your margin account. It usually ranges from 25 percent to 35 percent, and some requirements go as high as 70 percent of the purchase price. If we use 50 percent as an example, the Glovers would have to have $500 worth of stock held in margin.

Since Greg and Connie have $18,000 in equities, they can simply borrow the $1,000 to purchase the Sumatra shares. In doing so, the Glovers are creating leverage by borrowing against their assets. Instead of writing a check for $1,000, they pay the margin cost. Let's say the current margin interest rate is 4 percent, making their cost $40 per year or $20 for six months.

Leverage is designed to enhance the appreciation of an asset, but it can also work the other way. Let's look at two examples. Let's assume that Sumatra introduces a new method for decaffeinating coffee that is more cost effective; the stock goes through the roof, and in six months has doubled to $20 per share. The Glovers now have an investment worth $2,000 that has cost them only $20 in margin costs. Their gain is 1,000 percent versus 100 percent if they had paid cash.

On the other hand, let's assume that the Food and Drug Administration (FDA) finds that Sumatra's new process for decaffeination causes cancer in laboratory rats that drink more than two thimbles a day, and the stock plummets from $10 per share to $2 per share. If that happens, your Sumatra stock will now be valued at only $200, or $300 less than the amount required by the broker-dealer to maintain your margin account. When you don't have enough money in your account to cover the maintenance requirement, your broker-dealer or brokerage firm will issue a margin call. You must meet the call by adding money to your account or selling the stock to repay the loan and take a loss.

You must look at margin in the same manner as any other loan. Is the cost of capital (loan costs) and the risk associated with the investment worth the additional risk you are taking on? Margin is debt and must be actively managed for you to effectively achieve your retirement goals.

Investing Abroad

Living in an international world, we would be wise to look outside the boundaries of the United States for additional investment opportunities. One way of gaining international exposure is to buy the stock of U.S. companies that generate a significant amount of their revenue offshore. Companies like Coca-Cola, McDonald's, and Eastman Kodak are heavily reliant on international sales.

Recently, there has been an explosion in the technology world as foreign companies and countries are buying U.S. technology to modernize. In 2003, China entered into a software arrangement with Sun Microsystems to provide 200,000 copies of a Linux/Java software program and in the same year, Advanced Micro Systems announced its agreement to build a semiconductor manufacturing fabrication facility in Germany.

American Depository Receipt

While you can gain international exposure through the purchase of U.S. companies doing business abroad, you may also want to look at purely international stocks. If you're interested in trading non-U.S. securities, the most efficient way to do that is through buying and selling American Depository Receipts (ADRs), also known as shares. When you buy an ADR, you are buying it and selling it in U.S. dollars; a bank is serving as a clearinghouse for the shares and converts the U.S. dollar into the denomination of the country where the company is based. This means that you have the currency risk associated with that specific country in addition to the volatility of that stock.

Let's take the stock of Sony as an example. Sony is based in Japan but is one of the largest electronics companies in the world. As you may recall, the dollar was very strong against the yen during the late 1990s and into the early part of the first decade of the new millennium. If Sony's stock remained unchanged during that period, the value of the Sony ADR would have gone down based on the yen's value decrease as compared to the U.S. dollar during that period.

The opposite is true as well. During the six-month period from May 1, 2003, to October 31, 2003, Sony stock went from $24.36 to $35.20, a 44 percent increase. During that same period of time, the yen rose 8 percent, and roughly 20 percent of the increase during that time was based on the yen's value increase.

Utilities

Historically, people interested in income flocked to utilities. You couldn't go wrong with an investment in your gas or electric company. However, today, utility stocks should be looked at in the same manner that you would consider any investment you expect to receive income from. Look at the credit risk, look at the yield on the investment, and then compare it with similar investments in the market. Some people believe that the utility stocks have some greater exposure because of environmental concerns.

Risk Reward

As we look at the risk associated with each type of investment products, we put on our principal risk lens and apply relativity to the principal risk within an investment group. When we talk about the relative risk of one investment compared with another, we are not necessarily looking at the absolute risk associated with those investments—only how they relate to the others (see Figure 7–2).

For example, the relative risk of losing money on a share of General Electric stock is lower than the relative risk of losing money on a share of a micro-cap stock company. If we were to look at the relative risk of a share of General Electric stock to the absolute guarantee of principal associated with a U.S. Treasury Bill, we would see a fair amount of difference. These are subtle differences worth paying attention to in the world of investing—a world you are now a part of.

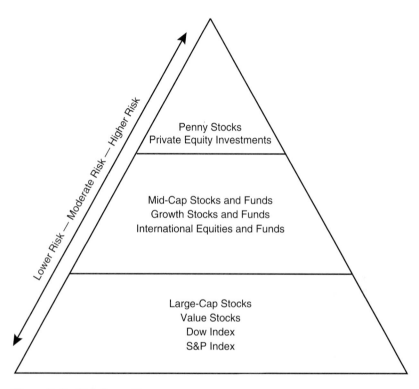

Figure 7–2   Risk Pyramid

As part of your risk reward strategy, you may want to utilize trading tools that are provided by almost all brokers. One example is a Limit Order, with which you authorize the purchase or sale of a stock based on certain parameters. Let's say that you consider Xerox a good buy at $20 per share, and you assign a target value of $25 per share, or a 25 percent increase. You can put in a Limit Order that will automatically sell Xerox at $25, locking in your gain if you are unable to monitor the market that closely. The same tool exists on the loss side of the equation where you can implement a Stop Order to sell the stock if a stock falls to a specified level.

Savings Tip

You may want to consider using a Dividend Reinvestment Plan (DRIP) instead of taking cash dividends. Many companies offer these plans as an alternative to cash by converting the cash dividend into shares or fractional shares of the company stock. As an added bonus, you don't pay commissions on DRIPs. You may want to check out *www.fool.com/DRIPPort/WhatAreDRIPs.htm* for more information.

Individual Stocks and Goal-Oriented Financial Planning

I have already laid out the cautionary issues you need to take into account when you decide to buy individual stocks. I understand you may still really need to feel directly connected to the market, and I know that at cocktail parties it's nice to be able to say, "Yeah, I bought that stock when it was selling for $3.50 a share." So let's look at how we can manage a portfolio of individual stocks as part of our investment strategy and tie it to specific objectives. Here's a checklist to help guide your decisions:

- ◆ Limit your individual stock exposure to not more than 10 percent of your portfolio, and make certain that you have good overall diversification.
- ◆ Try to avoid small-cap and micro-cap stocks altogether; you're better advised to pick those up in a mutual fund.
- ◆ Be careful of tips from a friend. In today's information age, it's hard to find new news. If you want to use the tip to research a company and that company meets your screens and needs, consider taking a flyer.
- ◆ Use "limit orders" to lock in gains or minimize losses. Remember that pigs get fat and hogs get slaughtered.
- ◆ Be thinking about the tax consequences of your investments. If you're buying individual stocks, you have better control over taxes than in a mutual fund. With that in mind, it may be better for you to keep your individual stock investments outside qualified plans.
- ◆ When we get to assigning assets to goals later in the book you'll see that individual investments are best suited to mid- to long-term goals.

Summary

We have covered the nuts and bolts of the equity market and what it takes to be a stock picker. This is no easy task if you want to really make educated stock purchases. As you will learn in Chapter 11, a much less risky path is to purchase mutual funds or buy stock indexes. I also have acknowledged that some people like to pick stocks and watch the market as a hobby. I don't want to discourage those efforts, but I believe that you need to set reasonable limits on the amount of your savings dollars you risk with individual stock purchases. Don't let ego get in the way of achieving your long-term goals.

Power Checklist

- ✔ Invest in companies that you are passionate about, but always be careful to do your homework before and after your purchase.
- ✔ If you choose to invest a percentage of your assets in individual stocks, be aware of all the risks.
- ✔ Since 1927, the Standard & Poor's 500 has shown an average annual compounded return on investment of 11.74 percent per year.
- ✔ You need to have a balance of large-, mid-, and small-cap stocks in your portfolio. One way to look at the distribution is to use a style box and look at the pattern created in the style box.
- ✔ Look at the risk-reward of any investment to make sure it will meet your goals.
- ✔ During low-interest-rate environments, dividends can be an alternative to other interest-bearing investments. You should deploy this strategy with caution and limit your investments to large-cap stocks with a strong dividend history.
- ✔ The SEC has been very busy over the past few years dealing with corporate greed issues and with mutual fund trading practices, and it will continue to be very active in protecting your rights, as will the attorney general of your state.

CHAPTER 8

Fixed Income Investments: Building a Bond

As an investor, you have a choice of being either an equity partner or a lending partner. If you purchase a stock or a stock mutual fund, you are purchasing equity in a company. If you purchase a bond or a bond fund, you are actually lending money to the company, government, or municipality for a certain period of time at a specified interest rate. As an equity owner, you have a say in how the company is run by being able to vote the power of your shares. As a bondholder, you don't have voting rights, but you stand in line ahead of stock holders if the company you're investing in goes out of business.

Bond performance goes through cycles just as equity performance does. The cycles of performance for these two investments rarely track together because of their different natures. In low-interest rate environments, stocks typically do well and bonds typically lag because of these lower interest rates. When interest rates are higher, the equity markets usually take a beating because higher interest rates bring higher inflation and a higher cost for businesses that need to borrow money.

Key Point

Since 1925, the average return on the S&P 500 has been 11 percent, and Treasury bills have averaged 3.8 percent. This illustrates the difference in risk between these two options.

There are, however, those rare occasions when the two product forces pass each other as market conditions change. When people see interest rates begin to drop, they feel more comfortable buying stocks and may try to take advantage of what's called "buying at the bottom of the trough." And if you're smart enough or lucky enough to buy bonds at the highest rates, you get a double bonus of high income and a great capital gain on the bond if you choose to sell it. But more often than not, the bond and equity markets keep slugging away, with the equity markets outperforming bonds over most long-term periods.

The 1990s, as an example, were not great years for bonds. Bond yields are a function of interest rates while bond prices are a function of the *volatility* of interest rates. Interest rates in the 1990s weren't too volatile, but they were very low, and low interest rates in a hot market translate to strong equity sales and weak bond sales.

Bonds and other fixed-income investments have historically been very popular tools in generating income, particularly at retirement. There are a number of strategies that people deploy to utilize bonds as income tools during retirement. I'll focus more on these strategies in Chapter 12 and leave this chapter to whet your appetite on these time-tested investment products.

Why People Buy Bonds

Fundamentally, there are four reasons people buy bonds: income, safety, diversification, and tax advantages. Although not all bonds share all of these characteristics, if you polled bond owners, you would find these four listed most frequently. However, in reality, you will find through the course of this chapter that bond income is typically not inflation proof, bond safety is relative, and tax advantaged bonds must be analyzed with respect to taxable alternatives. This doesn't mean that bonds (or bond funds) are inappropriate investments—quite the contrary. They need to be part of a balanced portfolio, and you'll use them as we begin to match assets to goals.

Bonds, Bonds, My Kingdom for a Bond

Since there are so many varieties of bonds to choose from, we have to pare them down into broader categories so that we can get our arms around them. I also want to provide you with a basic lesson on bond terms so that you have some background for our discussions on calculators and bond-price fluctuations. As an example, let's assume that Disney issues a 10-year corporate bond with a par value of $1,000 per bond, a coupon rate of 5 percent, and a maturity date of January 15, 2014. I'll use this example to provide any further explanation of terms:

◆ **Face amount.** Also known as par value, this is the amount of money that the bond issuer will pay at the maturity date. If you buy the bond at face amount, you receive your money back at maturity. If you pay more than the face amount for the bond, you are paying a premium; if you pay less than the face amount, you're getting a discount. Bonds are almost always sold in $1,000 increments. The Disney bond has a par value of $1,000. If it were trading at a 10 percent premium, it would sell for $11,000. If it were trading at a 10 percent discount it would be trading at $9,000.

◆ **Maturity.** This is the date that the bond matures. As you will hear from me repeatedly during this chapter, there are no maturity dates on bond funds, only on the bonds within the funds have maturity dates. Table 8–1 shows how maturities tie to the different classification of terms; that is, the types of time-specific bonds available for purchase. From this example we see that the Disney bond is a long-term bond.

Table 8–1   Bond Maturity Terms

Bond Maturity	Term
1 to 3 years	Short
4 to 10 years	Intermediate
Over 10 years	Long

◆ **Coupon.** The coupon is interest that the issuer pays on the bond. Most bonds pay interest biannually, so if you have a $1,000 bond that pays 5 percent a year as the Disney bond does, you'll receive two checks for $25 each for every $1,000 you have invested in the bond.

◆ **Current yield.** The yield is a little more complex of an element to understand. Theoretically, if you purchase the bond at face value and the valuation for the bond remains constant, the yield and the coupon are the same thing. Realistically, though, the bond value will fluctuate with interest rates and with the rating of the issuer. The current yield adjusts to these conditions by going up or going down. As interests and/or credit risk escalate, the price of the bond goes down and so does the current yield. Conversely, as interest rates go down and/or the credit risk lessens, the yield goes up.

◆ **Yield to maturity(YTM).** This calculates the principal plus the reinvestment of the income at some assumed rate and provides the total projected yield. YTM is used to compare the value of bonds with different issue and maturity dates, coupon rates, and par values. If you are able to reinvest the money you receive from Disney at 4 percent, your YTM would be 4.87 percent before taxes. If you were able to reinvest at 6 percent, your YTM would be 5.29 percent before taxes.

◆ **Duration.** The duration of a bond adjusts the amount of time it takes to return principal and interest based on changes in interest rates. If interest rates don't change at all during the term of the bond, duration will equal the maturity date. But since that rarely happens, the duration will increase or decrease depending on the impact that interest rates have on the bond.

◆ **Yield to call.** Most bonds have a call date. A call date is a time or a number of times over the course of the bond's life that the issuer can redeem the bond at face value. If your bond has a call provision, you may want to calculate your yield to call. This is the yield on the investment to the first possible call date. Bonds are typically called because of reductions in interest rates or the improved credit rating of the issuer. Let's say that the Disney bond has a right to call at 36 months, but Disney has to pay you 115 percent of the face value. Assuming we have been able to reinvest at the same 5 percent as the bond, your yield to call would be 8.69 percent before taxes.

Be Careful

Be on the lookout for *bearer bonds*. You might not find them because they've been illegal to sell since 1982, but bearer bonds have no owner information on them, so they are paid to the bearer. They are almost as liquid and transferable as cash. These bonds also have coupons that people would literally clip and take into a bank to cash. Yes, this is where the term "clipping coupons" came from. By the way, they aren't illegal to own, but they are no longer legal to issue.

Corporate Bonds

When corporations require capital, they can either borrow money or seek additional equity investors. The route that a business takes may be dictated by any number of factors, including the company's debt rating, the interest rate environment, and the general market for equity issues, to name a few. When companies go to the public for debt financing, they typically range from intermediate-term to long-term bond offerings. In the case of Disney, it floated a 100-year corporate bond, and only Disney could make that happen.

The interest rate yields on corporate bonds are higher than on government bonds and municipal bonds because the credit risk is greater and because the interest is taxable. To help you determine if owning a taxable bond will work in your favor, you'll need to calculate the equivalent yield by converting corporate yields to tax-free yields.

Let's say that you buy a tax-free municipal bond (muni bond) yielding 2.5 percent or a taxable AAA corporate bond yielding 4.50 percent. Assume that you're in a 41 percent combined state and federal tax bracket. Which is a better investment? To get the answer, subtract the taxes from the yield on the corporate bond and you have an after-tax yield of 2.66 percent, or 16 basis points greater than with the muni bond. There are 100 basis points in every percentage point.

Corporate bonds are affected by credit risk as well as by interest rate risk. Credit risk affects the pricing of the bond when it is issued, and changes in the credit risk will affect the value of the bond once it is issued.

Let's say that Motorola issues a 10-year corporate bond with a coupon of 6 percent. Assume that Motorola's credit rating at the time of issue is A. A couple of years go by, and you want to sell the bond. Now interest rates have risen from 6 percent to 7.5 percent and Motorola's credit rating has dropped two notches to BB. Your bond will take a 10 percent loss on the interest rate change alone, and you'll lose more as the market prices the credit rating at BB instead of A.

Savings Tip

If you plan to use taxable bonds to fund any part of your retirement, you may want to consider putting them into your IRA or 401(k) plan because they will shelter you from current income taxes. This allows you to enjoy compounding on interest that otherwise would have been taxed by Uncle Sam.

High Yield Bonds

High yield, or junk, bonds have been labeled as the bad boys of Wall Street. These are bonds issued from businesses whose debt is rated B or lower by the major rating agencies. A bond can either start out as a junk bond or be reclassified as junk when a rating agency downgrades it. As a result, some of the companies making up this category climb up the ratings ladder and some move the other way. However, just because a bond is downgraded by the rating agencies doesn't mean that it stays down. Chrysler was down and almost out in 1980, and its bonds were the lowest of junk. Today, Chrysler bonds are investment grade. But the checkered past of the junk bond industry has no better icon than that of a man named Michael Milken.

Almost everyone in the investment industry has heard of Michael Milken and the infamous junk bond scandal of the late 1980s and early 1990s. Milken made billions by getting corporations and financial institutions to purchase junk bonds as the spread (the difference) between junk bonds and other bonds was steep. Milken was not convinced that the ratings agencies were doing an effective job of rating all but the lowest-risk companies' debt. This means that the price, or yield, of the junk bond was attractive enough to override concerns about the company issuing the debt.

Though the story is long and the scandal quite extensive (Milken served time for securities fraud and paid a $1.1 billion fine), Milken did change the perception of junk bonds in the long term. These issues were no longer considered castaways but rather opportunities to take a managed risk for additional reward. There are a number of good and easy-to-find books on Milken if you want to read more on the topic.

The bottom line on junk bonds is that they may have a place in your portfolio. If you're willing to take the additional risk of principal to get a better rate of return on your investment and you're on the right side of an investment in a junk bond or a junk bond fund, you can benefit from the higher credit rate and the appreciation of the bond, assuming that the rating is upgraded.

Government Bonds

The federal government issues a variety of Treasury bills, bonds, and notes to raise money to fund government operations. These three have certain common elements: They all are guaranteed by the federal government, they cannot be called as corporate bonds can, the income is free from state and local taxes, and you can purchase them for as little as $1,000.

Key Point

Go to *www.publicdebt.treas.gov* for more information on Savings Bonds and Treasury issues directly from Uncle Sam.

Descriptions of government securities are as follows:

◆ **Treasury bills.** U.S. Treasury bills are issued in durations, which don't exceed one year. Unlike notes and bonds, these are purchased at a discount to their face value (par), and the face value is paid on maturity. For example, if you purchased a 26-week Treasury bill with a face amount of $1,000, you may pay $925 for the bill and receive $1,000 in 26 weeks.

◆ **Treasury notes and bonds.** U.S. Treasury notes are issued in durations from one to 10 years and are sold at face value. Bonds mature in more than 10 years from their issue date. Notes and bonds pay semiannual interest.

◆ **U.S. Savings Bonds.** U.S. Savings Bonds are somewhat different from the note and bonds just described. I remember U.S. Savings Bonds as the ones my grandmother would give me on my birthday, and my mother would put them into a safety deposit box. I'm still not certain what happened to them after that. In any event, these Savings Bonds are available in Series EE or Series I. Series EE are bought at a discount just like Treasury bills, and Series I are bought at face value and inflation adjusted to the Consumer Price Index (CPI). Unlike the other bills, notes, and bonds we have discussed, Savings Bonds are issued to a person and cannot be traded.

Key Point

U.S Treasury securities are the safest of all investments, but to ensure that you get back your principal, you need to hold on to them until maturity. If you sell the Treasury security before its maturity, it will be valued to the market, meaning you could get back more or less than you originally invested.

Municipal Bonds

It's no secret that state and local governments rarely operate with a surplus. Even when they operate with a balanced cash flow statement (they take in as much as they spend), governments need to fund major projects like building schools, maintaining roadways, and providing other valuable services to their constituents. To achieve these needs, they float bonds and raise capital from you and me and through a lot of pension funds across the country.

The major draw for municipal bonds (known as munis) is the income that they generate is tax free. The extent to which they are tax free depends on which muni you buy.

Let's say that you live in Los Gatos, California, and the city floats a $10 million bond offering to build a new high school. That bond is automatically free from federal income tax. For you, it's also free from state income tax and city taxes because you live in Los Gatos. However, if you lived in New York and bought the Los Gatos school bond, you would avoid only federal taxes.

Because munis are free from federal taxes, the yield on these bonds will be less than the yield on a corporate bond. It will be less for two reasons: because munis have the tax-free advantage we just discussed and because they are generally regarded as safer investments than corporate bonds. To compare munis with taxable bonds, you'll need to convert the munis' yield into a taxable yield.

Be Careful

I can just hear Jim Nabors who played Gomer Pyle on the *Andy Griffith* show saying, "Surprise, surprise, surprise!" You may pay taxes on your Municipal Bond! This can happen in two ways. If you sell your bond at a profit, you'll pay capital gain income taxes on any gain. The other way you may get stuck with a tax bill is if you buy a muni bond fund. The manager will likely be trading the bonds and passing along capital losses and gains or losses. Also, be aware that the Alternative Minimum Tax (AMT) may be applied to certain munis. Ask whoever sells them to you if they are excluded from the AMT.

Let's look at an example. You have an opportunity to buy either a muni yielding 6.5 percent tax free or a AAA corporate bond yielding 10.0 percent. I'll explain this in a way that might drive a numbers person crazy but that is easy to follow. The first thing you do is take your income tax and move the decimal point two places to the left. If your income tax is 35.00 percent, it becomes 0.35 percent. Then you subtract that number from 1.00, which makes the adjusted income tax number 0.65. The next step is to take the yield on the muni and repeat the first part of the previous step. If the muni is yielding 6.5 percent, it becomes 0.065 percent. The final step is to divide the adjusted muni percent by the adjusted income tax percent. That means you take 0.065 and divide by 0.65, and—voila—you have 0.10, or 10 percent. So, a taxable bond would have to yield more than 10 percent to beat the muni on yield alone, not taking into account relative safety. For the record, here's the formula without the explanation:

$$\text{Taxable equivalent yield} = \text{tax exempt yield}/(1\text{-income tax rate})$$
$$10 = .065/.65$$

Munis are not for everyone. It's important that you do the above calculation to see if they are right for you. If your tax bracket is 15 percent, the numbers look a whole lot different. By doing the math, you'll find that the tax equivalent yield on the muni for someone in the 15 percent tax bracket is only 7.7 percent, making the 10.0 percent AAA corporate bond a much better choice.

Zero Coupon Bonds

Zeros, as zero coupon bonds are called, get their name from the process of stripping the income from the bond. That might sound peculiar, but if you think about it, a bond is two parts: one part principal and one part interest. Zero coupon bonds are either issued at a discount (like Treasury bills) when they are purchased since they pay no interest or packaged as traditional bonds. A financial institution will split the interest and principal and repackage them separately, with the principal piece being the zero coupon bond.

 Key Point

Zero coupon bonds are purchased at a discount, but you'll pay taxes on the interest each year you own them just as if you had received the interest. Your best bet is to keep these in a qualified retirement plan where you won't have to pay current taxes.

These bonds can be very volatile because there are no interest payments to reduce the impact of interest rate changes. And the longer the duration of the bond, the more volatile the price tends to be. Bond price fluctuation has always been an enigma to me. When interest rates are high, bond prices are low; when interest rates are low, bond prices are high. It's kind of like flushing a toilet in Australia where the water runs the opposite way. It took me a long time to understand how bonds work, so if you're like me, maybe the following logic will help you put everything into perspective.

Let's say that you buy a 10-year Treasury note for $10,000 and the yield on the note is 6.0 percent. You're happy because for the next two years, you receive your interest payments and enjoy the safety of a note backed by the government. But in the third year that you own the note, interest rates start to rise and you notice that the new 10-year Treasury notes are paying 8.0 percent.

All of a sudden, your 6.0 percent is looking like four-day old leftovers, and you are hungry for the 8.0 percent interest rate. You can go out and buy a new note yielding 8.0 percent, but you first want to sell your old note. The best way to understand the impact of interest rates on bonds is to ask yourself the following question: How much would you pay someone for a 10-year Treasury bond yielding 6.0 percent interest when you could buy one paying 8.0 percent interest? The answer will certainly not be $10,000; it is roughly $8,700. The moral of this story is that as interest rates go up, the prices of bonds go down. Conversely, as interest rates go down, the prices of bonds go up.

Be Careful

Some bonds have a "call" provision, which means that the issuer can pay off the bond early. This typically occurs when the current cost of money is cheaper than the coupon on the bond you own because of lower interest rates or a change in the rating of the underlying company. Either way, you're left with the money to reinvest, and likely at a lower interest rate.

Convertible Bonds

A convertible bond is one that looks like a bond, but it can also become an equity. These hybrid bond/equity products are both interesting and peculiar. They are interesting in that they provide you with income, albeit at a lower interest rate than a bond that was not convertible. They also provide you the right to convert the bond at any time to equity in the company at a rate that is disclosed through an indenture. (The indenture is part of the bond and spells out the terms of the conversion.) Here are some points to note if you're interested in convertible bonds:

◆ As the price of the stock increases, the bond value increases even though interest rates may not have changed.

◆ They will most likely have a "forced conversion" clause that allows the company to convert the debt to equity at its discretion.

◆ You may want to consider a mutual fund that buys convertibles.

Inflation Indexed Bonds

Perhaps the biggest downside to bonds is that they provide no protection from inflation. If you buy a long-term bond, the semiannual interest rate won't change as inflation erodes the buying power of your investment. With the introduction of Treasury Inflation-Protected Securities (TIPS), you gain the advantage of a government-issued note with inflation protection. Here's the way TIPS work: You purchase a 10-year TIPS note and receive the regular semiannual payment of interest. Your principal amount is adjusted for inflation, so the interest being paid is on the inflation-adjusted amount of the note, not the original amount.

Be Careful

TIPS are inflation adjusted, so that knife can cut both ways. It is very rare for us to have a deflationary economy in the United States, but remember that the Japanese have been in a deflationary economy since 1991. If we did have deflation, your TIPS would continue to pay the stated coupon, but there would be an adjustment made at maturity to compensate for any long-term impact from deflation.

With TIPS you need to be aware of the following:

◆ During the 10-year period, you receive only the interest that your note bears, not the inflation-adjusted amount. When the note matures, you receive the inflated principal and the interest over and above the coupon on the note.

♦ This "gotcha" is the big one: Although you won't receive the additional interest you earn on the TIPS, you will receive a tax bill, and each year, you'll have to pay the taxes on the adjusted amount.

Bond Funds

You always have the alternative of purchasing bond funds instead of individual bonds. Just as we discussed in the chapter on equities, the advantages are similar. Bond funds provide greater diversification, and they also provide professional money management. The cost of managing bond funds is less on average than the cost of managing an equity mutual fund, with the average cost for bond funds running .90 percent per year.

The key point on bond mutual funds is that unlike an individual bond that has a specific maturity date, bond funds comprise multiple bonds with varying maturity dates, and the fund managers may actively buy and sell bonds within the portfolio. This means two important things: There is no maturity date, and you will likely have annual gains and losses on the fund that are passed on to you as the investor.

How Bonds Are Rated

In Chapter 6, we discussed the concept of risk management and the various types of risk that are associated with any investment. One of several risks associated with bonds and bond funds is the risk of principal. Stated another way, there is a chance that you will not get back some (or all) of your hard-earned money that you lent to the business or government agency. Table 8–2 is the same as Table 6–1, which illustrates the manner in which Standard & Poor's and Moody's rate bond issues.

Table 8–2   Rating Bond Issues

Bond Ratings	S&P	Moody's
Highest quality	AAA	Aaa
High quality	AA	Aa
Upper medium quality	A	A

Table 8–2   Rating Bond Issues *(Continued)*

Bond Ratings	S&P	Moody's
Medium grade	BBB	Baa
Somewhat speculative	BB	Ba
Low grade, speculative	B	B
Low grade, default possible	CCC	Caa
Low grade, partial recovery possible	CC	Ca
Default, recovery unlikely	C	C

It may be helpful to note the general pecking order of risk ratings that range from the most secure to least secure ratings (see Figure 8–1).

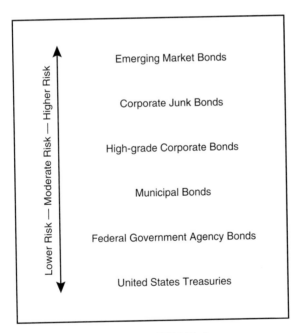

Figure 8–1   Pecking Order of Risk Ratings

Bonds and Loss of Principal

Regardless of how highly rated your bond may be, companies—even governments—have financial trouble and go out of business. Clearly, it is rare that a city or county government declares bankruptcy, but it has happened.

In December 1994, Orange County in California filed for bankruptcy protection, having caved under the burden of $1.64 billion in losses on bonds that the county treasurer had purchased on margin with a bet that interest rates would not rise. When they rose by more than 3 percent, the county was not able to meet the margin call on the investment, and it filed for protection under the bankruptcy laws.

When companies file for bankruptcy, there is either a reorganization of the company or an orderly distribution of remaining assets. Bondholders stand in front of equity investors if a company goes out of business. If you have bought the bond of a company that goes bankrupt, you are likely to be represented by all bondholders and receive whatever negotiated settlement is due to the bondholders. There are different classes of bondholders, and those with the highest order of preference will be first to collect on any court-ordered distributions.

Laddering Bonds

Another way to create a steady income flow is to buy a series of bonds that have scheduled maturities and stagger them so that you have a bond maturing each year over a period of time. Typically, people do this with zero coupon bonds, purchasing 10 years of bonds with varying maturities. This eliminates the interest rate risk associated with bonds, which is discussed later in the book, and provides steady and predictable income. Laddering can be an effective means of generating predictable income. It does not, however, provide you with inflation protection, so you'll need to limit this strategy to part of your retirement income solution if you like the concept.

Risk Reward

Figure 8–2 shows our principal risk pyramid focused on bond investments.

More Information

INFORMATION

Here are three bond sites you may find of interest:
www.bondmarkets.com
www.investinginbonds.com
www.bondsonline.com

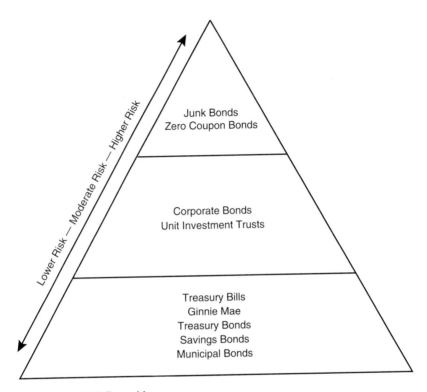

Figure 8–2   Risk Pyramid

Summary

You will find that bonds will play more of a role in your retirement income strategy than they will in your asset accumulation strategy. The reason is simple: Bonds are designed for income, not accumulation, and their historic returns have paled by comparison to those for equities. Interestingly, since 1925, the average compound return on large cap stocks has been 10.2 percent compared with 5.5 percent on long-term government bonds and 3.8 percent on U.S. Treasury bills.

But bonds are also a safe haven when the markets are rough, so you may find yourself sitting on the equity sidelines periodically, enjoying a lower return while knowing that your principal is safe.

Power Checklist

- ✔ In low-interest-rate environments, stocks typically do well and bonds typically lag because of the lower interest rates.
- ✔ People buy bonds for three fundamental reasons: income, safety, and tax advantages.
- ✔ The interest rate yields on corporate bonds are higher than on government bonds or municipal bonds because they carry more of a credit risk and because the interest is taxable.
- ✔ Junk bonds may have a place in your portfolio if you're willing to take the additional risk of principal to get a better rate of return on your investment.
- ✔ The major draw for municipal bonds is that the income they generate is tax free.
- ✔ Although zero coupon bonds are purchased at a discount, you'll pay taxes on the interest each year you own them as if you had just received the interest. Your best bet would be to keep these in a qualified retirement plan where you won't have to pay current taxes.
- ✔ A convertible bond is one that has two personalities; it looks like a bond, but it can also become an equity.
- ✔ Perhaps the biggest downside to bonds is that they provide no protection from inflation.
- ✔ With the introduction of Treasury Inflation-Protected Securities (TIPS), you gain the advantage of a government-issued note with inflation protection.

CHAPTER 9

Insurance and Annuities

Insurance! I'm certain that the topic renders you speechless and engenders the warmest of feelings in the deepest recesses of your body. Mom, America, apple pie, and insurance—it just rolls off your tongue, doesn't it? Why is it that we love to hate insurance and all that it stands for? I think it's actually fairly easy to explain. If you think about the reasons you don't like insurance, you'll most likely find yourself boiling it down to this statement: "I hate insurance because I get paid only after something really bad has happened, it's too difficult to understand, and I always feel that I'm being taken advantage when it's being sold to me." Does that pretty well sum it up?

My goal in this chapter is to change the way you think about insurance to the extent I can. I know that I can show you that not all insurance products pay out only when something bad happens. I can provide you with ways to make insurance less complex and easier to understand. I hope that I can also give you some guidance to help you find the right resources and ensure that you'll feel comfortable with the manner in which these products are applied to our approach to goal-oriented financial planning.

Insurance is very popular to sell for one main reason: Everyone requires insurance. Therefore, it's an easy way for businesses to leverage their customer base for additional revenue. Let's say that you buy a car and you're pitched the extra warranty. That's a form of insurance underwritten by either the car manufacturer or a reinsurance company. If you've ever taken out a loan, you've likely been offered loan insurance, which is nothing more exotic than decreasing term-life insurance.

It's amazing how many different types of people sell insurance and how many different places you can buy insurance. You can buy insurance from an insurance agent, a banks sales rep, a stockbroker, a financial planner, and even a CPA or an attorney. You can buy insurance from your employer and many other places too. Recently, I was at Costco, one of the national warehouse merchandisers, and found out that you can buy life insurance from a store that also sells bulk paper towels. And you know what—it wasn't a bad deal.

As I have disclosed before and will reiterate, I've been in the financial services industry for 25 years. I've been in senior management at an insurance company and at a major bank. I've designed numerous insurance and annuity products and trained thousands of people in various professions who sell these products. And I've spent my most precious time listening to and being a consumer.

As a consumer, I've dealt with insurance agents and others selling insurance products, and I know the subject can be challenging to understand. I also know that while you want to be trusting, you will likely be concerned about the motivation of those who are selling you these products. There are so many products and there is so much to learn and understand, and you'll find that many of the outlets that market insurance rely on specialists who focus on just certain aspects of the market, or certain products.

For example, I fully understand life insurance and annuity products. As a matter of fact, I co-authored a book called *Annuities* that was used by the Supreme Court in a ruling on banks selling annuities, and I provide expert testimony on annuities. But as much time as I have spent in the insurance business, I'm sure many of you know more than I do about car insurance or perhaps home owners' insurance. There's just too much to learn and keep up on in the business to know everything about all types of insurance.

Let's put insurance into perspective. Insurance is a way for you to share the cost of unexpected experiences with others who wish to do the same. We expect things in life to work right and to proceed in a manner that has an expected result. When the result is unexpected and creates financial hardship, we have the option of self-insuring or insuring the loss. That's the concept of insurance in its most simple form. Insurance companies pool and assess risk, charge premiums based on a combination of real experience and actuarial formulas, pay claims, and ultimately make a profit on that process.

Determining the Need for Insurance

As consumers, we have to decide which risks we want to fully insure, which risks we want to partially insure, and which risks we want to self-insure. Some risks are more catastrophic than others. We are constantly balancing these risks to determine what we can afford because it is nearly impossible for us to insure 100 percent of the risk in our lives. If you want to do a healthy exercise, create a list of risks and assess their impact on your life financially. For instance, what would be the financial implications if:

- You died or became disabled?
- Your spouse died or became disabled?
- Your home were lost in a fire or burglarized?
- Your car were totaled, stolen, or vandalized?
- You didn't save enough for retirement?

Once you have completed your own list, you can force rank the items from the most expensive replacement cost to the least expensive replacement cost. The next step is to determine the cost of insuring each of these risks and then put the two together to do a cost-benefit analysis. To recap, you can apply this concept to any form of risk and make an educated buying decision by following these steps:

- Assess the risk.
- Put the risk into perspective relative to other risks.
- Quantify the cost of reducing or eliminating the risk.
- Validate the cost and the terms of the product used to reduce or eliminate the risk.

Risk Choices

As we dig further into the area of insurance, let me make a statement that will help guide you through the fundamentals. You insure assets, not liabilities. This can sometimes be a difficult and emotional pill to swallow. I know a lot of parents who have fallen prey to the misguided statement that you need to insure your children. Let me be clear on this: You do not need to insure your child, and you should slam the door on anyone whose foot is still in it after making that assertion.

Yes, it may feel like the right thing to do, especially when some commission-hungry sales rep is trying to lay a guilt trip on you by using your own children to generate a sale, but it is an unnecessary expense. Children are a financial drain until they are self-sufficient, so there is no need to insure them. What you should be insuring is the life of whoever is raising the children and running the household, which is a risk that you may not be in a position to manage.

Insuring Preretirement Needs

You may find it easier to break risks down into preretirement and post-retirement categories. Take life insurance as an example. Life insurance is most necessary during the years when you and/or your spouse are generating income and you have children who need clothing, shelter, and education. This is when the need for life insurance is typically at its peak because there is a dire need to fund ongoing responsibilities should someone die prematurely.

Bring back the point I made earlier—you don't insure liabilities, you insure assets. As you grow older and you build assets, those assets can offset the need for insurance unless you want to protect the assets in your estate because your life insurance needs could remain constant. Estate planning is a critical part of your overall financial plan but not a primary focus in this book, other than funding any estate needs that impact your retirement planning. You'll learn more about the need for estate planning in Chapter 12.

Be aware that other risk expenses also transition during your lifetime. The need for homeowners and auto insurance tend to be higher during your working years than in retirement as many couples downsize their family residence and drive less expensive cars for longer periods of time. As we get older, we try to simplify our lives, resulting in an overall reduction of risk and therefore a cost reduction as well.

Postretirement risks are clearly led by health insurance and related expenses such as long-term care insurance, nursing-home insurance, and other expenses not covered by Medicare. Another big risk is that you'll outlive your money. It's fascinating to me that so little is written about outliving your income and possible solutions that guarantee continuity in cash flow. This is where the insurance industry has missed a terrific opportunity to bring value to consumers.

As I discussed earlier in the book, we reduce risks all the time, from wearing seat belts when we drive to brushing and flossing our teeth to prevent dental disease to wearing life preservers on a boat. For ages, the insurance industry has offered what I call "income insurance" or "insured income," and what the industry calls annuitization. Annuitization is simply a stream of guaranteed payments. Gee, with a name like annuitization, you wonder why it doesn't fly off the shelves!

In all fairness, though, historically, the income insurance offered by the industry has not been nearly as attractive as it is today. As a result, product distributors like broker dealers and banks didn't focus their attention on the product in the past. You'll see that income insurance should be a key piece of the strategy as we move into discussions on matching investment products with our retirement goals.

Annuities

An annuity is an agreement between you and an insurance company. That agreement can take many forms and can be as complex or as simple as the underlying need. Fundamentally, an annuity contract is a vehicle used to accumulate assets for retirement and a vehicle for distributing income during retirement. You can buy an annuity with a single payment or you can fund the annuity with ongoing deposits, much like a mutual fund or savings account. The annuity is tax efficient because assets within the contract that are accumulating for retirement are not subject to current income taxes. That's an important point, as you will come to find out shortly.

Annuities have been around for centuries, dating back to the Romans who paid out annuity benefits long before the insurance industry opened its doors. The first insurance annuity was issued in 1759 to a group of Presbyterian ministers, but it wasn't until the early 1970s that annuities took flight as an investment tool. Before then, the focus was more on establishing retirement income, not accumulating assets for retirement. Both are offered today through hundreds of annuities with sales in excess of $200 million a year. Total annuity assets exceeded $2 trillion in 2002.

Key Point

The annuity is a contract with the insurance company. There are three parties named in the contract:

The owner has full contractual rights to the contract.

The annuitant is the life that the contract is based on.

The beneficiary is the party or parties who will receive the benefit in the event of the death of the annuitant or owner.

The annuity comes in two basic flavors (it's so much more appealing to think of them as flavors): fixed and variable. In each category, you can use the annuity to accumulate assets or distribute income. We'll cover each of these in some detail as we learn how these products can be applied to our efforts to save for retirement. The concept behind using an annuity to save for retirement is very straightforward—why pay taxes each year on money that you have earmarked for retirement? The concept for using annuities to fund retirement is also a straightforward proposition. By using the annuity as income insurance, you can create an income that you cannot outlive.

You will find that the fundamental underpinning of all annuities comes from the inherent guarantees offered in these products. Clearly, one of the main advantages of an annuity is tax deferral, the same advantage you are affording in 401(k)s and many of the other qualified plans we discussed in Chapter 4. There are other benefits as well, including principal guarantees on fixed annuities, living benefits, and death benefits on variable annuities and lifetime income from immediate annuities. In addition, almost all annuities allow for some percentage of the account value to be withdrawn without penalty during years when there is a surrender charge. Although most annuities have a surrender charge that is applied for a specific number of years, more and more annuities are being sold without any surrender charges by fee-based financial planners.

The annuity offers investors the ability to enjoy compounded tax-deferred growth. Albert Einstein, who discovered the Theory of Relativity, also understood the value of compound interest when he declared, "It is the greatest mathematical discovery of all time." In the case of annuities, you receive interest or earnings credited to your account. Since you don't pay current taxes, the interest that you would have sent to Uncle Sam is working instead for your benefit. Let's see how compounding and tax deferral combined compare with compounding alone by looking at $50,000 on a taxable and on a tax deferred basis. We'll assume an interest rate of 8 percent and an assumed state and federal income tax of 40 percent (see Table 9–1).

Table 9–1   Compounding and Tax Deferral

End of Year	Taxable Value	Tax-Deferred Value
10	$79,906	$107,946
20	$127,701	$233,048
25	**$161,436**	**$342,423**

As you can see, there is a dramatic difference in accumulated values. To be fair, the money in the tax-deferred account will have to be taxed at some time, and you'll find that the SEC will require a worst-case scenario to be illustrated for potential buyers. But let's take it a step a further and look at the liquidated and nonliquidated values shown in Table 9–2. We've already shown that you can accumulate more on a tax-deferred basis, so why after 25 years would you just elect to pay your taxes and not continue to enjoy the tax benefits on this account?

The income comparison in Table 9–2 shows what happens if you use the 25-year value to produce income at the same rate of return used to accumulate the account value. In the taxable account, we generate $12,915 of taxable income, in the tax deferred account on which we have paid our taxes we generate $18,036 in taxable income, and in our tax-deferred account we generate a whopping $27,394.

Table 9–2   Liquidated and Nonliquidated Income

Taxable	Tax Deferred and Liquidated	Tax Deferred and Nonliquidated
Value after 25 years	$161,436	$342,423
$342,423	Liquidated value	$161,436
$225,454	NA	Annual income @ 8 %
$12,915	$18,036	$27,394

I have oversimplified this picture purposely to illustrate my point. When you oversimplify, you tend to leave yourself open to criticism, so let me close up any loopholes. In doing any comparison of products or concepts, it's important that you understand all the costs associated with the products so that you get a fair comparison. For example, you'll find that variable annuities have management and insurance costs that can make them more expensive than other investment products depending on what you're comparing. Fixed annuities don't have the same cost structure, so it's somewhat easier to compare fixed annuities with other safe investments. You should do your homework, but the point here is the same—compounding and tax deferral over a long period time tends to outperform the taxable alternatives.

In addition to the advantage of tax deferral, most annuity contracts are not subject to probate as long as the beneficiary of the contract is living. This means that at the death of the annuitant, the beneficiaries don't have to deal with the cost, delays, and publicity of the probate process. The AARP did a national survey some years ago and determined that probate costs run on average 2 to 10 percent of a person's estate. People can save some real money by keeping assets out of the probate process.

Fixed Annuities

Fixed annuities are products designed for those who don't like market risk. These are interest-bearing accounts with the insurance company. The length of the interest rate guarantee and the manner in which the rate is credited vary from product to product and company to company. You'll find single-year guarantees and multiple-year guarantees. You'll also find increasing rates, maybe 3 percent in the first year, guaranteed to go up by half of 1 percent each year for the next two years.

Key Point

Fixed annuities are not subject to market risk because the insurance company is guaranteeing the contract. You need to be comfortable with the stability of the company issuing the contract, but you need not worry about the market risk.

Some of these are promotional tools that don't mean much in the long run. If an insurance company can credit you 4 percent on your money but chooses to start off by paying you 3 percent and guaranteeing to increase by half of 1 percent a year for two years, it's not much different than paying you 4 percent for three years, but it may sound better. Hey, I can't fault insurance companies or any other businesses involved in marketing their products for varying the manner in which they position their products— that's the American way—as long as no one is misled in the process.

Key Point

Avoid annuity contracts that credit substantial up-front bonuses. Be very suspicious of anything over 3 or 4 percent. These contracts normally have very long surrender charges and very short guaranteed interest periods.

There are typically no costs to buy a fixed annuity. One hundred percent of the money received goes to work for you immediately, but there are typically liquidation fees for some period of time, usually for the first five to seven years. The liquidation fees, also called "surrender fees" or "contingent deferred sales charges," provide for two things: the commission on the sale of the product and a disincentive for you to liquidate the contract prematurely. Even if you were to strip out the commission and buy a true no-load fixed annuity, you would have either a very low rate of return or some surrender charge. That's because credited rates on fixed annuities track pretty closely with intermediate term bonds.

The way an insurance company invests your money is predicated on the type of underlying guarantees offered in the contract. For example, most annuities have a minimum lifetime guaranteed interest rate of 2 percent.

That means that you'll never receive less than 2 percent on the money deposited with the insurance company. But some contracts guarantee you three to five years of interest at much higher rates than you can get on CDs, money market funds, or Treasury bills. Since the insurance company is investing for an intermediate term, it can't afford to liquidate the portfolio prematurely without assessing surrender charges.

Key Point

If you have an older fixed annuity contract, don't surrender it! Some of these contracts have contractually guaranteed interest rate as high as 4.5 percent—you can't beat that as a guaranteed rate of return on a low-risk investment.

Another type of fixed annuity is called an "equity indexed annuity." In these annuity contracts, the insurance company offers you a fixed rate of interest that is tied to an equity index. I'm proud to say that I worked on the first design of these products in 1992. When we designed this contract, we were attempting to provide the upside of the stock market with the protection of the fixed annuity contract.

These contracts work in a variety of ways, but they have the same fundamental principles of crediting your account with interest based on the performance of the underlying index. In almost all equity-indexed annuities, the index is the S&P 500. Unlike traditional fixed annuities, which have a 100 percent guarantee return of principal, the equity index annuities guarantee 90 percent of your principal accruing at 3 percent each year. This concept requires an example.

Tom and Dawn decide they want to purchase an equity indexed fixed annuity. They make a $25,000 premium into the contract, which states that they get 80 percent of the average monthly increase in the S&P 500 over a one-year period. In the first year of the contract, the average monthly increase in the S&P 500 is 8 percent. Eighty percent of that is 6.4 percent, so that's what Tom and Dawn earn that year. The following year the market is ugly, and the S&P 500 is down 5 percent. The good news is that even though the market was down, Tom and Dawn didn't lose a penny. They also didn't make a penny, but given the alternative, it's not too shabby.

Key Point

Equity linked annuities are a great way to enjoy the upside of the market without the downside risk.

Equity indexed annuities are designed for those people who don't have very high risk tolerance and who don't have a problem giving up some of the upside of the index in return for some downside protection. If you're interested in equity linked fixed products, and I underscore the *fixed* part of this statement, be sure you read all the fine print and understand exactly how the index operates. These contracts can be confusing, and you're better off not buying something if you don't understand it. Equity indexes in variable annuities are quite different and I think very desirable, but we'll cover those products later in this chapter.

Fixed annuities do not require the individual selling them to have a securities license. That means that anyone with a state insurance license can sell this product to you. I struggle with my thoughts on whether this is good or bad. Ultimately, I don't think you should dismiss buying these products from non-securities-licensed reps, but I think that you have to be comfortable that the person you're buying the product from is knowledgeable and cares about how this product fits into your overall strategy. I won't discuss this any further at this point because we will spend a fair amount of time in Chapter 13 on this topic.

Let's summarize fixed annuities so that they are properly positioned in your mind. Fixed annuities are for anyone looking for a secure alternative to market risk. They provide a guarantee of principal, access to a percentage of your account during the surrender charge years for emergencies, and a variety of interest rate options for you to choose from. They compare favorably to CDs, intermediate term bond funds and muni bonds discussed in Chapter 8. You should also know that virtually all variable annuities offer a fixed component to provide a safe alternative to the markets.

Variable Annuities

Many of the concepts we covered in our general discussion of annuities and in our discussion of fixed annuities will also apply to variable annuities. The key difference between fixed and variable annuities is that variable annuities allow you to invest in portfolios of stocks and bonds called subaccounts, which are just like mutual funds. They do have some differences, and the SEC likes the industry to refer to them as subaccounts.

Investment Options

Variable annuities typically offer a variety of investment options, including numerous subaccounts, a money market account, and a fixed account. The latter two are homes for safe investing, whereas the subaccounts allow you to step out into the bond and equity markets. Most variable annuities offer at least 10 subaccount options, and you can find as many as 50 in some products.

Subaccount options are just as varied as the mutual fund industry, meaning that you can find a subaccount that invests in almost any market segment. Since annuities are typically used in the accumulation phase for growth, you see more assets invested in equity subaccounts than in bond subaccounts. You also will find index subaccounts that mirror the S&P 500. Figure 9–1 shows the distribution of assets in variable annuities as of the end of 2002. As you can see, equity subaccounts have almost as much in assets as the other categories combined.

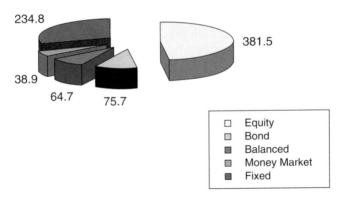

Figure 9–1   Distribution of Variable Annuity Assets, 2002 ($ million)

In many cases, you will find that the money management firm has simply replicated or cloned its mutual funds and has the same manager for both the fund and the subaccount. However, you may find that the actual investments differ in these two accounts because the annuity and the mutual fund are taxed differently.

Savings Tip

The average mutual fund turns over 50 percent of its portfolio each year. Some can turn over 200 percent or more, generating significant short-term tax gains. Variable annuity subaccounts can turn over as much as they want, and the taxes aren't passed along to you, allowing your money to compound instead of going to Uncle Sam.

Let's say that American Funds has a small cap equity mutual fund and also a small cap subaccount that it offers in variable annuities. The manager may buy the same stocks for both in the same proportion, use different proportions, or choose not to have a stock in one or the other. The strategies vary from fund company to fund company and from manager to manager. As a result, you can have a fund outperform a subaccount or a subaccount outperform a fund. You'll find that a number of subaccounts outperform the mutual fund primarily because of expenses, which will be covered shortly.

Insurance companies usually provide a choice of fund families in their products. This type of variable annuity is called a multimanager product, and its big advantage is access to a number of different fund managers, all within one product. There are also single-manager products that offer only one fund family. There isn't a right or wrong approach here—just different marketing philosophies. In practical applications in the market, you see more sales in multimanager products, but again, you should look at any product from the perspective of how it meets your overall requirements and how it's priced to the market.

Death Benefit Options

All variable annuities have a basic death benefit. This benefit insures the underlying money that you deposit into the contract. In essence, this guarantee provides your beneficiary with the greater of the account value or the premiums paid. If you die at a time when the account value has decreased because of market returns, your beneficiary is paid back the amount invested in the contract. Over the past decade, the insurance industry has vastly improved the death benefits in variable contracts, and most policies have one of the enhanced death benefits described below. Some of these are available at no cost; others may come at an optional cost from 0.15 percent to 0.40 percent each year.

◆ **Stepped-up death benefit.** The stepped-up death benefit looks at the account value periodically, such as every five years, and adjusts the death benefit based on the higher of the account value on the fifth anniversary or the premiums paid into the contract.

This sets the bar for the next five-year period during which the death benefit is adjusted once again.

◆ **Highest anniversary death benefit.** This death benefit is like the five-year step-up, except that it's adjusted every year.

Be Careful

You must read the fine print on all contracts. Some death benefit resets renew only up to a certain age and then revert to the greater of the account value or the premiums paid. Don't just ask—have your sales rep show you the language covering the death benefits.

Income Guarantees and Withdrawal Features

Some people will elect to convert their accumulated value in an annuity to "income insurance," and others may elect to take periodic withdrawals to fund their retirement. Many insurers are rewarding existing customers and encouraging new customers by offering living benefits. These include income and withdrawal benefits offered at an optional cost to the consumer. Some examples are:

◆ **Guaranteed minimum income benefits (GMIBs).** The GMIB feature guarantees the premiums are paid when the owner converts from the accumulation phase to income insurance (annuitization). When the owner is ready to receive income, if the account value is less that the premiums deposited, the insurance company uses the premiums deposited to determine the amount of income generated.

◆ **Guaranteed minimum account benefits (GMABs).** This benefit provides security that the premiums are guaranteed as long as the owner leaves the money invested for some period of time, usually eight years. It also may require the owner to have a diversified portfolio.

◆ **Guaranteed minimum withdrawal benefits (GMWBs).** This benefit allows the owner to make a limited fixed withdrawal annually and guarantees the premiums invested. Let's say that you deposit $100,000 in the contract. The GMWB allows you to begin taking 5 percent to 7 percent each year and guarantees that you'll get your premiums back regardless of market performance.

Subaccount Transfers Within the Annuity

All variable annuities offer you the ability to move your funds from one investment to another without paying additional cost and without incurring taxes. If you think that the market is heading down, you can run for cover in the fixed account, the money market fund, or perhaps a short-term bond fund. Some companies limit the number of transfers per year, but most allow you to switch as many times as you feel necessary. One thing to keep in mind is that money moved in the fixed account (also known as the general account) may have to stay there for a minimum period of time. Otherwise, it could be subject to a market value adjustment because the insurance company typically invests that money for a longer period than one year.

Savings Tip

When you transfer money from one subaccount to another within an annuity contract, it does not result in a taxable event. When you move money within a mutual fund family or from one family to another, you create a taxable event unless the assets were in a qualified plan.

Cost of Annuities

Much noise has been made in the press about the cost of annuities. I have my own views on why the press is so slanted against annuities, and I'll provide those a little later in this chapter.

There are fees associated with annuities, but most apply to variable annuities. Fixed annuities generally have a cost only for premature liquidations. For variable annuities, some costs are realized each month or year, and some are not realized unless you withdraw your money. The fees fall into the following categories:

- ◆ **Policy fee.** This fee typically applies only to small policies and is normally $25 per year.
- ◆ **Management fee.** This is the fee charged by the fund managers to provide their investment oversight. Management fees are often lower in variable annuities than in mutual funds because the costs are lower, and they can range from 0.25 percent to 2 percent or more for some highly specialized subaccounts.

◆ **Administrative and mortality fees.** These are fees charged by the insurance company to administer the policy and to provide insurance benefits. These costs range from 0.30 percent to 1.5 percent, depending on the extent of the guarantees.

◆ **Optional benefit fee.** The optional benefits are mostly related to guarantees of living benefits ranging from 0.35 to 55 percent.

◆ **Contingent deferred sales charge (CDSC).** This is commonly known as the surrender charge. It is not assessed unless the contract is surrendered prematurely. Run for the hills if the insurer is charging these fees for more than 10 years because the average is five to seven years.

Comparison of Annuity and Mutual Funds Costs

The cost structure of annuities is more complex than that for mutual funds, so you really have to be diligent when comparing the two. To do an accurate comparison, try to quantify the value of the insurance elements in the contract. You need to look at the features of each product and the cost of the features, and then you have to ask yourself how tax efficient these two products are. What you will find is that if you move your money around frequently and pay more in short-term capital gains than you do in long-term capital gains, the annuity performs well. If, on the other hand, you buy and hold mutual funds and those funds have very little turnover, you may be better suited to the mutual fund.

Turnover is the single most overlooked factor in comparisons of annuities and mutual funds. When fund managers buy and sell investments, they create taxable events. The turnover for a mutual fund is expressed as the percentage of the portfolio that is bought and sold each year. Most of the comparisons I have seen in the press assume long-term buy-and-hold strategy. Although these look good on paper, they are not consistent with the manner in which people manage their money. Because it is human nature to act and react, the average no-load mutual is held for less than four years. Also keep in mind that even with a buy-and-hold strategy, you can generate significant taxes.

According to Morningstar, the average domestic equity mutual fund turns over its portfolio 110 percent annually. The average domestic bond mutual fund turns over its portfolio 159 percent annually. This high level of turnover generates taxes that must be paid and taken into account when the mutual fund is compared with the annuity. The nice thing about doing these comparisons is that you don't go into them with any predisposition; let the more effective investment be the one you buy.

Insured Income

At the start of this chapter, I told you that not all insurance requires something bad to happen before something good happens. With income insurance, something very good happens when you retire: The insurance continues your income for a period that you define based on your situation. When you create an insured income stream, you also get to take advantage of the exclusion ratio, as long as the income you are receiving is not coming from an annuity in a qualified plan. When you use the exclusion ratio, each insured income check is part interest and part principal. You pay taxes on only the interest.

We discussed the advantages of insured income and the concepts of fixed and variable annuitization in Chapter 3. We also covered the broad types of payouts you can generate through annuitization. Fundamentally, you have to decide if you want to generate fixed or variable income payments and select a period of time. Once you have made those decisions, you can begin to play with various allocations between fixed and variable annuitization to provide you the right combination of income. Remember that fixed annuitization provides a guaranteed income that will not change, and variable annuitization will result in an income stream that parallels the markets in which you have chosen to invest. I'm an advocate of combining these two and keeping some portion of your assets liquid to maintain some degree of flexibility.

Table 9–2 shows a few of the more popular forms of insured income. Most insurance companies have many more options available. Figure 9–2 represents the amount of income guaranteed assuming a 60-year-old deposited $100,000 into each of these insured income options.

Over the years, I have spent countless hours with couples discussing income strategies and the differences between annuitization payments and systematic withdrawals from other investments. My position has always been to diversify income sources and never buy a fixed income annuity only because the inflation risk is simply too great. We always have to remember, though, that sometimes people don't want to implement the clear and obviously better choice. Let me share a particularly applicable story.

I received a call one day from a stockbroker who had participated in one of my income seminars. He was frantic because he had an older Swiss client whose husband had recently passed away, and she was looking for a guaranteed-income stream. She was interested in only one form of income and wanted a fixed-rate immediate annuity. I reviewed all my

Table 9–3   Popular Forms of Insured Income

Type of Insured Income	Description
Lifetime income with period certain	Benefits are paid for the life of the annuitant or a certain period of time, whichever is greater. If the annuitant dies before the time period has ended, the remainder of the payments for the time period are made to a beneficiary.
Lifetime income	This option allows for the highest lifetime benefit payments or lowest premium for a specific lifetime payment because there is no guaranteed number of payments. Payments continue for life and end on the death of the annuitant.
Period certain	Benefits will continue for a guaranteed certain period from 5 to 50 years. If the annuitant (usually the owner of the annuity) dies before the period is over, the remainder of the payments for the period of time will be made to a beneficiary. If the annuity contains after-tax dollars, the specified period of time plus the annuitant's age cannot exceed the age of 100. If the annuity contains pre-tax dollars, the time period cannot exceed the annuitant's life expectancy.
Life income with cash refund	Benefits can continue for life. If the annuitant dies before the premium amount is paid, the remainder of the "unearned" premium is paid to a beneficiary as a single lump sum.
Life income with installment refund	Benefits can continue for life. If the annuitant dies before the initial premium is recovered, the annuity payments will continue to be made to the beneficiary in installments until the balance of the premium has been refunded.

talking points about inflation protection and liquidity needs. He said that he had shared them all with her and she was adamant about her choice.

The following day, he arranged for the three of us to get together. I reiterated all the points the broker had shared with her, but she wanted nothing other than a fixed, guaranteed-income stream for the rest of her life. She wanted to be certain that the money was going to be in the bank, no matter what. How can you convince someone who has made up her mind and decides something that isn't in her best interest?

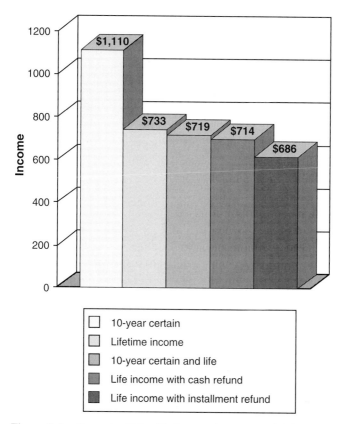

Figure 9–2   Guaranteed Monthly Income Amounts on $100,000

Fortunately, the decision she made, while not in her best interest, did provide her the protection she needed, and she agreed with me that she would increase the amount of income to compensate for inflation over her remaining life expectancy. The moral of this story is that what makes perfect logical sense in theory means nothing to someone with an overriding emotional driver.

Health and Insured Income

Speaking of life expectancy, it's important for us to cover a heath-related aspect of insured income pricing. Insurance companies' price insured income products use broad tables of life expectancy. If the table says that you will live longer, the insurance company will pay less each month because it will be paying out for a longer period of time.

Many people have life-shortening factors that, when taken into account, could dramatically increase the amount of money the insurance company would be willing to pay. Morbid thought, you say. Yes, it is— and certainly not one you would strive to achieve, but Mother Nature isn't as generous with some people as with others. The genetic track can produce diseases like diabetes, while not life threatening, do impact mortality. Some insurance companies are willing to underwrite insured income and provide enhanced payouts to those with life expectancies less than those used in the traditional tables.

1035 Tax-Free Exchanges

In real estate, when you sell your home, you have just over six months to purchase a home of equal or greater value and avoid having to pay capital gains tax. The tax-free exchange of real estate is treated under section 1031 of the IRS code. Annuities are afforded that same right through what is called a 1035 tax-free exchange (section 1035 of the IRS code). That means that you are allowed to move from one annuity contract to another without paying income taxes on the gain as long as you don't take *constructive receipt* of the money. In other words, if the money is sent from one company to another (or endorsed by you to the new company without being cashed), your gain is protected.

The SEC and the various state insurance departments have been cracking down on what they consider excessive or unnecessary 1035 exchange activity. These are exchanges that are not warranted for any reason other than to generate a new commission for the salesperson. It's a good thing that there has been a crackdown on these exchanges, and you should keep your eyes out for anyone trying to convince you to exchange your contract without a solid reason.

However, there are very good reasons to move your money, and it's important that your right to do so is preserved. As new features become available that make one product better than another, you need to have the freedom to choose. If the existing product has not provided sufficient subaccount choices or if the performance in your view is not up to expectations, you should be able to move your money. Use caution when making these exchanges because the insurance company holding your money is not likely to waive the surrender fees on the contract if they still exist.

The Press and Annuities

I told you at the outset that I would tell it like is, and I believe I have been doing so. If you recall early on in the book, I expressed a lack of tolerance for people who exaggerate and make broad blanket statements that just can't be true. They simply want to make a point and be heard so that they make the most extreme and absolute sentence they can. So when I hear someone quoted as saying, "An annuity is *never* a proper investment for anyone," I get suspicious. Imagine if I said, "You should never wash your car; it's just a conspiracy by Procter and Gamble to sell soap, and rainwater works even better."

A variation of this type of hyperbole is being used by critics who don't like annuities, and the popular press is reporting these exaggerations as if they were factual. I struggled with saying anything on this subject, but I read too many articles full of half-truths written by reporters who are not provided a balanced report. Clearly, if there is only one side to an issue, reporting one side is appropriate, but in this case, the reporting has not been balanced or fair. Annuities are not for everyone, and people must review their goals and ensure that the annuity is a proper match for their situation. With tax law changes that have lowered the maximum capital gains rate to 15 percent, the deferred annuity must be held for a longer period of time to merit consideration. However, income insurance tends to get painted with the same brush, which is unfortunate for those people requiring an income they can't outlive.

Be careful to look into the motives that are expressed by those who criticize any product. Do they have a vested interest that may be benefited by the negative coverage that follows the publication of their views? Are they making blanket generalized statements that are difficult to believe?

I realize that I'm not going to change the manner in which editors edit, and I'm not going to be able to keep people from making self-serving statements at the expense of any product or industry. The insurance industry is not without blame for the manner in which people view products, but it is not even close to what the press makes it out to be. Just as all attorneys are not like those portrayed as ambulance chasers, and not all doctors are like those portrayed as caring more about their golf game than their patients.

Don't believe everything you read and do challenge statements that include all-encompassing words like everything, nothing, nobody, everybody, all the time, or none of the time. Bear in mind that the vast majority of newspapers and magazines are *for-profit* businesses that need to sell their products to stay in business. Remember the famous quote by Sir

Winston Churchill: "A lie gets halfway around the world before the truth has a chance to get its pants on."

Life Insurance

Life insurance is one of those necessary evils that we avoid discussing and avoid facing. I can tell you from personal experience that life insurance needs to be one of the most important risks that you protect. Remember earlier when I said that you have to evaluate each risk you face and choose which risks you can afford to assume and which risks you cannot afford? Life insurance is the granddaddy of risk protection. Ask those who lost their spouses in 9/11 whether they could afford to lose their spouses. Ask the spouses or parents of soldiers who shipped off to Iraq or any other conflict where they put their lives on the line.

My personal experience isn't about life and death; it's about how life experiences can impact your ability to buy insurance. I was born with a congenital heart defect. My aortic valve was only partially formed, allowing blood to flow back into my heart once my ventricle pumped the blood through my heart and out the aorta. With only a partially formed aortic valve, my heart became enlarged over time because of the additional strain. I learned that I had this congenital defect when I was 30 years old. If I had purchased life insurance before that period of time, it would have been very inexpensive. But like a great number of us, I chose to wait, to procrastinate. After my diagnosis, which included having to have my heart valve replaced within 20 years, the cost of insurance skyrocketed. Actually, most carriers flat out turned me down. Back to our old adage: Forewarned is forearmed.

The following discussion of life and health insurance is abbreviated and supplements the discussion in Chapter 6 on risk management. These are important topics, but there are many books written on insurance. The following sections focus only on those issues that relate specifically to your retirement or will impact your ability to save for retirement.

Be Careful

Avoid buying all the specialty insurance products like mortgage insurance or burial insurance. They are marked up because they are convenience sales that play on your emotions, and usually at a weak moment.

Term Insurance

Term insurance is insurance in its purest form. You pay a premium and the insurance company pays a benefit if you die while the policy is in force. There are some choices on riders that can modify the product slightly, but otherwise, term insurance is straightforward. Because term insurance is so easy to understand, you see everyone advertising term insurance on the Internet (those irritating pop-up advertisements) and through direct mail. You can buy term insurance in several forms, with the most popular being:

Key Point

Riders are additional benefits that carry an additional cost. The most common is waiver of premium, which waives the premium in the event of disability, also called a disability waiver. The other is accidental death, which normally doubles the face amount, and this is sometimes called double indemnity.

♦ **Annual renewal term.** This form of term insurance increases in cost each year, and the benefit stays the same. The premiums are cheap when you're young and get progressively more expensive as you age.

♦ **Level term.** This form of term insurance creates level premiums over any number of periods from five to 30 years. This is helpful for those individuals who don't like to see annual increases in their premium. Keep in mind that with levelized premiums, you are overpaying in the early years and underpaying in the later years.

♦ **Decreasing term.** This type of term insurance is usually sold with mortgages or other forms of debt. You can buy a variety of term lengths to match your liability if you are buying to pay off a mortgage or loan. Personally, I don't like this insurance because it tends to be very expensive and is marketed as an impulse buy. The finance person at the car dealership or the loan officer at the bank sells it to you. Convenience sales are almost always the worst buy for a consumer.

Whole Life Insurance

Whole life, also known as ordinary life, bundles the cost of insurance (term insurance) with a savings plan (cash value). The premiums are fixed, and conceptually, it works sort of like a mortgage. With a mortgage, the bulk of your early payments are interest and little goes to principal. With whole life, your cash value is next to nothing for the early years and grows significantly in the later years. This is a rudimentary explanation to convey the concept, but it works. You don't see nearly as much whole life sold these days. When you do, it's normally in conjunction with corporately owned life insurance or business life insurance.

Fundamentally, most whole life policies include your cash value in the death benefit, so make sure that you understand this point well: For every dollar in cash that you accumulate in your policy, you have one dollar less in pure insurance coverage.

Let's say that you have been paying premiums for 25 years on a $100,000 whole life policy. At that point, your cash value is $40,000. If you die, your beneficiary gets $100,000, not $140,000. If you don't like that concept, and many don't, look at other forms of insurance such as universal life or variable universal life.

Indeterminate Premium Life Insurance

Indeterminate premium life insurance is a catch-all phrase for insurance with premiums that can fluctuate based on its underlying assumptions. There are really three main products in this area: universal life, variable universal life, and interest-sensitive whole life. All three use assumptions on interest rates or performance to determine a single premium, a level premium for life, or a level premium for some number of years. What you must be comfortable with is that the underlying assumptions are just that: assumptions alone. If the interest rate or performance assumptions do not pan out, you'll end up paying more premiums.

All in all, though, these are good policies. Both forms of universal life actually differentiate the cost of insurance, administrative and policy fees, and account savings on a statement so that you can see how much of your premium is going to policy costs and how much is growing on a tax-deferred basis. Universal life also allows you to choose a death benefit that includes your cash savings or allows your cash savings to sit in addition to the insurance benefit. If you go back to the earlier example of premium payments for 25 years on a $100,000 whole life policy and elect the savings element to sit on top of the death benefit, $140,000 would be paid out.

Life Insurance and the Glovers

Assume the Glovers are interested in $100,000 of term insurance coverage for which the premium payment would be level for 20 years. They would pay in the following ranges for an average 20-year level term policy at current rates.

- ◆ Dennis Glover: $603–884

- ◆ Mary Glover: $363–549

- ◆ Greg Glover: $127–218

- ◆ Connie Glover: $120–199

Other Forms of Insurance

In addition to life insurance and annuities, you should review and assess other forms of risk protection. The topics discussed in the following sections were also covered extensively in Chapter 6.

Health Insurance

Many people have relatively low-cost heath insurance during their working years, but postretirement health insurance can cost a bundle. The two main areas of health insurance coverage are major medical and long-term care (LTC). As you reach retirement, you may want to continue your health coverage with your current provider or you may want to convert to the Social Security Medicare program or a MediGap policy. The cost-effectiveness of these options must be evaluated based on your own personal health care needs.

You may also want to look at buying long-term care insurance at an earlier age when the premiums are lower. If you consider this, do a little cost-benefit analysis and look at the difference between the premium cost at your age today and the premiums you would pay if you waited until your retirement age to buy the coverage. As I mentioned in Chapter 6, LTC coverage can cost up to $8,000 a year. For example, if Dennis and Mary Glover wanted to purchase an LTC policy that paid them $200 per day after a 90-day elimination period and paid that benefit for the rest of both of their lives, it would cost $3,790 today.

Disability Insurance

Disability is a form of risk protection that most people don't look at. It's expensive, but when you need it you *really* need it. If your employer doesn't offer disability insurance, check with your state to find out about coverage so that you know how much you'll receive if you become disabled. If you choose not to have disability coverage, your emergency fund *must* take into account the possibility of disability. If your emergency fund is normally three to six months of expenses, you need to increase it to one year to cover yourself in the event of an unexpected disability.

The Safety of the Insurance Industry

When you consider investing your money in products offered by insurance companies, you need to understand what they provide you in terms of relative safety. The answer is that your money is very safe if it rests in the hands of the insurance company in a product like a fixed annuity or the general account of a variable annuity. But you are often asking the insurance company to administer assets that you are directing into other investments, and they are subject to market risk. Those investments, primarily in variable annuities and variable life, are only as safe as the underlying investments that you have chosen.

The insurance industry itself is incredibly sound and one of the most highly regulated industries in the country. Each of the 50 states regulates insurance. In addition, the National Association of Insurance Commissioners (NAIC) acts to set uniform standards that are typically adopted and enforced by the States.

INFORMATION

More Information

Here are a couple of insurance regulatory Web sites:

www.naic.org

www.sec.gov

When you are investing money in a fixed annuity or the general account of a variable annuity, this issue of relative safety is important.

Most of the major distributors of annuity contracts will not sell products from an insurance company whose rating is lower than single A.

That's why third-party rating agencies like A.M Best, Standard & Poor's, and Moody's all rate insurance companies. These are similar to the ratings that we discussed earlier on corporate debt and generally range from AAA down to unrated companies.

Most of the annuity products offered by lower-rated insurance companies tend to be high-commission products and not very consumer friendly. The bottom line is that insurance companies in general are very safe, and for every dollar you put into an annuity, more than one dollar is put into reserves by the carrier to ensure your safety. My recommendation is to stay with the highly-rated companies for maximum security, and you shouldn't have a problem.

Summary

Risk management can make or break you as you prepare for retirement. It is imperative that you assess your risks and make educated decisions relative to how you want to deal with risk, as part of goal-oriented retirement planning. Define the risk, assess the options to minimize the risk, and fund the risk so that you can meet your goals.

Power Checklist

- ✔ If you think about the reasons you don't like insurance, you'll most likely find yourself saying, "I hate insurance because I get paid only after something really bad has happened, it's too difficult to understand, and I always feel that I'm being taken advantage when it's being sold to me."

- ✔ Insurance is a way for you to share the cost of unexpected experiences with others who wish to do the same.

- ✔ As consumers, we have to decide which risks we want to fully insure, which risks we want to partially insure, and which risks we want to self-insure.

- ✔ When faced with managing risk and making an educated buying decision, follow these steps: assess the risk, put the risk into perspective relative to other risks, quantify the cost of reducing or eliminating the risk, and validate the cost and the terms of the product used to reduce or eliminate the risk.

✔ You insure assets, not liabilities. This can sometimes be a difficult and emotional pill to swallow.

✔ Income insurance replaces up to 100 percent of your preretirement income and can guarantee that income for the rest of your life.

✔ Fundamentally, an annuity contract is a tax-advantaged vehicle used to accumulate assets for retirement and a vehicle for distributing income during retirement.

✔ Annuities avoid the cost, delay, and publicity associated with the probate process.

✔ Annuities can be fixed, variable, or immediate.

✔ All annuities enjoy tax-deferred growth. You pay taxes only when you make withdrawals or begin insured income payments.

✔ There are typically no costs to buy a fixed annuity; 100 percent of the money received goes to work for you immediately, but there are liquidation fees, usually for the first five to seven years.

CHAPTER 10

Real Estate and Other Investments

So far in the book, we have discussed investments with varying degrees of volatility, but with fairly good liquidity. This chapter brings our focus to investments that are typically much less liquid, though they can be very worthwhile investments—particularly when considered over the long-term. The granddaddy in this category is real estate and the various ways that you can invest in real estate. They are followed distantly by gold and other precious metals, and collectibles.

Key Point

Volatility defines the extent to which an investment moves up and down. The greater the volatility, the more likely an investment is to have wide swings in prices.

Liquidity defines the ability to quickly sell an investment with the least chance of losing money.

With the exception of some of the mortgage-backed securities, a common thread that runs through the rest of these investments is the lack of regulatory oversight. The real estate market does have oversight and legal protection, but in my opinion, it pales in comparison with the markets regulated by the SEC and National Association of Securities Dealers (NASD). The lack of comparative oversight to the securities industry makes investments in categories like gold and precious metals, numismatic (rare) coins, and other collectibles ripe for con artists and fly-by-night organizations that could care less about whether you achieve your goals. My advice? Treat them with a similar attitude. There's a difference between creating a win-win scenario and being hustled into an investment that is "too good to be true." Here is where technology presents us with the opportunity to reduce the risk associated with the historical pitfalls of investing in collectibles and ensure that we are at least receiving competitive pricing on the items we buy.

Real Estate and Related Investments

Real estate captures and holds our attention for any number of reasons. It's "cool" to own real estate, and it's tangible property that we can see and touch. And unlike equity in a stock over which you have next to no control, you have almost absolute control over the real estate you own.

There is also a limited amount of real estate and an even more limited choice of prime real estate. On top of all this, you are provided with some nice tax benefits, and real estate can provide income if you're buying and renting real estate properties.

But perhaps one of the best advantages of real estate is that it is a leveraged investment. Let me explain. With a stock or a bond, you generally put in $10,000 to get $10,000 of value and 100 percent of the growth of the investment. With real estate, on the other hand, you may put in as little as $500 to control 100 percent of the growth of the investment. In other words, real estate allows you to leverage your investment for the cost of your loan to buy the property.

For many years, people have bought real estate as a hedge against inflation, and it's done well in that regard. Since 1972, real estate investment trusts have provided their owners an average annual growth rate of 10.18 percent, well above the average inflation rate of 4.98 percent.

As with all investments, there are trade-offs. Real estate is not highly liquid and it's not a highly regulated industry from the perspective of protecting investor rights. If you need to sell your real estate quickly, you'll likely pay the price by receiving a lower value. On the other hand, real estate is tax efficient, so you don't pay taxes until you sell the property, and then you receive favorable capital gains treatment. You can also utilize a 1031 tax-free exchange to preserve the gain as long as you aren't liquidating the asset.

The 1031 tax-free exchange allows you to sell one property and buy one of equal or greater value without having to recognize any tax gain on the sale. You have 45 days after the sale of the first property to identify another property and 180 days after that to close the sale and preserve the exchange.

Real estate provides other tax advantages as well: Any expenses that you incur in managing your real estate investment are deductible as business expenses as long as the property is not used as a personal residence. You are also allowed to depreciate your real estate investment over time. This means that you are allowed to write off a percentage of the remaining value of the real estate each year until the depreciated value is zero.

Let's say that you buy a property for $100,000 and you have to depreciate it over 27.5 years. You are entitled to the tax benefit of depreciating your property by $3,636 each year. You can actually depreciate some of the purchase even faster for items like appliances and carpeting.

As you consider buying real estate for income or for growth, ask yourself if you have the patience and the dedication it takes to be a property owner and whether the effort is worth the return. With real estate in general, and rental properties in particular, you need to be comfortable with the ongoing maintenance, the cost of insurance and accounting, and the stress of dealing with tenants and their idiosyncrasies. Finally, the real estate market is not nearly as efficient as the stock and bond markets, making liquidity an important concern, as we discussed earlier.

Real Estate to Avoid

At the outset of this chapter, I expressed concern regarding the unregulated nature of the real estate, precious metals, and collectibles markets, which sometimes attract salespeople in the way hospitals attract personal injury attorneys. I don't mean to suggest that all real estate salespeople are less than ethical—quite the contrary. They are like any other profession with a mix of both good and bad.

What I'm saying is that there are elements of any business that attract the sleazy sales reps, and in the case of real estate, those areas tend to be limited partnerships and real estate time shares. While I'm not a big advocate of more government intervention, I do believe the government should protect the rights of its citizens, especially when businesses won't police their own representatives. The manner in which time shares and limited partnerships are hawked is a clear indication of a product segment in need of regulatory attention to protect consumer rights.

Be Careful

Real estate limited partnerships and time shares are not liquid investments, and the secondary market for these is not fluid at all. In addition, expenses can easily chew up any gain in value.

Several years ago my wife and I were in Hawaii for a vacation when we received a flyer touting a wonderful time share that encouraged us to sit through a one hour "no-pressure" sales presentation. I'm the kind of person who occasionally talks to telemarketers just to hear what they are pitching and how they are pitching it, so I thought it would be interesting to hear the presentation. I won't give you all the gory details, but suffice it to say the presentation was all about pressure, and the sales rep lost all credibility with me by *guaranteeing* double-digit returns and *guaranteeing* that if we wanted to trade our time for a different location, there would be no problem.

If you really want to test their promises, just tell them you want everything guaranteed in writing by an officer of the company and see how fast they backtrack. By the way, in the event that they give you those guarantees, you still should find a way to say no. Both real estate limited partnerships and real estate time shares are high cost, low return propositions. On a final note, I'm not saying that you shouldn't buy into a time share for your personal enjoyment, I'm saying that as an investment don't count on them for adding much value to your retirement.

Real Estate Investment Trusts

A real estate investment trust (REIT) is to real estate as a mutual fund is to an equity. A REIT (rhymes with neat) offers investors the benefits of owning real estate without the hassle and pressure associated with buying properties directly. Instead of purchasing and managing your own portfolio of real estate, you buy shares of the REIT and enjoy the income and growth through dividends and share growth. The advent of REITs has made it possible to have an investment in a shopping mall without having to be a millionaire.

In the forty years that REITs have been available to investors, they have grown to 10 percent of the $3.5 trillion real estate market. There are lots of different types of REITs, and they have their own distinct differences. These include the following:

Key Point

REITs are required by law to pay out at least 90 percent of their net income exclusive of capital gains to shareholders, avoiding much of the double taxation that can accompany stocks.

♦ **Equity REIT.** Equity REITs purchase and manage real estate for their shareholders. Since these are regulated investments that are traded on the major exchanges, REITs are very liquid. The types of properties that they purchase are wide ranging, and equity REITs make up 96 percent of all REIT sales. You can invest in general REITs or specialized REITS. Specialized REITS include regional

REITs with a focus on a state, such as California, or a region, like the Southwest. They can also specialize in shopping centers, apartments, and health care facilities, to name a few. The more specialized the REIT, the greater the diversification risk. If you own a healthcare REIT and the healthcare market goes down, your entire portfolio is likely to react. If, by comparison, you were invested in a more diversified REIT, only that sector would likely be affected.

Savings Tip

As with equities and bonds, you may choose to invest in REIT mutual funds as opposed to the REIT itself. By investing in the fund, you get an extra layer of due diligence on the REIT and additional diversification. It comes with an additional cost as well.

◆ **Mortgage REITs.** These are REITs that invest in mortgages, not in real estate, and typically lend money to real estate developers. Mortgage REITs are significantly more volatile than equity REITs because they are really loan instruments paying interest, not income-producing properties. When interest rates are low, they are not a good investment. They represent 2 percent of all REITs, with the final 2 percent in Hybrid REITs.

◆ **Hybrid REITs.** These are a combination of equity and mortgage REITS.

Federal Agency Mortgage-Backed Securities

Mortgage-backed securities are actually a bond type of investment backed by real estate loans. There are three forms of mortgage-backed investments that all have government or quasi-government backing, making them very safe investments. However, they are a bit unpredictable... but more on that later.

The government wanted to ensure that there would always be a readily available pool of money for individuals to purchase homes. In 1968, the Government National Mortgage Association (also known as Ginnie Mae) was created to serve low- to moderate-income homeowners. Ginnie Mae takes enormous numbers of mortgages issued through the

Veterans Administration and Federal Housing Authority and packages them up to sell to large institutional investors.

Prior to the creation of Ginnie Mae, the government had taken steps to create a method for private corporations to buy and sell government-insured mortgages in conjunction with the government. The first and only such corporation to be set up was created in 1938 and is now called the Federal National Mortgage Association, otherwise known as Fannie Mae. Since that time, Fannie Mae has changed from a government-owned entity to a mixed ownership (1954) and then to a privately owned company (1968) when the government formed Ginnie Mae.

In 1970, Congress created another privately held entity to continue to support the growing real estate market to make matters even more confusing. The government felt that the demand for loans exceeded the capacity of both Ginnie Mae and Fannie Mae, so it created the Federal Home Loan Mortgage Corporation Act (Freddie Mac), whose function is to purchase mortgages from lenders across the country and package them into securities to be sold to investors around the world. Freddie Mac doesn't always sell the loan packages. Sometimes, it retains them in their own portfolio. Let's take a closer look at each of these entities to see the differences.

Ginnie Mae Securities

Perhaps the best way for us to look at a Ginnie Mae pool of mortgages is to see how they are created. Let's say that Preston and Naomi are recent newlyweds looking to buy their first home. They find a lovely little two-bedroom home in a nice neighborhood and settle on a price of $275,000. They go into Nantucket Bank and Loan and secure a loan for $220,000. Nantucket Bank and Loan then pools Preston and Naomi's loan with five other loans of similar amounts and goes to Ginnie Mae and sells the loan pool to Ginnie Mae, which adds those properties to others so that the pool contains 50 mortgages. Finally, Ginnie Mae turns around and sells the loan pool it bought from Nantucket Bank and Loan to a broker dealer who in turn sells it to investors looking to buy mortgage-backed securities. There you have it—a long and winding road that explains how these mortgaged-back securities work.

When you buy a Ginnie Mae, you are buying an income stream paid to you on a monthly basis. Part of the payment is the interest, and part is a return of principal because each payment results when Preston and Naomi (and others in the pool) make their payments to the bank. And since Preston and Naomi have an amortized loan, most of their initial payments is interest, not principal, so the bulk of the payments that you'll receive will be interest.

Ginnie Mae

Each month you'll receive a statement with your payment showing principal and interest paid, and you'll notice over time that the payments will vary in both their amounts and the proportion of principal and interest. If you think about the underlying investments, you'll understand why. Let's look at Preston and Naomi along with their 49 other loan friends to see what type of events could drive these changes in these payments:

- ◆ Interest could go down, and they could choose to refinance.

- ◆ They could find out that they are having quadruplets and decide to move.

- ◆ They could choose to accelerate their payments.

Each of these events will have an effect on the payment you ultimately receive. That's one of the reasons that people don't buy these mortgage-backed securities. Although they are very safe, their income streams can be unpredictable and the reinvestment risk is high. You may very well find yourself having to reinvest the money you receive from these when interest rates are low because the pool has been paid off. The average Ginnie Mae is paid out in 12 years, faster when interest rates are falling and slower when interest rates are rising.

Since your Ginnie Mae pays out part principal and part interest, the interest is taxable and the principal is returned tax free. Ginnie Maes are sold in $25,000 increments, but you can buy them through mutual funds at $1,000 per unit.

Key Point

Amortization of a loan spreads out the payments of a specified period of time, with a part of each payment going to interest and a part to principal. At the start of the amortization, the bulk of the payment is interest, but at the end, the bulk of the payment is principal.

Freddie Mac and Fannie Mae Securities

Much of what we have covered in discussing Ginnie Maes also applies to Freddie Mac and Fannie Mae. However, you'll need to understand a few differences if you're considering putting these in your portfolio.

Unlike Ginnie Maes, which consist of government-guaranteed loans, the pools you'll find in Freddie Mac and Fannie Mae mortgages are not directly insured by the government. That said, these loans are considered the moral obligation of the United States government and are considered very safe. Because these loans do not have the direct guarantee of the government, the yields on Freddie and Fannie are a bit higher than those on Ginnie, sometimes as much as half of a percent. The other key difference is that Freddie and Fannie are much larger pools, typically containing over 1,000 loans compared with 50 loans in the Ginnie Mae. The greater the number of mortgages, the more stable the income streams because the effect of one or two prepayments on 1,000 loans is significantly less than the impact on 50.

More Information

INFORMATION You'll find valuable information on mortgage-backed securities at these sites:

www.ginniemae.gov
www.freddiemac.com
www.fanniemae.com

Collaterized Mortgage Obligations

Remember our discussion in Chapter 8 of zero coupon bonds for which you separate the coupon from the bond? Collaterized mortgage obligations (CMOs) are similar in that they do the same thing to pools of mortgage-backed securities, creating what are called tranches (French for slices). CMOs are generally purchased by large institutions that buy the best slices, leaving the less desirable slice for you and me. Let's eat someplace else.

Gold and Other Precious Resources

Our monetary system stopped using gold as the standard for U.S. currency in 1976. When President Nixon severed the formal ties between gold and the value of the dollar, he made gold a commodity investment. You may still hear people tell you to buy gold as a hedge against inflation. My own personal belief is that real estate is a better hedge against inflation than gold, and it can produce income, which is something gold cannot do. Also, depending on the manner in which you buy gold or other precious resources, you can get taken to the cleaners by the salespeople offering these investments. The markups are very high, and unless you're an expert, you can't be certain of the quality if you're buying gold directly.

Gold can be purchased any number of ways, including as a gift of a lovely gold ring or necklace. While you're certain to be fondly remembered for your gift, I'd love to be a fly on the wall when you try to convince your spouse or significant other that it's time to sell the gold necklace for your retirement. However, you can also purchase gold in bullion form, gold coins, gold stocks, gold futures, or gold certificates.

If you feel that gold or precious resources such as diamonds, silver, or platinum should be a part of your investment portfolio, I would strongly urge you to buy them through a mutual fund that specializes in these types of investments. There is just too much to learn for you as an individual investor and too much ongoing work to protect any direct investments in this area.

Collectibles

Our final look at other investments is the area of collectibles. This includes the buying and selling of art (note that our art patrons above don't quite know a real Da Vinci from a fake De Vinci), numismatic coins,

vintage sports cards, dolls, and anything else there is a market to buy and sell. A 1928 vintage Babe Ruth baseball card recently drew over $2,000 on eBay. Clearly, there are people who make a living buying and selling collectibles, as evidenced by the worldwide conventions for just about all of the collectibles that I mentioned.

Lessons from eBay

One of the most incredible successes of the dot-com era is eBay. eBay was founded in 1995, and since its humble beginnings, it has grown to boast over 10 million users buying and selling goods and services online. On any given day, more than 16 million are items listed on eBay across 27,000 categories, and over $14.87 billion in annualized gross merchandise sales were transacted in 2002. eBay stock went public in a frenzied IPO in September 1998, and since hitting the market at $18 per share, eBay's stock price has ranged from a low of $3.76 to a high of $61.60.

eBay has driven a lot of change in the way people buy goods ands services. Aside from creating the world's largest online garage sale, the company has also found a way to legitimize the sale of goods and services through a simple tool called "feedback." Whenever you buy or sell an item on eBay, you are given the opportunity (and encouraged) to provide feedback on the person you dealt with in the transaction. This system of feedback is better than any Better Business Bureau data I have ever seen. eBay also provides other forms of buyer protection, but I believe the feedback mechanism is the best. You don't have to buy from anyone whose feedback is negative or has insufficient feedback to make you feel comfortable. In this manner, eBay legitimizes the sale of goods and services through a simple "honor system."

To tie this whole eBay discussion to the point, my wife and I were tasked (deemed more a labor of love) with finding a rare antique seltzer bottle for a friend. We did a search on eBay and found a number of possible items, and then we did research on the sellers by reviewing their feedback. We dismissed some off the cuff, and with others, we began an email exchange to ask questions and learn more. Those who responded quickly and who communicated clearly won our trust and got our bid. In three years of buying and selling on eBay, we have rarely been disappointed with the result. But back to the point—eBay has provided collectors with a system that allows them to trade their collectibles in a relatively safe environment. For an investment to be worthy of your consideration, there must be a ready market and a measurable means of protecting your investment.

Liquidity and Market Value

Any time you make an investment, you must take into account liquidity and market value risk. With collectibles, this risk is considerably higher than with other securities such as stocks and bonds. Usually, the market for collectibles is not very liquid and amateur collectors can lose money on their investments quickly. This is very common with investments in art and numismatic coins for which you are often dealing with individual buyers and sellers. This is a big reason for the success of eBay. With competitive markets, prices are more easily verified.

Another way to look at market value is in buying or selling a used car. The most popular provider of comparative information on cars is the Kelley Blue Book. Before the Internet, you had to find someone who subscribed to the Kelley Blue Book to find the wholesale and retail values of cars. Today, that information is widely available, making the market much more stable and affording you the ability to see what similar cars with similar features are selling for.

To give you an example of how collectors might utilize resources to ensure they are not overpaying, let's look at those who collect rare books.

Before the Internet, you had to get your hands on a copy of a book called *Used Book Price Guide.* From that book, you could see comparable pricing on rare books based on their condition and the overall market. Today, you can more easily do that research by going to *www. Alibris.com.*

Liquidity is another factor in making money on your investments, particularly real estate. The best example is trend for an average price of a home and the average length of time it takes to sell the home. The average price is an indicator of market value, and the average time it takes to sell the home is a function of liquidity. You may be able to sell your home at a given price, but you may have to wait longer to get that price. The more you require liquidity, the greater the potential loss of value.

If you like collectibles, I suggest that you consider this a hobby, and if it pays for itself, great. After you retire, you may want to get more serious about using collectibles to generate some retirement income. In fact, you can combine your postretirement avocation with travel and have very legitimate business expense deductions.

Let's say that you love to collect and trade antique dolls. Although I would never suggest that you build your retirement reliance on this as a business, you certainly can have some fun, make a few bucks, and generate some legitimate business write-offs on your taxes. Be sure to work with a tax specialist if you do this to make sure that you don't run into problems with the IRS. Thousands of people have legitimate small hobby businesses, though I don't think such a business should ever be more than a very small part of your overall investment picture.

Summary

Although we discussed a variety of investments in this category, my strong suggestion for your investment portfolio is to consider committing only a very small percentage of your assets, or ongoing savings, to this category. For those dollars, you may want to focus more on real estate and mortgage-backed securities.

I want to share with you a quote from another one of my favorite Broadway musicals, *Guys and Dolls.* One of Damon Runyon's finest efforts, it's about a gangster named Sky Masterson who runs an underground crap game in New York and falls in love with Sister Sarah, who runs the local Salvation Army. Yes, he falls in love with her and becomes redeemed, and the show has a happy ending.

During the show, Sky regales us with some advice from his wise, albeit poor, father.

On the day when I left home to make my way in the world, my daddy took me to one side. "Son," my daddy says to me, "I am sorry I am not able to bankroll you to a large start, but not having the necessary lettuce [money] to get you rolling, instead I'm going to stake you to some very valuable advice. One of these days in your travels, a guy is going to show you a brand-new deck of cards on which the seal is not yet broken. Then this guy is going to offer to bet you that he can make the jack of spades jump out of this brand-new deck of cards and squirt cider in your ear. But, son, do not accept this bet, because as sure as you stand there, you're going to wind up with an ear full of cider."

That's the best advice I can share because when it appears that things are too good to be true, they probably are.

Power Checklist

- ✔ Mortgage-backed securities are very safe investments, but the checks that they generate may vary significantly.

- ✔ For an investment to be worthy of your consideration, there has to be a ready market and a measurable means of protecting your investment.

- ✔ Real estate is typically much less liquid, though it can be a good investment, particularly when considered over the long-term.

- ✔ Perhaps one of the best advantages of real estate is that it is a leveraged investment. You put down 10–20 percent and get 100 percent of the growth.

- ✔ Real estate limited partnerships and time shares are not liquid investments, and the secondary market for these is not fluid at all. In addition, expenses can easily chew up any gain in value.

- ✔ Since 1972, real estate investment trusts have provided their owners an average annual growth rate of 10.18 percent, well above the average inflation rate of 4.98 percent.

- ✔ My personal belief is that real estate is a much better hedge against inflation than gold is, and it can produce income, which gold does not.

CHAPTER 11

Mutual Funds

History of Mutual Funds

Mutual funds are pooled investments working toward the goal of providing their owners with diversification and cost efficiencies. The idea for this concept of pooling investments began in Europe in the mid-1800s and took root in the United States in 1893 when a group of Harvard faculty and staff created a pooled fund. It wasn't until March 21, 1924, that three Boston securities executives pooled their money and created the Massachusetts Investors Trust—the first mutual fund born in the United States. That fund, part of the huge MFS family of mutual funds, is still around today, with assets in excess of $6.6 billion and a lifetime annual return in excess of 9 percent.

There are more than 8,300 mutual funds in the United States today, with a combined asset value of $7.1 trillion. The Investment Company Institute (ICI, *www.ici.org*) tracks the mutual fund industry and publishes an annual *Mutual Fund Fact Book*. According to the ICI, at yearend 2002, there was $2.7 trillion in equity funds, $327 billion in hybrid funds, $1.3 billion in bond funds, and $2.3 trillion in money market funds. Figure 11–1 shows how mutual fund assets grew from 1993to 2002.

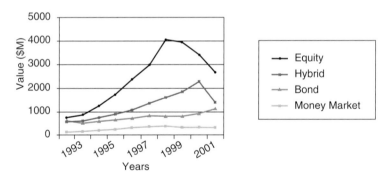

Figure 11–1 Mutual Fund Growth by Type, 1993–2002

Closed-Ended Funds

Closed-end mutual funds are a lot like individual stocks. The mutual fund company sells only a certain number of shares, and following the initial public offering, the only way to buy the fund is to buy the shares on the open market. When you buy a closed-end fund after it has been on the market, you'll buy it either at face value, at a premium, or at a discount.

Unit Investment Trusts

A unit investment trust (UIT) is similar to a closed-ended mutual fund in that it is passively managed and has specific time horizons after which the assets are sold. At this time, the UIT pays out any final benefits to shareholders. UITs are *goal specific,* meaning that you can find UITs that are designed for capital appreciation or for income. UITs are low in cost because the portfolio is not actively traded. This is a concept called passive management wherein the manager doesn't actively buy or sell during the term of the UIT. You'll read more about passive management later in this chapter. These products are typically sold through major banks, wirehouses such as Morgan Stanley, and independent financial planning firms.

Open-Ended Funds

Most mutual funds are open-ended funds. There is no set limit on the number of shares that can be issued and no limit on the amount of money put into the fund. A fund can sometimes get so big that it closes itself off to new investors; however, this is not a closed-end mutual fund but simply a fund that has chosen to limit the amount of money being invested. Over 97 percent of mutual funds are open-ended funds.

Key Point

Some open-ended mutual funds have had to close off the funds to new investors periodically if they don't have viable places to invest the money. Peter Lynch, legendary former manager of the Fidelity Magellan Fund, could create a huge effect on a company by buying or selling the stock as part of the Magellan Funds portfolio. Some funds have a history of opening and closing periodically to control the assets in the fund. Over the past several years, with assets going down in the mutual fund market based on the market losses, some funds with very attractive track records have reopened to new investors.

The ICI classifies U.S. mutual funds into five categories, with over 33 different investment objectives. The broad objectives are:

◆ Equity funds

◆ Hybrid funds

◆ Taxable- bond funds

◆ Tax-free bond funds

◆ Money market funds

From these broad categories, the ICI divides them into more finite objectives.

As you do your research and compare sources, you will find that not everyone uses the same definitions for investment objectives. This will sometimes drive money managers and consumers a bit crazy as they try to figure out how a given fund is benchmarked and analyzed. Benchmarking is the act of comparing an investment to a standard. For example, a large cap mutual fund may want to be benchmarked for performance against the S&P 500.

Key Point

Morningstar *(www.morningstar.com)* is an independent source for information on mutual funds.

Morningstar has created a ranking system for mutual funds that credits them with stars. One star is the lowest rating and five stars is the highest rating. The problem is that sometimes Morningstar will classify a fund in a certain category and then apply its star ratings, which are relative within that category. If fund managers feel that they are not being classified correctly, they have to try to get the fund reclassified, which can be quite a cumbersome process.

Equity Funds

Equity funds, as their name suggests, are mutual funds that invest primarily in equities. Using the ICI classes, equity funds are further defined and categorized as follows:

◆ **Aggressive growth funds.** These funds invest primarily in common stocks of small, growth-oriented companies.

◆ **Growth funds.** These funds invest primarily in common stocks of well-established companies.

◆ **Sector funds.** These funds invest primarily in companies in related fields, such as health care and technology.

◆ **Total return funds.** These funds seek a combination of current income and capital appreciation.

◆ **Growth and income funds.** These funds invest primarily in common stocks of established companies with the potential for growth and a consistent record of dividend payments.

◆ **Income-equity funds.** These funds invest primarily in equity securities of companies with a consistent record of dividend payments. They tend to seek income more than capital appreciation.

◆ **World equity funds.** These funds invest primarily in stocks of foreign companies.

◆ **Emerging market funds.** These funds invest primarily in companies based in developing regions of the world.

 Key Point

It's easy to confuse global funds and international funds. Global funds invest in companies from around the world, including companies in the United States. International funds invest only in foreign securities, not U.S. securities.

◆ **Global equity funds.** These funds invest primarily in equity securities traded worldwide, including those of U.S. companies.

◆ **International equity funds.** These funds invest primarily in equity securities of companies located outside the United States.

◆ **Regional equity funds.** These funds invest in companies based in a specific part of the world, such as the Pacific Rim or Eastern Europe.

Hybrid Funds

Hybrid Funds typically invest in a mix of equities, fixed-income securities, and derivative instruments. Derivatives include futures and options that money managers may use to enhance growth or reduce risk. These funds include:

- **Asset allocation funds.** These funds invest in various asset classes, including equities, fixed-income securities, and money market instruments. They seek a high total return by maintaining precise weightings in asset classes. These funds have become very important as the story on asset allocation is told. We will revisit this subject in Chapter 12 as we consider how to deploy our strategy for matching assets to goals.

- **Global asset allocation funds.** These funds invest in a mix of equity and debt securities issued worldwide, including in the United States.

- **Balanced funds.** These funds invest in a mix of equity securities and bonds with the three-part objective of conserving principal, providing income, and achieving long-term growth of both principal and income.

- **Flexible portfolio funds.** These funds invest in common stocks, bonds, other debt securities, and money market securities to provide high total return. These funds may invest up to 100 percent in any one type of security and may easily change weightings depending upon market conditions.

- **Income-mixed funds.** These funds invest in a variety of income-producing securities, including equities and fixed-income instruments. They seek a high level of current income without regard for capital appreciation.

Taxable Bond Funds

Taxable bond funds are corporate bond funds, and they seek current income by investing in high-quality debt securities issued by U.S. corporations. The following are taxable bond funds:

◆ **Corporate bond funds—general.** These funds invest two-thirds or more of their portfolios in U.S. corporate bonds with no explicit restrictions on average maturity.

◆ **Corporate bond funds—intermediate term.** These funds invest two-thirds or more of their portfolios in U.S. corporate bonds with an average maturity of 5 to 10 years. These funds seek a high level of income with less price volatility than longer-term bond funds.

◆ **Corporate bond funds—short term.** These funds invest two-thirds or more of their portfolios in U.S. corporate bonds with an average maturity of one to five years. These funds seek a high level of income with less price volatility than intermediate-term bond funds.

◆ **High-yield funds.** These funds invest two-thirds or more of their portfolios in lower-rated U.S. corporate bonds (Baa or lower by Moody's and BBB or lower by Standard and Poor's rating services).

◆ **Global bond funds—general.** These funds invest in debt securities worldwide, with no stated average maturity or an average maturity of five years or more. These funds may invest up to 25 percent of assets in companies located in the United States.

More Information

INFORMATION   Another great source for mutual fund information is Lipper, a division of Reuters. You can find more information at *www.lipperweb.com.*

◆ **Global bond funds—short term.** These funds invest in debt securities worldwide with an average maturity of one to five years. These funds may invest up to 25 percent of assets in companies located in the United States.

◆ **World bond funds.** These funds invest in foreign government and corporate debt instruments such as international bond and emerging market debt. Two-thirds of an international bond fund's portfolio must be invested outside the United States. Emerging market debt funds invest primarily in debt from underdeveloped regions of the world.

◆ **Government bond funds.** These funds invest in U.S. government bonds of varying maturities and seek high current income.

- **Government bond funds—general.** These funds invest two-thirds or more of their portfolios in U.S. government securities of a nonstated average maturity. Securities utilized by investment managers may change with market conditions.

- **Government bond funds—intermediate-term.** These funds invest two-thirds or more of their portfolios in U.S. government securities with an average maturity of 5 to 10 years. Securities utilized by investment managers may change with market conditions.

- **Government bond funds—short-term.** These funds invest two-thirds or more of their portfolios in U.S. government securities with an average maturity of one to five years. Securities utilized by investment managers may change with market conditions.

- **Mortgage-backed funds.** These funds invest two-thirds or more of their portfolios in pooled mortgage-backed securities.

- **Strategic income funds.** These funds invest in a combination of U.S. fixed-income securities for the purpose of providing a high level of current income.

Tax-Free Bond Funds

Among the tax-free bond funds are the following:

- **State municipal bond funds.** These funds invest primarily in municipal bonds issued by a particular state. These funds seek high after-tax income for residents of individual states.

- **State municipal bond funds—general.** These funds invest primarily in single-state municipal bonds with an average maturity of more than five years or no specific stated maturity. The income from these funds is largely exempt from federal as well as state income tax for residents of the state.

- **State municipal bond funds—short-term.** These funds invest primarily in single-state municipal bonds with an average maturity of one to five years. The income of these funds is largely exempt from federal as well as state income tax for residents of the state.

- **National municipal bond funds.** These funds invest primarily in the bonds of various municipal issuers in the United States. These funds seek high current income free from federal tax.

- ◆ **National municipal bond funds—general.** These funds invest primarily in municipal bonds with an average maturity of more than five years or no specific stated maturity.

- ◆ **National municipal bond funds—short-term.** These funds invest primarily in municipal bonds with an average maturity of one to five years.

Money Market Funds

Money markets have been interesting funds to follow for the past several years. With the markets in turmoil during 1999–2002, people were fleeing traditional equity funds and flocking to money market funds. Money market fund (MMF) assets rose steadily from $1.6 billion in 1999 to $2.3 billion in 2001, and then people began to look at their yields. After comparing the yield to that for fixed annuities and short-term bond funds, many people moved away from MMFs and these alternative investments. In 2003, yields on MMFs dropped to less than .50 percent, and the equity markets came back after three horrible years. At this point, people continued pulling money out of their money market accounts and invested in the equity markets. MMFs include the following:

- ◆ **Taxable money market funds.** These invest in short-term, high-grade money market securities and must have an average maturity of 90 days or less. These funds seek the highest level of income consistent with preservation of capital (i.e., maintaining a stable share price).

- ◆ **Taxable money market funds—government.** These funds invest primarily in U.S. Treasury obligations and other financial instruments issued or guaranteed by the U.S. government or its agencies.

- ◆ **Taxable money market funds—nongovernment.** These funds invest primarily in a variety of money market instruments, including certificates of deposit from large banks, commercial paper, and bankers' acceptances. In other words, they are all very safe, short-term investments.

- ◆ **Tax-exempt money market funds.** These funds invest in short-term municipal securities and must have an average maturity of 90 days or less. These funds seek the highest level of income— free from federal and, in some cases, state and local taxes—consistent with the preservation of capital.

Be Careful

Money market funds offer a safe haven when you want an alternative to equities or bonds. Be careful, though; in low-interest-rate environments, you can actually lose money invested in a money market fund if the fund management fee and expenses exceed the credited rate. Check the prospectus because some funds may waive fees under some circumstances.

◆ **National tax-exempt money market funds.** These funds invest in short-term securities of various U.S. municipal issuers.

◆ **State tax-exempt money market funds.** These funds invest primarily in short-term securities of municipal issuers in a single state to achieve the highest level of tax-free income for residents of that state.

More Information

INFORMATION   A wonderful source for information on mutual funds is the Investment Company Institute. It has tons of information at *www.ici.org.*

Style Boxes

In Chapter 7 we discussed how equities have certain characteristics that ultimately help us to classify them so that we can get different views of our portfolio. Morningstar's style boxes help us classify stocks, bonds, and mutual funds based on their capitalization and management style. The top-left box is for large-cap value funds and the bottom-right box is for small-cap growth funds. As you can see from the two examples in Figure 11–2, you can deploy very different approaches with different resulting risk profiles. The first portfolio is fairly well balanced and of moderate risk, whereas the second portfolio is heavily weighted to small- and mid-cap funds and has greater risk. Using the Style Boxes gives us a better understanding of our overall portfolio.

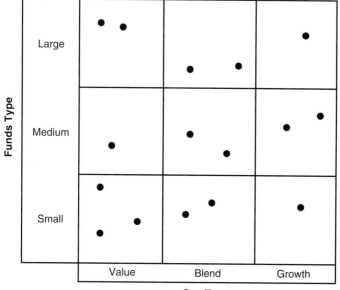

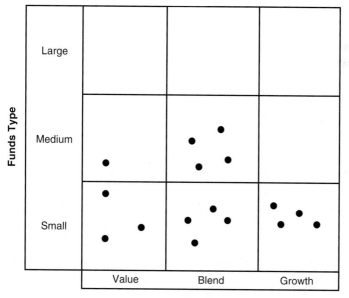

Figure 11–2   Morningstar Style Boxes

Equity Indices

In 1976, John C. Bogle, the man generally credited with turning Vanguard into a powerhouse mutual fund company, opened the first retail index fund called the First Index Investment Trust. That fund is now called the Vanguard 500 Index fund *(www.vanguard.com),* and in October 2003, its assets were a whopping $79 billion. It has more assets than any other mutual fund on the market. Since Vanguard introduced its S&P 500 index, over 678 funds have been introduced. Most track the S&P 500, but some track the Europe, Australia, and Far East Index (EAFE) while others track the Russell 2000 or other popular indices.

There are two clear advantages to investing in index funds: lower fees and tax efficiency. The management fees and the trade costs for index funds are dirt cheap. For example, the Vanguard 500 Index fund charges only 0.18 percent per year. That's less than 2/10 of 1 percent. Index funds are very tax efficient because they are passively managed, which means they buy or sell a security only when one is added or deleted from the underlying index. This tax efficiency is a critical issue to those in high tax brackets.

You will also find "enhanced index funds." There is nothing wrong with these funds, but you have to understand that their objective is to out-perform the underlying index. The managers do this primarily through the use of derivative investments like put and call options on the underlying index. These can be rewarding, but they are more risky and require greater management, hence higher management fees.

Socially Responsible Investment Funds

Socially responsible investment (SRI) funds have been around for a very long time. Although they are not their own fund class or category, you'll find dozens of them to choose from. These are mutual funds that screen investments to exclude companies that don't meet their standards. The screening process may exclude companies that pollute the environment, tobacco companies, gaming companies, or those that exploit third-world labor. There is even a fund whose objective is to match the Domini 400 Social Index of 400 companies that meet the rigorous screening applied by Domini. That fund, the Domini Social Equity Fund, was started in June 1991, and since its inception, it has a 9.80 percent average annual return compared with the 10.12 percent, which the S&P 500 returned over that same period. Many other fund managers offer SRI funds, with the largest and oldest being The Calvert Group at *www.calvertgroup.com*. You can also log onto *www.socialinvest.org* for good information on socially responsible investing.

Turmoil in the Industry

In 2003, the mutual fund industry was turned on its side by allegations of violations of securities laws. These allegations have led to a major shakeup in the industry, with many fund companies reducing management and marketing fees and providing greater clarification of the charges and expenses that impact the fund's performance. At its core are three pervasive issues:

◆ Late trading

◆ Market timing

◆ The use of 12(b)(1) fees

Late trading is the illegal practice of allowing exceptions to the rule that cuts off trading of mutual funds at the close of business, 4:00 p.m. Eastern time. This cutoff time provides for an orderly and consistent method of determining closing prices on the funds. Any trade made after 4:00 p.m. is supposed to be priced at the closing price the following day at 4:00 p.m. Late trading violations were created when some fund companies allowing preferred clients to settle trades after the 4:00 p.m. close. The Securities and Exchange Commission and some state officials have charged several mutual funds with allowing hedge funds and other large investors to break the rule repeatedly and knowingly.

The second area of abuse is called market timing, and although these activities are not necessarily illegal, they are generally considered unfair and unethical. Market timing is rapid, in-and-out trading to take advantage of differences between the fund's share price, which is set once a day, and current market conditions that may change frequently during the day. As I said, it's not technically illegal, but most fund companies have policies prohibiting it. For example, the European markets close before the U.S. markets do, and a market timer may be allowed to buy at the closing price in Europe and then sell, based on the closing price in the United States.

Finally, a number of mutual fund companies and broker dealers who distribute their products have been chided recently for failing to inform consumers when marketing allowances paid to the broker dealer have not been disclosed. The practice of mutual fund companies' paying to be preferred sponsors is not unique to this or any other industry.

Manufacturers pay distributors to showcase their products all the time. These arrangements are not always paid for directly with cash; they are often the result of enhanced services that differentiate one manufacturer from another. Let's say that you were buying a gas fireplace and went to a local store to look at the products it offered. The sales representative showed you several models from Heat-N-Glo and one model from Empire. They products had similar features, similar prices, and similar service records. Yet the sales representative clearly was more enthusiastic about the Heat-N-Glo line. Perhaps he was being paid more by Heat-N-Glo to push its products or the Heat-N-Glo regional representative was more helpful in teaching the sales representative about new developments in the fireplace market. The point is that as a consumer, you need to ask questions, and one question would be, "Do you make more on Heat-N-Glo than you do on Empire?" The sales representative may say the store does, but the consumer is not paying any more for the Heat-N-Glo product then for the Empire product.

Now back to mutual funds and the financial services industry. In the financial services industry, many of the major broker dealers have preferred status relationships with mutual fund companies. A mutual fund company may even divert fees collected from the consumer to the broker dealer in return for the broker dealer's focused efforts to market its funds. But these are fees that the consumer would pay regardless of whether the fund manager paid the broker dealer or not. They are fees that are fully disclosed in the prospectus customers receive before making an investment. It is important for consumers to know if the preferred status has an explicit cost to the consumer—that's a very fair question. Clearly, the recommendation of any fund must be first predicated on your need.

Mutual Fund Expenses

Mutual funds have their expenses divided into four possible areas: sales charges, management fees, fund expenses, and 12(b)(1) fees. The specific charges associated with a fund will be found in the prospectus and should be clearly stated. In fact, by law, the fund's fees and expenses must be clearly disclosed to investors in a standardized fee table at the front of the fund's prospectus. The fee table breaks out the fees and shareholder expenses and allows investors to easily compare the cost of investing in different funds. If it takes an attorney who doubles as a rocket scientist to understand the charges, you are well advised to proceed with caution.

Be Careful

Some mutual funds, particularly younger funds without a lot of assets, will waive the management fee for a period of time or until the fund reaches a certain level of assets. This is not a bad thing, but you should understand that it is not likely that the management fee will be waived forever.

The prospectus must be delivered *before* the sale is made to all individuals who purchase a mutual fund. All funds will have management fees and expenses, but not all funds will have sales charges or 12(b)(1) fees; it depends on the class of shares being purchased. The following sections offer a brief description of these charges.

Mutual Fund Share Classes and Charges

The following are the share classes of mutual funds:

- ◆ **"A" shares.** These are funds with front-end loads. Historically, these funds were sold only by commissioned sales reps. The argument was that although they had a front-end load, the overall fund expenses were lower than those for other types of shares. "A" shares also have breakpoints that reduce the load on larger sales. Typically, "A" shares start with a 5.5 percent load taken out of the investment and reduce down to 1 percent or less for large deposits.

Be Careful

Classes of shares can be confusing. You should check the prospectus for exact details on any of these expenses associated with its share class.

- ◆ **"B" shares.** These are funds that have a back-end load. That means that 100 percent of your investment goes to work immediately. However, there is a redemption fee, also known as a contingent deferred sales charge (CDSC), that usually runs for five years. In most funds today, it is a declining charge that is reduced by 1 percent a year so that after the fifth year there is no charge. This is one of the most common share classes sold. Investors pay higher annual 12(b)(1) fees for class "B" shares than class "A" shares. Typically, after the CDSC, "B" shares revert to "A" shares and enjoy lower expenses.

- ◆ **"C" shares.** These shares have a limited back-end load that is assessed for a shorter period of time than "B" shares. If you sell "C" shares within 12–18 months of purchase, a 1 percent CDSC is assessed. "C" shares usually charge a higher 12(b)(1) fee than "A" shares, and these typically do not convert into "A" shares at any time. "C" shares may be appropriate for investors with short- to intermediate-term goals. A higher 12(b)(1) fee is paid, but there is no CDSC after 12–18 months. Investors can then redeem shares without a charge after a shorter period of time, unlike with "B" shares.

- ◆ **"H" shares.** These are sometimes called hybrid shares because they combine a low front-end sales charge with a low back-end sales charge (CDSC) that is assessed if shares are redeemed within 12–18 months. As with "C" shares, there are higher 12(b)(1) fees than with "A" shares, and "H" shares do not convert into "A" shares at any time.

Key Point

Mutual fund prices are called the NAV, which stands for net asset value. To calculate the NAV, take the fund assets from the close of the previous day, subtract the expenses, and then divide by the outstanding shares. The NAV can be found in *The Wall Street Journal*, in most daily newspapers, and at various online locations. Your best source may be your broker or the fund family Web site.

- ◆ **"I" shares.** These shares are sometimes called institutional shares because they are intended only for financial institutions purchasing shares for their own or their clients' accounts. Class

"I" shares have no front-end sales charge, have low annual operating expenses, and cannot be purchased by the general public.

◆ **"R" shares.** These shares are sometimes called retirement shares because they were designed for retirement plan investors. "R" shares have a low back-end sales charge. If you sell "R" shares within 12–18 months of purchase, a small CDSC is assessed. This usually is about 0.75 percent but sometimes can be as high as 1.00 percent or as low as 0.50 percent. "R" shares have a lower 12(b)(1) fee than other back-end loaded share types and do not convert into "A" shares at any time. "R" shares are typically offered only in sponsored qualified plans or in IRA accounts.

12(b)(1) Fees

12(b)(1) fees were made possible through the passage of the 1980 Investment Company Act. When applied, which is often, this fee is deducted from fund assets to compensate sales professionals for providing investment advice and ongoing services to mutual fund shareholders as well as to pay fund marketing and advertising expenses.

Mutual Fund Expense Fees

Every mutual fund has operational expenses outside the management of the fund. For example, if you own shares of a mutual fund, the fund is required by law to provide you with certain types of information. That requirement results in printing costs, mailing costs, transfer agent costs, and a host of other expenses. Funds also have to pay for the execution of trades, which is included in this fee.

Mutual Fund Management Expense

The single biggest cost of running a mutual fund is the management of the fund assets. The funds investment strategy is led by professional money managers who have significant experience in managing money. Different mutual fund companies have different styles of management, some preferring a single manager who has a team working for him or her. Other fund companies take a full-team approach in which investments are agreed upon by a group of professionals and no one person is responsible for the funds asset management.

Depending on the type of fund you purchase, the fees could range from a low of 0.25 percent to a high in excess of 2.5 percent (see Table 11–1). The cost of management fees is a function of any number of variables, but in general terms, the harder it is for the manager to get information or acquire securities, the higher the cost. Money market funds are the least expensive to manage, and international and technology funds tend to be the most expensive.

Table 11–1   Types of Funds and Their Fees[a]

Type of Fund	Average Management Expense
Equity	1.28%
Bond	0.90%
Money market	0.36%

[a] Source: Investment Company Institute 2002 Mutual Fund Fact Book

Mutual Funds and Goal-Oriented Financial Planning

Mutual funds are great investment tools for goal-oriented financial planning (GOFP). The big advantage to using mutual funds for GOFP is that you can get very specific with the objectives of a mutual fund and match it very closely to the goals and characteristics of your own list in your GOFP.

Summary

Mutual funds offer a variety of advantages as you look at constructing your portfolio of assets. The key advantages of funds include a wide assortment of choices, the diversification of the fund assets, and professional money management. And mutual funds offer so many different investment options, you can get everything from traditional bond and equity funds to sector-specific funds for people who want to get very granular in their investing without taking all the risk associated with individual stock investments.

Power Checklist

- ✔ There are over 8,300 mutual funds today in the United States, with a combined asset value of $7.1 trillion.

- ✔ Over 97 percent of mutual funds are open-ended funds that allow you to make additional investments as you choose.

- ✔ U.S. mutual funds are divided into five categories, with over 33 different investment objectives.

- ✔ Be sure that you understand the class of mutual fund shares that you are buying because each type has its own cost structure.

- ✔ You may want to look at investing in an indexed mutual fund. These are very low cost and are designed to mirror their underlying index.

- ✔ SRI funds are mutual funds that invest only in companies that meet certain screens designed to ensure that they are managed by good corporate citizens. Approximately $2 trillion of investment assets are screened today.

CHAPTER 12

Managing Your Investments

NEVER CHARGE WHEN THE
WIND IS BLOWING

> "'Tis the part of a wise man to keep himself today for tomorrow, and not venture all his eggs in one basket."
> Miguel de Cervantes
> in *Don Quixote de la Mancha,* 1605

And you've been wondering all this time where the saying "Don't put all your eggs in one basket" came from. While I can't be certain that Don Quixote de la Mancha was the first to utter these famous words, their truth is undeniable. In this important chapter, we begin the process of linking your retirement goals with your assets. We also review the various strategies and approaches to managing your investments. When we're done with this chapter, you should be able to leverage the book's lessons so far to help you point to the best way to utilize GORP.

I'll provide the framework necessary for you to be able to determine how much more you need to save to reach your goals and give you techniques to choose which investments are best suited to you. Remember, we are separating goals and assets so that we don't get confused. Goals have unique characteristics and so do assets—they must match and be monitored to ensure success.

Chasing Returns

For you to achieve your goals, you must actively manage the risk-reward relationship, the relationship of risk to performance. The greater the risk, the greater the potential for reward. While all of this can be calculated out mathematically, we often go with our gut instincts and buy or sell based on emotional data points, not scientific ones. In this chapter, I'll review some of each. After all, there is more than one way to climb a mountain and more then one way to achieve financial success.

An interesting way to start this discussion is to look at how the S&P 500 has responded to recessions. Table 12–1 shows the gain in the S&P 500 for the 6- and 12-month periods following major down markets.

Investing Is Not a Two-Dimensional Process

Earlier in the book, we talked about investments being three-dimensional. This remains an important concept as we look at managing assets. The first

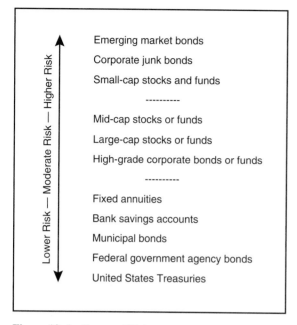

Figure 12–1   Range of Risk

* Variable annuities offer almost all of these investments, so the risk
  is the risk of the underlying investment, not the annuity itself.

Table 12–1   S&P Gains Following Market Bottoms

Market Bottom	6 Months	12 Months
1969–1970	24.02%	43.73%
1973–1975	30.88%	38.01%
1981–1982	45.41%	58.33%
1990–1991	27.81%	29.10%
1999–2002	10.50%	26.38%

two dimensions are time and returns (value). Time itself is one dimensional,
meaning that we don't influence time—we can't speed it up, and we can't
slow it down. Returns are not one dimensional. Because they can be
affected by any number of factors, some macro-economic (like how our
country or the world is faring) and some micro-economic (like the status of
a given industry or market sector). As you consider risk and return, try to
consider this dimensional element of investing, and keep it as a visual.

From this point, we'll move on and take a look at a variety of issues that impact the manner in which you or an outside professional would manage your assets.

Identifying the Right Mix of Securities in Your Portfolio

The research on the right mix of securities in a portfolio is very broad, as you might expect, but a common theme emerges. Everyone has an opinion on how you should allocate your assets among stock and bonds, whether it is 50/50, 75/25, or any other combination. What you need to be concerned about is that you are basing your asset weighting not on someone's general theory of asset allocation but on what you need to achieve your goals. Let's learn more about asset allocation.

Asset Allocation

Asset allocation is a tool by which we reduce diversification risk by spreading assets into different classes. Typically, you will complete a questionnaire about your risk tolerance and time horizons and then look at a suggested portfolio of asset classes to appropriately allocate your assets among equities, bonds, and cash. Some asset allocation programs get really granular and subdivide into dozens of smaller asset classes.

Savings Tip

You might want to consider a simple rule of thumb that is often used in asset allocation. Subtract your age from 100 and invest the result in equities with the difference going into bonds. If you were 50 years old, you would subtract 50 from 100 and half of your investments would go into equities and half into bonds. A 30-year-old's portfolio would be 70 percent equity and 30 percent bonds, and so on.

There really isn't a right or wrong method, although those who get more granular in their approach become very territorial when you suggest their systems are a bit like shooting a gnat with an elephant gun. Table 12–2 shows some recommended asset allocation strategies.

Table 12–2   Recommended Allocation Strategies by Term and Risk Type

Term, Risk	Investment	Percent
Short term, low risk	Cash/CD/Treasury	25
	Bonds	45
	Equities	30
Short term, moderate risk	Cash/CD/Treasury	20
	Bonds	45
	Equities	35
Short term, high risk	Cash/CD/Treasury	20
	Bonds	40
	Equities	40
Moderate term, low risk	Cash/CD/Treasury	15
	Bonds	35
	Equities	50
Moderate term, moderate risk	Cash/CD/Treasury	15
	Bonds	30
	Equities	55
Moderate term, high risk	Cash/CD/Treasury	15
	Bonds	25
	Equities	60
Long term, low risk	Cash/CD/Treasury	10
	Bonds	20
	Equities	70
Long term, moderate risk	Cash/CD/Treasury	5
	Bonds	25
	Equities	70
Long term, high risk	Cash/CD/Treasury	5
	Bonds	10
	Equities	85

As you look at asset allocation, you'll realize that GORP is, in many ways, a form of allocating assets. The nature of the specific goal will limit the investment choices based on time horizon and liquidity needs. In many circumstances, that will dictate the asset choices available.

If you determine a specific goal that can be met only with short-term assets, you might want to combine your entire short-term objectives and do an asset allocation among these assets.

Let's say that you have 10 retirement objectives and two of them are short term, each one being a $25,000 objective. Instead of investing $25,000 in a CD for one objective and $25,000 in a Treasury bill for the other objective, diversify further by splitting the $50,000 total into three rather than two investments. Buy a CD, a Treasury bond, and a short-term muni bond fund for $16,666 each and allocate half of each of them to the two goals requiring short-term assets. It's just a simple way to diversify your plan further.

Dollar Cost Averaging

Dollar cost averaging (DCA) allows you to systematically make investments. For those who prescribe to its concept, DCA is a disciplined way to save. Mathematically, DCA will result in a lower average cost than the average price of the investment during that period. This is because when the price is high, you buy less, and when the price is low, you buy more.

If it doesn't sound as if I'm too convinced, I'm not. I'm a true believer in asset allocation, but I have my doubts about DCA. I do believe in systematic investing—that's what you're doing with your 401(k) and any other regular savings program. But there is an ever-growing volume of data that suggests that DCA is no better than actively managing your portfolio and moving into and out of the market as conditions fluctuate and warrant. Table 12–3 shows how DCA works.

More Information

For more detail on the controversy over dollar cost averaging, go to your favorite search engine and type in "studies on dollar cost averaging." There's plenty of reading material

As you can see from the numbers in Table 12–3, the average price of the investment as it traded on the market was $45 per share.

Table 12–3   Dollar Cost Averaging at Work

Month	Investment Amount ($)	Price per Share ($)	Total Shares Bought
1	100	50	2
2	100	40	2.5
3	100	30	3.33
4	100	40	2.5
5	100	50	2
6	100	60	1.67
Totals	**Average Price**	**Total Shares**	**Average Per Share**
600	45	14	42.86

When using DCA, we set a systematic amount that we invest in each month in whichever investment we choose. By investing the same amount each month, we buy more shares when the share price is low. For example, compare month three when we buy 3.33 shares with month six when we only buy 1.67 shares. As a result, over the six-month period, our average cost is $42.86, or $2.14 less than the average price of the investment over that period of time.

Savings Tip

Dollar cost averaging is available as a systematic investment program from most mutual fund companies and from insurance companies through their variable annuity products. You can also do it own your own, but it will increase the amount of time you have to spend managing your investments.

Portfolio Rebalancing

As time goes by, your investments will not yield the same return, nor are they supposed to. Remember, we have short-term, intermediate-term, and long-term goals, and each calls for a different approaches to investing. As a result, you will find that your portfolio of investments will become overweighted to riskier investments. This will make more sense when we see what happens to a portfolio through an illustration.

Let's assume we have $100,000 invested as shown in Table 12–4.

Table 12–4   Initial Optimal Allocation of $100,000 Investment

Investment Term	Yield	Amount	Percent of Total
Short	2.5%	$20,000	20%
Intermediate	4.0%	$35,000	35%
Long	6.0%	$45,000	45%

Table 12–5 shows the account totals you can expect, their new percentage on the overall portfolio, and the difference in five years.

Table 12–5   New Percentages on Overall Portfolio After Five Years

Investment Term	Yield	Original Value	5-Year Value	% of Total	% Change
Short	2.5%	$20,000	$22,628	18%	-2%
Intermediate	4.0%	$35,000	$45,583	34%	-1%
Long	6.0%	$45,000	$60,220	48%	3%

We're really pleased that our portfolio has grown to $128,431, but look at our allocation percentages. We now have close to 50 percent in high-risk investments. Periodic portfolio rebalancing simply readjusts the assets in our portfolio to the original allocation and our original goal.

What's really important to remember about portfolio rebalancing is that the younger you are, the less frequently you need to reset your goals that underlie the rebalancing that you do. Remember, you rebalance an allocation. As long as the allocation doesn't change, you'll always rebalance the same percentage allocations.

It's time to share another experience from the personal archives: I was meeting with a financial planner and one of her new clients, a couple in their 60s. They had switched their account to this planner because they felt that their previous planner was taking too much risk with their money. They had just completed an asset review, and I realized that they were probably taking a bit too much risk. We talked about asset allocation and portfolio rebalancing, both concepts they knew by less technical terms. Their previous planner had indeed been doing portfolio rebalancing, but he hadn't been changing the underlying assumption frequently enough. The take-away point from my story is to remind yourself that the older you get, the more frequently you need to revisit the underlying allocation to make certain that you're not taking too much risk, just as this couple did.

Standard Deviation

Standard deviation is one of those phrases that just sounds too complicated. When I was studying investments to get my Securities License and my Certified Financial Planner designation years ago, I finally realized why I had chosen theatre voice and not mathematics as a minor in college. After many years, much graying of the hairs, and work with countless spreadsheets, the concept of standard deviation is far less daunting to me, and arguably interesting. It helps to have a clear understanding of it, so let me try my hand at simplifying this mathematical term.

First, let's define standard deviation by example, not by the dictionary. Then we can see how its use can help us assess risk. Let's say that you wanted to look at the batting averages of the top 100 major league baseball players. You would want to map out the batting average for the 2003 season and then plot the batting averages on a graph so that it can start to tell a story. Let's say that the lowest of the top 100 was .267 and the highest was .395. When you look at the end points on a graph, as in Figure 12–2, you notice that there are a few batters in the top 20 percent and a few in the bottom 20 percent, with 60 percent somewhere in the middle.

This grouping of batters in the middle also tells us a lot. The group in the middle represents what statisticians call the "normal distribution" of batters. When you think about it, it makes sense. Not every batter can be a Ty Cobb, so the grouping containing the most batters' averages is the norm, and the extremes on either side are deviations from the norm.

Next, look at the slope of the curve. In graph A of Figure 12–2, you see a looser grouping of averages, so the arch is less severe. In the graph B of Figure 12–2, the groupings are much tighter and arch more severely. As a matter of fact, there is no one outside the 1st deviation in graph B. When the end points are spread apart, as in graph A, the standard deviation is larger; conversely, when the end points are tighter, as in graph B, the standard deviation is smaller.

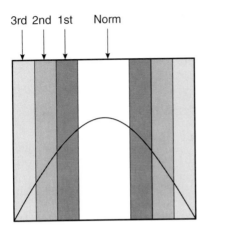
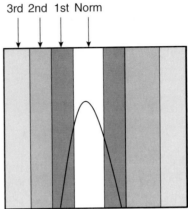

Graph A

Graph B

Figure 12–2   Standard Deviation

One standard deviation away from the mean (dark gray) in either direction accounts for somewhere around 68 percent of the batters in this group. Two standard deviations away from the mean (dark and medium gray) accounts for roughly 95 percent of the batters. And three standard deviations (the dark, medium and light gray colored areas) account for about 99 percent of the batters.

After all of this, you can now attend a holiday party or a family gathering and wow everyone with your mathematical genius. Try going up to a big drinker at a party and saying, "I've noticed the amount of alcohol you've consumed, and you fall in the third standard deviation and are likely to become ill."

From an investment standpoint, we can use this information in researching investments. If you're looking at investing in the S&P 500, it would be nice to know what the standard deviation is and what the expected return will be. Over the past 33 years, the S&P 500 has had a standard deviation of 15. If we expect to generate a 9 percent return, the S&P is likely to range plus or minus 15 percent of our expected return. This means that in any given year, assuming 9 percent, the S&P could be –6 to +24. Quite a spread, but that is the nature of the equity market. Bonds have a much lower standard deviation, and CDs and Treasuries have a standard deviation of 0.

Passive Management Versus Active Management

Our discussion point here is the manner in which you invest your money. There is a wide variety of strategies that professionals and do-it-yourselfers use, and they fall into two broad categories: passive management and active management. Understanding these two options is very easy and worthwhile.

The philosophy of passive management is that you put money away in indexed investments. Other than adjusting for changes in your asset allocations based on lifestyle changes or life events, you pretty much leave things alone. Those who endorse passive investing point to much lower costs because you're not actively trading and also point out that passive management has significantly outperformed active management, partly because of those lower costs. For example, a 1996 study by Vanguard looked at a 10-year period ending December 31, 1996. In that study, Vanguard found that out of 273 growth and value funds, only 14 percent beat the compound return on the S&P 500 Index. In other words, only 14 funds beat the average by more than 2 percent while 147 underperformed by 2 percent.

Richard Gosnell, head of the index and absolute return funds of Nedbank Treasury Asset Management, says, "It is a mathematical certainty that the average active investor will underperform the average passive investor." He continues by saying, "The active investor has higher management fees and transaction costs, and thus the average active investor will see a lower rate of return than passive investors." Finally, he suggests that over a 40-year period, the additional costs of an actively managed fund can eat away as much as 50 percent of the final portfolio value.

INFORMATION

More Information

A couple of Web sites are dedicated to passive investing.
www.indexinvestor.com
www.indexfunds.com

For those who believe that passive investing is the way to go, there are plenty of indexes to choose from. In addition to the obvious choices of the S&P 500, the Dow Industrials and the NASDAQ 100, there are the Russell 3000, the Lehman Brothers Aggregate Bond index, and dozens more.

Those on the other side of this debate believe that active management is the preferred choice for the serious investor. The argument for active management is that you get professional oversight and rigorous research. In addition, because active managers are working at the performance every day, they can make quick corrections ahead of the market. If their indicators point to a market decline, they can deploy defensive strategies to minimize losses and to actuate their performance relative to the index. Conversely, if they see signs that the market is moving up quickly, they can take advantage of that by using derivatives and hedging techniques if the fund objectives allow.

The disadvantages of active investing are primarily cost related. Active management will typically cost at least three times as much as passive investing and sometimes can cost 10 times as much. In addition to costs, the investment style of a particular manager may not run consistent with the market, which can result in much lower returns.

Ultimately, you'll have to decide which philosophy is more consistent with your style. If you want someone watching over your money on a regular basis and feel that that person can adequately deliver an acceptable return on your money, perhaps you want to use active investing. On the other hand, if the expenses seem too high or the historic performance of the active managers you are investigating has failed to beat the indexes, you may choose to elect passive management. As with all decisions that have two viable alternatives, perhaps you should consider splitting your portfolio and having a little of both. Balance is key throughout your life, in every investment you make.

Repositioning Assets

It's interesting to see how much pride of ownership people take in their investments. I can understand the attachment that you may have to the investments that you have purchased; however, I do want to make the point that you may want to look at repositioning some of your assets if they don't meet your retirement goals. It's amazing that you can pick up percentage points just by changing where you currently have your assets invested. It's even more amazing to see the impact of that 1 or 2 percent compounded over time.

For example, let's say that you have created a long-term goal of taking four vacations a year after you retire at age 65. You do the math and determine the assets required to generate enough income to cover your goal for four vacations a year over your remaining life expectancy. Assuming historic inflation and a current cost of $8,000 a year for the vacations, the inflation adjusted amount for a 45-year-old retiring at age 65 would be roughly $15,000 a year at age 65. When you run the numbers, you'll see that you will need $250,000 to fund this one goal.

As you take your next step, you review your existing assets and find that you have $54,000 currently invested in an intermediate-term bond fund yielding 6 percent. In 20 years, assuming the 6 percent as the average return, you'll have $173,000. Although you'd like to use this asset to meet your goal, it is currently falling $77,000 short. One suggestion would be to move this into a long-term asset class. Assuming that you could earn 8 percent (instead of 6 percent), you'll have the $250,000 at retirement.

As you consider repositioning your assets, look beyond the term and yield on the asset to the tax implications. This is where an annuity or an indexed stock fund might be better suited to your goal. The annuity defers taxes until you require the income. An index fund is perhaps even more efficient because it rarely generate capital gains.

Dogs of the Dow: Top 10 Dividend-Paying Stocks

Among the various investment theories, there is a very interesting one called the *Dog of the Dow*. First introduced in the 1992 book, *Beating the Dow* (Michael O'Higgins and John Downes, HarperCollins Publishing, 2000), the theory behind the Dogs of the Dow is that if you buy the highest-paying dividend stocks in the Dow Jones Industrial Average, you are getting two possible advantages. First, you're getting the dividend yield on blue chip stocks, which can serve as a very safe and attractive alternative to bonds or bond funds. Second, you get the added possible upside of a stock that is likely undervalued by the market (that's why they call them the dogs).

To fully grasp this concept, you have to understand the relationship of dividends to price. As a stock price falls, the dividend usually remains the same, so the dividend expressed as a percentage of the share value goes up. The further the stock drops, the more the dividend yield grows. If you buy the stock at a trough (the low point), you get the highest dividend yield and the upside potential if the stock recovers.

Let's say that you are watching Bank of America (BAC) stock and you notice that following Bank of America's announcement to buy Fleet Bank, the stock price dropped from $86 per share to $73 per share. The dividend on BAC is $3.20 per share. With the stock at $86 per share, the dividend as a percentage of the stock price would have been 3.7 percent. With the stock at $73 per share, the dividend as a percentage of the stock price would be 4.4 percent. In a nutshell, that is the Dogs of the Dow theory.

The Web site *www.dogsofthedow.com* explains it well: "Investing in the Dogs of the Dow is relatively simple. After the stock market closes on the last day of the year, of the 30 stocks that make up the Dow Jones Industrial Average, select the 10 stocks which have the highest dividend yield. Then simply get in touch with your broker and invest an equal dollar amount in each of these 10 high yield stocks. Then hold these 10 'Dogs of the Dow' for one year. Repeat these steps each and every year. That's it!"

In terms of performance, the Dogs of the Dow strategy has made some impressive returns during bear markets but much less so during bull markets. Table 12–6 compares the Dogs with the S&P 500, the Dow, and the NASDAQ indices over the five-year period from 1998 to 2002.

Table 12–6   Stock Market Returns by Index, 1998–2002

Year	Dogs (%)	S&P 500 (%)	Dow (%)	NASDAQ (%)
1998	10.7	26.67	16.10	39.63
1999	4.0	19.53	25.22	85.59
2000	6.4	–10.10	–6.10	–39.29
2001	–4.9	–13.04	–7.10	–21.05
2002	8.9	–23.37	–16.76	31.53

There is also a small version of the Dogs, often called the *Puppies of the Dow*. There is a greater diversification risk and the rewards can be impressive. Historically, the average annual return of the Puppies from 1973 to 1996 was 20.9 percent. To identify the Puppies on the last day of any given year, select the 10 highest yielding stocks in the Dow 30. Of these 10 Dogs, select the five Dogs with the lowest stock price, and you will have what we call the *Small Dogs of the Dow*. For the investment year ending December 31, 2003, the Dogs were those companies shown in Table 12–7.

Efficient Frontier and Portfolio Diversification

Another measuring stick, if you will, is the concept of modern portfolio theory, also called the *Efficient Frontier*. Do you see what you're missing by not sitting in meetings with asset managers and quantitative analysts? Sarcasm aside, you can also see how time consuming and difficult it can be to manage your own retirement planning and investing. Of course, you could just throw darts at the stock section of the *Wall Street Journal*, but

Table 12–7   2003 Dogs of the Dow

Symbol	Company	Price ($) 12/31/03	Yield
MO	Altria	54.42	5.00%
SBC	SBC Communications	26.07	4.79%
T	AT&T	20.30	4.68%
GM	General Motors	53.40	3.75%
JPM	JP Morgan Chase	36.73	3.70%
MRK	Merck	46.20	3.20%
DD	DuPont	45.89	3.05%
C	Citigroup	48.54	2.88%
GE	General Electric	30.98	2.58%
XOM	ExxonMobil	41.00	2.44%

most of us realize that to reach our goals, we need to take this task seriously because the consequences have such a great impact. Let's go back to the Efficient Frontier.

The essence of Efficient Frontier is an investment strategy based on the relationship of several risk factors applied to an overall portfolio of investments. The analysis is called optimizing your portfolio and analyzes an investment's alpha, beta, and r-squared compared with the other investments in a given portfolio. In other words, this theory suggests that the risk of a particular investment should not be looked at on a stand-alone basis, but rather in relation to how that particular investment's price varies with the price of the entire portfolio. Now let's try to make some sense of this all, briefly.

INFORMATION

More Information

Alpha measures the risk-adjusted performance of a specific security and not the overall market. A large alpha indicates that the security has performed better than would be predicted given its beta.

Beta is a means of measuring the volatility of a security in comparison with the market as a whole.

r-squared measures how closely a security's performance tracks with the performance of a benchmark index such as the S&P 500. Values for r-squared range from 0 to 1, where 0 indicates there is no correlation to the benchmark and 1 indicates a perfect correlation.

The whole point of this theory is to reduce the volatility of your portfolio. Any time that you can reduce volatility, you can increase the predictability of an investment's return and reduce your risk. That's a good thing because investing in low-risk securities will make it harder to achieve your retirement goals. With the Efficient Frontier, you can achieve greater performance without greater risk. If this is a concept that you are interested in, either work directly with a financial planner or (if you're more adventuresome) invest in Efficient Frontier software to help you optimize your investments using this theory.

Lifestyle Investing

Of the many ways to look at investing, the traditional method was to choose your investments and then plot them into the investment pyramid, a graphic you have seen frequently in this book. The problem with the investment pyramid is that it's overly one-dimensional and difficult to apply to your retirement planning because you will typically go through phases. To more broadly accommodate the manner in which you invest, it can often be easier to approach investing from the angle of a lifestyle preference.

Applying this concept, we all go through three phases in our lives: accumulation to preservation to distribution. These are not defined by age per se; they can also be defined by your emotional state of mind. Taking risk as an example, I will illustrate my point, but first let's look a bit more closely at each of these phases.

The accumulation phase is as its name suggests. If you look at this phase from an age standpoint, accumulation typically runs from post-college years through age 50 or 55, approximately. These are the years where you can take more risk because you have more time to recover from market swings or simply bad choices. If we looked at this phase from the perspective of asset allocation, you would be heavily weighted to equities because of your active lifestyle.

The next phase is the preservation phase, which follows chronologically (after age 55), up to the age you choose to retire. During this phase, you are much more interested in getting to the finish line without having to start over or endure critical setbacks. From our asset allocation perspective, this would be a higher mix of low-risk investments (but still intermediate in duration), a fair amount of moderate-risk investments, and very few high-risk investments.

The third phase is the distribution phase, during which we start living off our assets and must continue to do so for the rest of our lives. During this phase, we become fairly conservative because we have the least amount of time to recover from losses. The asset allocations would be very high in shorter-term and safer investments. Although you may be looking at 20 to 30 years of life expectancy, you just don't know for certain, so you pull the reins in a bit.

Now that we have a basic understanding of the lifestyle philosophy, let me get clarify the point I was making earlier using risk as an example of how a state of mind can impact these phases.

It's time to introduce you to my Uncle Ernie. Ernie is 84-years old and still in the accumulation phase of his life. I don't think Ernie will ever be in the preservation or distribution phase. There isn't a thing wrong with that, and I admire his love of life and his optimistic outlook. He still runs his own business and makes his money by buying and selling stainless steel. The point here is that these phases are not a point in time, but a state of mind.

Investing and Relationships

Often couples differ in their approaches to saving and investing. Usually these differences focus on how much money to save and how much risk to take. Regardless of which partner wants to take more risk, the difference can and does cause problems that require open communications, particularly when one partner perceives a specific point in their lifestyle as accumulation while the other partner perceives it as preservation. Rarely do people confuse distribution, though many couples disagree on the timing of distributions.

It is imperative for couples to sit down and agree on their investment style and philosophy up front and then review them on a regular basis to ensure continuing consensus. This will sometimes result in their having to confront their differences and negotiate compromises. Couples are faced with these compromises regularly, but how we confront and resolve them usually sets the tone for the underlying volatility of the relationship. Remember, the number one reason that couples divorce is money issues.

As it relates to this book, I would strongly suggest that you reach an agreement on goals and assets assigned to those goals, working as a team. Have one person own certain goals and another own different goals. Research each of these separately and then share with each other the results of your findings. You'll see these words again in the book, so put in an anchor when you read this next sentence. If you're working with an advisor to assist you in achieving your goals be *open and honest* with that person so that the advisor can truly be of assistance.

So many couples play games with themselves and with others, making it very difficult to clearly see the issues. You really have to watch out for ego and competition as you work together on retirement. I realize how difficult it is to trust someone enough to share (what you may perceive as) intellectual weakness or poor savings habits. My advice is to face these issues head-on if you want to reach your retirement goals. Once you select an advisor, let that person help you work through the issues. More often than not, a clear explanation of a difficult concept can change someone's perspective, allowing for an agreement to be reached.

More Information

INFORMATION

For further research on money and marriage go to *http://marriage .about.com/cs/finances/.*

Divorce and Its Impact on Your Retirement

Unfortunately, divorce is a factor in our lives with which we need to contend. The Census Bureau predicted that 50 percent of marriages in 2002 would end in divorce. This means that half of the people who were married that year will need to deal with the equitable distributions of assets. I can't and won't turn this segment into more than what it needs to be because there are plenty of books written on the topic by people far more studied in this area. It took me three attempts to find the person I will spend the rest of my life with, so I know how painful divorce can be. In this next segment, I address the ways divorce affects financial issues.

To begin, consider that each state treats divorce differently, but its treatment is also founded on a few principles: community property, separate property, or quasi community property. The latter occurs when the assets of a couple are in more than one state with different rules. Since I'm not an attorney, I'm not going to venture into greater detail. Regardless of how the state requires assets to be distributed, there are some things to watch for and protect.

More Information

INFORMATION

There is a wonderful article written by family development specialist Mary K. Lawler, RN, Ph.D. that I hope it will be on the Web for a long time. It divides divorce into six phases: emotional, legal, economic, co-parental, community, and psychological. You can find the article at *http://pearl.agcomm.okstate.edu/fci/family/coparenting/t-2234.pdf.*

Most people will tell you to separate your emotions from the financial issues when going through a divorce. To that I say, *ha!* It's wonderful advice and it should be taken, but it rarely is. When two people are trying to protect themselves, the result is a very protective environment with a lack of trust as the underpinning of the relationship until emotions are vented and constructive dialogue begins. Don't mistake what I'm saying—you should absolutely endeavor to contain your emotions and think thrice, say once. The financial reality of anger is that it costs money. The more time it takes for you to bring anger under control, the more costly the legal bill and the more long-term damage can destroy your relationship and the relationship with any children.

To minimize the acrimony, you may want to consider hiring a CPA to assist in quantifying and defining assets. You can actually hire forensic CPAs who can find assets that one party may not have exposed. You may also want to consider working with a financial planner or a CPA who also has a certified divorce planner (CDP) designation. These folks will apply some of the tools we discussed earlier in this chapter to evaluate assets for your future.

Key Point

Be mindful of insurance in a divorce, particularly when financial support is involved. Life insurance and disability insurance should be strongly considered.

When a divorce occurs, one of the key items becomes the pension or qualified plan assets. Spouses are required to be beneficiaries of qualified plan assets unless they specifically have signed away that right; however, they are not automatically guaranteed ownership rights. A court will have to issue a qualified domestic relations order (QDRO) to solidify these rights. This order will stipulate the rights of the spouse so that the plan administrator can properly split the account in half. Subsequently, the (now) ex-spouse typically moves the money into an IRA to become disassociated themselves from the ex-spouse.

Savings Tip

An ex-spouse who gains rights to qualified plan assets may need some of the money to supplement other income. That spouse can take advantage of an exception to the IRS rules that penalize pre-59.5 distributions from retirement plans. However, if the ex-spouse rolls the money over into an IRA, the exception no longer applies and any distribution would have to fall into the exception rules for qualified plans that are quite complex and limiting. If you need money, take what you need before the rollover is executed.

Relationships and Investing

This book is about people and how people manage their way to a secure and lasting retirement. Through the writing this book, I have tried to keep blinders on and treat women and men as people, not a generalized universal population of species. I don't see how it would help you to hear me explain broadly about men and women when what really matters is how two people in a relationship manage these goals respectively and independently.

Potentially, two people hold different goals, different investment interests, and different levels of risk tolerance. Remember, these are not static issues—you may wake up one morning and find that your partner has become more conservative or may perceive life expectancy in a different frame of mind. Regardless of whether this is the result of the differences between the sexes, it's a process of ongoing management between the two of you that needs to be acknowledged and respected. And it can be further complicated when the two are really four or six or eight as happens from the union of two people who were married before, with children from the previous marriages.

Be Careful

When there are ex-spouses and children from a previous marriage, you may want to consider a qualified terminable interest property trust (QTIP). A QTIP trust provides for the distribution of a biological parent's selected assets in a manner that keeps his or her children from fighting with the surviving stepparent.

That doesn't mean that I don't recognize the potential differences between sexes; I believe it needs to be simply another data point in this process. In addition, I have shied away from presuming only traditional male-female relationships. It is much wiser for all of us to face the variety of issues based on our circumstances. If you're single, you have one perspective, and if you have a partner, you will have another perspective.

I should also add that my assumption is that regardless of how you ultimately parcel out responsibilities for this process, you must behave as partners. I have always been disappointed when I have met with advisors and their prospective or existing clients and heard, "I take care of all the investments, and you don't have to explain it to my spouse." The follow-up to that statement by the advisor should be, "We have a fundamental difference in our approach to this process that we need to work out."

My final thought on this topic is that each partner must understand what the goals and objectives are for their joint plan. When all is said and done, both partners have to understand, share, and agree to the path that you take, regardless of who does the legwork. We are talking about the financial future of two people who choose to meld their lives together and share common goals. This comes with certain responsibilities that, as mature people, we are obligated to consider.

Ultimately, some couples will not be able to agree on common goals or a shared investment path. If this happens in a relationship, you have four choices:

◆ You both compromise.

◆ One of you acquiesces to the other.

◆ You agree to disagree and then establish independent goals and separately agreed-upon assets to manage and achieve those goals.

◆ You agree to disagree on the essence of your union and take separate life paths.

I have ordered these in the way that I would approach the problem. I hope that regardless of the way you would initiate the order, my last alternative would always be the last on your list as well. In fact, some couples will not consider divorce under any circumstances because of religious beliefs, nonreligious spiritual beliefs, or just a strong bond of love that they will not allow to die. Whatever your personal reasons, order the choices according to your beliefs and solve the problem as quickly and as fairly as possible. Time is our friend when we are looking at retirement issues only if we have a lot of it.

Estate Planning and Retirement

This book cannot do justice to all facets of retirement and financial planning. I've said this as it relates to tax issues and insurance issues, and I reiterate it here as we look briefly at probate and estate issues.

Probate

All assets of a decedent go through the probate court unless the assets' ownership is structured to bypass the probate process. Joint ownership and living trusts are two popular means of avoiding the probate process. The probate court is the arm of our judicial system charged with managing the liquidation of estates of people who have a will or die intestate (without a will). The probate process, as I mentioned earlier, is public and lengthy. It's also expensive because attorneys representing those with claims will battle it out through the judicial system.

Among famous people whose lives have been subject to public viewing through the will and probate process were Howard Hughes and Andy Warhol. Their deaths resulted in highly contentious court battles that cost their estates millions and millions of dollars, in part because the ownership of assets was subject to interpretation, and those assets were not kept out of the probate court. It's not difficult to avoid probate—trust documents are not difficult to create, and you have a choice of sitting down with an attorney, working with an online legal service, or buying a form from a local stationery store. Obviously, the more complex your situation the more important it is to meet with an attorney and address any other estate issues.

You can also utilize a health care directive and a durable power of attorney, which allows you to have a third party manage your assets in the event of your death or incapacitation. This is much more common today with life expectancy and the possibility of living incapacitated increasing. A living trust can help to provide continuity in an estate plan. Wills and trusts are typically drafted and revised simultaneously unless the trust is irrevocable. Finally, you can preserve assets outside probate by having joint owners on any asset. Most married couples own their homes as joint tenants with rights of survivorship for this very purpose, though many states now treat joint assets in this manner automatically.

Estate Issues

By law, an individual is allowed to pass up to $1 million in assets without the imposition of federal estate taxes. If they plan properly, a husband and wife can pass $2 million tax free to their children. In 2006, that number jumps to $2 million apiece, or $4 million combined, and after 2010 there will be no estate tax. This assumes, of course that there are no changes to these laws—which is highly unlikely, but a nice goal. Between now and 2010, you expect that any assets above the maximum will be taxed at roughly 50 percent. The exposure to estate taxes is the reason that many consumers seek to purchase life insurance. For the cost of the premiums, the insured individuals can take comfort that the assets they have accumulated will reach their designated beneficiaries intact.

Unfortunately, some states apply their own estate taxes, either as a direct form of a percentage of assets or in a complex arrangement of credits with the federal government. As those credits are being phased out by the federal government, additional states are adding direct estate taxes to replace the lost revenue. It is estimated that the states lost $6 billion in revenue as a result of the federal estate tax phase-out in 2003 alone.

Summary

There are multiple paths to ascend the mountain, and the choices can sometimes be confusing. Some of the paths lead nowhere, some will take you on a pleasant gliding path to your destination, and some will be downright ornery. This explains why you don't just put on your backpack and start hiking. You buy a trail book, you study the weather conditions, you map out your strategy, and you develop contingency plans and determine alternate routes—at least that's the proper way to do it. Alternatively, you can be a free spirit and just ride wherever the trail takes you. The choice is yours and so are the results.

Power Checklist

- ✔ Goals and assets have characteristics, and they must be matched and monitored to ensure success.
- ✔ To achieve your goals, you will have to actively manage the risk-reward relationship.
- ✔ As you look at asset allocation, you'll realize that GORP is, in many ways, a form of allocating assets.
- ✔ Dollar cost averaging provides for the systematic purchase of a security in a manner that ensures that you get the lowest average price.

✔ The older you get, the more frequently you need to revisit the underlying allocation to make certain that you're not taking too much risk.

✔ Standard deviation is volatility of a security relative to other comparable securities. The greater the standard deviation, the further the range is from the mean.

✔ The philosophy of passive management is that you put money away in indexed investments. Aside from adjusting changes in your asset allocations based on lifestyle changes or life events, you pretty much leave things alone.

✔ The philosophy of active management is that through timely professional management, you can outperform the index.

✔ Sometimes you can pick up 2 or 3 percent return simply by repositioning an asset. That means that you may be able to make more with less capital.

✔ The lifestyle method of risk management uses three phases of life to determine risk tolerance: accumulation, preservation, and distribution.

✔ The lifestyle phases of accumulation, preservation, and distribution are not points in time but states of mind.

✔ Regardless of the style of investing and managing risk, it is imperative for couples to agree on their philosophy up front and review it on a regular basis to ensure ongoing consensus.

✔ Couples are faced with these compromises regularly, but how they confront and resolve them usually sets the tone for the underlying volatility of the relationship.

✔ An integral aspect of retirement planning is the manner in which an estate is protected via a will and other estate planning techniques.

✔ Time is our friend when we are looking at retirement issues only if we have a lot of it.

PART III

TAKE ACTION *NOW* TO GET THE LIFE YOU WANT

CHAPTER 13

Finding the Right Path for You

We're at a point in the book where you should start thinking about how you will deploy your plan. Do you have the time to define your goals, research your options, implement your strategy, and do all the ongoing research to maintain and fine-tune your plan? Are you qualified to do all this without the perspective of someone whose life's profession is these issues? If a life event occurs that has a significant impact on your goals, will you have the time and emotional commitment to modify both the goals and the underlying assets to reset your plan? If you do, you may be one of the few people who can enjoy retirement without the benefit of professional assistance.

We all have egos, and those egos can take us to the highest of highs and the lowest of lows. As we mature, we learn to pick our battles and seek the wisdom of others with greater experience, taking care to trust and verify. We trust people to a certain level, and we periodically verify to ensure that we are on the right path.

Going back to our analogy of mountain climbing, you will find that mountain climbers respect the mountain and respect the leader of the expedition. What the leader says goes. Such blind faith need not carry over to retirement planning, but the core concept is sound. The more complex the issue, the more we must either commit the necessary time or delegate and manage the process to leverage our time.

The statistics have shown that most people who engage in their own financial planning will either knowingly or unknowingly compromise their goals, their investments, or both. That doesn't mean that they will fail; they will simply compromise. The fact of the matter is that most of us don't think we need any help with anything until someone, or something, proves otherwise. At each step of the process, I have noted that this point hinges on the successful execution of those actions that complete that specific step. Failure to succeed at any step can result in increased risk of not achieving 100 percent of your goal.

This step, choosing the right path for you, is just as important, if not more so, as any other step in the process. You need to be honest and ask yourself what drives the instinct to tackle problems without assistance. If that answer is lack of trust, I encourage you to read this chapter thoroughly and keep an open mind. If the reason is that you are the kind of person who loves this field and feels you have the time to establish and manage these goals, it may be worth trying to do. Just allow yourself to be open to working with an advisor if you find that you are not meeting your time goals or investment objectives.

Perhaps it is the male mystique that drives the to do-it-yourself urge, because many more women than men seek assistance. Regardless, with the vast majority of adults in relationships for a good portion of their lives, we have to consider the path couples take together, not necessarily the path dictated by their individual characteristics. In other words, rather than seek assistance, one party will try to carry the load only to find out at some point that the load is too heavy and the road too long and difficult. By the time help is sought, valuable time that cannot be recaptured is no longer available. Again, time is your friend if only you have a lot of it.

I'm not mandating or presuming that you must work with a planner or advisor (I'm using these terms interchangeably). I can help you look at your options and make suggestions that can make you more efficient with your retirement plan. I can also provide you with resources that will pave your goal-setting and achievement path, making the process a bit smoother. All this assumes that you have the necessary time and skill sets described above to manage the process. But if you ask my opinion, you'd be making a mistake to tackle this one on your own. This chapter is all about finding the path to assistance.

Throughout the course of this book, I have compared the planning process with climbing a mountain. I want to review that element here as we discuss the different paths. Before you go mountain climbing or trail hiking, you prepare in a number of ways. You make certain you are physically fit, you research the intended path, you pack the proper supplies and equipment, and you make certain you have time to accomplish the climb. If a particular route is difficult or unknown, perhaps you seek a guide. Guides help you make the right decision because they have been on the path many times before, and you are paying for their experience. The same preparation should be true of the help you receive with your financial and retirement planning.

Even the Best Athletes Have Coaches

When Tiger Woods is not playing golf competitively, he is practicing. And when Tiger Woods is practicing, you can bet that when he needs help, his coach Butch Harmon is right there. Butch has been Tiger's coach for a very long time, and Tiger follows Butch's advice to fine-tune his game.

The reality is that Butch probably does not tell Tiger how to play golf; rather, he coaches him on those things that he could do to improve his game with minor adjustments. Those minor adjustments can make the difference between success and failure.

It's also important to know that a great coach doesn't have to be a great player. Butch played professionally in the 1970s, and although he wasn't atop the leader board enough to be remembered as a great golfer, he is without doubt a great coach. It has always baffled me that everyone isn't able to accept the fact that some people are better coaches than they are players.

Andre Agassi's coach, Brad Gilbert, is a solid former professional tennis player whom many regard as a great coach. I could go on with the list, but the point has been made: If it makes sense for professionals to use coaches, why wouldn't it make sense for you to have a coach as you plan your retirement?

Key Point

Coaching is different from teaching. Coaches work with those who have a core understanding and help them improve basic skill sets that they have developed. Teachers help those who don't know how to do something to learn and then do it. It is also important to note that some people do both, though teaching and coaching are different.

Paths to Choose

The paths that you have available to you are very easy to identify. You can do it yourself, work with an advisor, or do a combination of the two. The next section will help you to choose the most appropriate path, or combination, to pursue.

Doing It Yourself

Let me first be very clear on this topic. There is no reason that you can't do retirement planning yourself, but it is my belief that you won't do it yourself. If you choose to go down this path and find it to be successful, please prove me wrong. Nothing would make me happier than if you sent an email to me at *david@retirementcountdown.com* and told me how off the mark I was. I also want to say that I don't believe the reason you won't do it has anything to do with intelligence, thought process, or will. For most people, the outside influences are simply too distracting to keep us on track, and guess what—we also run out of time.

Set Your Goals Clearly   As we discussed in Chapter 5, GORP can be expanded to cover the entire financial planning process. What you will see over the course of the next few pages is the process that you'll have to pull together to do this on your own. I'll qualify that somewhat: This is the process that you should go through to best ensure that you meet your goals. You may be able to meet them with less effort, but only time will tell. I also have to tell you that this chapter can't go into the depth that I would like for the do-it-yourself planner. That would be a book unto itself. What you can expect is that I will be your architect, but you'll have to build the house yourself or hire a contractor. Just to see how in-depth the certified financial planner (CFP) coursework is, go to *http://www.cfp.net/downloads/ guide_FPTopics.pdf* and review the seven areas of expertise covered by the designation. This seven-page document will open your eyes to the complexities of involved financial planning.

Let's start with the five steps to creating and managing your way to retirement. These are the criteria used by the Certified Financial Planning Association and are the underpinnings of achieving the designation. They are important for you to understand because these disciplines will be woven throughout your plan, so get used to seeing them:

1. Gather data, including your goals.

2. Analyze and evaluate your financial status.

3. Develop your own list of recommendations.

4. Implement your recommendations.

5. Monitor and modify your plan.

Gather Data, Including Your Goals   The process begins with the collection of all relevant information that will be needed to develop your plan. You will need to sit down, either alone or with your partner, and pull together a snapshot of your life to determine what can and can't be used in the planning process. Start by listing just your family members and any others you may need to provide for in the plan.

Next, start gathering and reviewing quantitative financial information, such as your assets and liabilities. This will help you put together a comprehensive net-worth statement, statement of income and expenses, and a budget. You'll also need to gather all of your insurance policies so that you can be prepared for the risk-management element of your planning.

The final group of necessary documents relates to your investment, tax, and estate information. Pull together tax returns, wills, powers of attorney, a comprehensive list of your investment portfolio, your employee benefit booklets covering retirement-related information, trust agreements, and pension statements. You'll now have a picture of your current status so that you can plan for your future.

You now need to add the goals that you have. This step seeks to identify both financial and personal goals and objectives. After you identify and list them, prioritize your goals and objectives to facilitate the allocation of the available resources to the highest concerns on this list of yours. It is of primary importance that the financial goals are measurable so that you can track success and provide feedback and then fine-tune your strategies. Go back to Chapter 5 and use GORP to clarify and develop your list of goals.

Analyze and Evaluate Your Financial Status To manage your way to retirement, you need to put together the picture laid out in the first step. This means you have to develop your budget, analyze all of your investments, and then start applying your findings to see where the holes are in achieving your goals. This element uncovers potential obstacles to your plan, such as time. You may find that this leads you to either redefine your goals or modify the risk you are willing to take to achieve them. Obviously, you must identify problems before you can find a solution.

You will soon discover in this stage that you'll need a good understanding of the math that goes into the time value of money concepts and calculations. You'll be doing present and future value calculations, studying irregular cash flows, and assessing tax equivalent yields and other financial formulas imperative to the planning and retirement process.

This is also the stage at which you'd look at various mortgage options to determine if you should pay off your mortgage or put the money into additional savings. Paying off your mortgage reduces your debt, but it also reduces your ability to leverage real estate through low-cost tax-deductible financing. Remember that real estate loans create leverage, which can offer you enhanced returns, but not without risk.

You'll also start evaluating possible investments to fund your goals, as well as look at repositioning inefficient assets to gain more yield and get closer to achieving your goals. To effectively do this, you'll need to understand and apply all the characteristics of investments that we discussed in the last chapter.

Develop Your Own List of Recommendations Now you are ready to develop your own list of recommendations. This is the portfolio of assets that you'll be managing to ensure that you reach your goals. In GOFP, this is where you assign assets to goals and define any shortfalls that you have to make up by saving more money.

If you are doing it yourself, review the section in the last chapter on passive and active management. Passive investing is something for the do-it-yourself planner to consider. It may make it infinitely easier for you to invest in low-cost passive index funds so that you don't need to spend as much of your time staying current with the markets.

Implement Your Recommendations   Finally, it's time to implement the plan. You should evaluate all the various options that you have for making investments. Even though you are doing it yourself, you may want to set up a brokerage account with a full-service broker dealer, but you'll more likely want to set up an account at a discount brokerage firm like Fidelity, Schwab, or TD Waterhouse. Full-service broker dealers can charge $100 or more for a stock trade whereas discount firms have standard charges around $20 per trade. You can actually trade as cheaply as $8 per trade with some deep discount brokerage firms like Ameritrade, and even the full-service firms are now offering discount trading services, albeit at a small premium.

More Information

INFORMATION

To evaluate both discount and full-service banks and brokerage firms, check out these Web sites:

www.gomez.com

www.businessweek.com

www.fool.com

www.kiplinger.com

Monitor and Modify Your Plan   The final step in the financial planning process is the ongoing monitoring that is required to fine-tune the financial plan and to ensure the successful attainment of the specified financial objectives. You'll want to perform regular reviews and updates because life has a way of changing on a regular basis. You'll also want to take notice of any life event that could significantly impact your plan. The birth of a child, an elderly parent's dependence on you, or the untimely death of a spouse can make a difference and require a major modification to your plan.

In addition, you'll have to take into account the macro and micro changes in our economy, shifts in the markets, and any other external forces of change that can impact the plan. You may find that your risk tolerance has changed and you need to revamp your investment portfolio to accommodate new perspectives.

Getting Help from a Professional

The television show *Nip/Tuck*, which premiered in 2003, has generated a considerable amount of attention. The Golden Globe–winning drama centers on the lives of two plastic surgeons and their exploits. The show starts with the two surgeons doing a consultation with a new client, and one of the doctors begins each episode with the question, "What don't you like about yourself?"

The correlation to retirement planning is that any meeting should begin with an assessment of your needs. "What don't you like about your retirement plan?" is the *Nip/Tuck* equivalent in the retirement planning world, and if you choose to work with a professional, establish your needs as the fundamental issue at hand. All roads must lead to the achievement of your goals.

As you seek the assistance of an advisor who lives and breathes these issues day in and day out, you are likely to have a long list of people interested in helping you. But let me add that you may not need an advisor for *every* element of your plan. You may feel that you need an advisor for only certain aspects. Assistance may include professionals like an investment advisor, tax advisor, estate planner, or an insurance advisor.

Be Careful

Although I suggest that you consider a specialist like an insurance advisor, in reality, I'm not certain that such a person exists. Theoretically, you should be able to pay a fee and get advice on risk management, but I don't think the industry has developed a model for that type of fee-based assistance at the consumer level. Clearly, tax, investment, and estate advice is readily available on a fee basis.

The list of professionals who would generally be happy to help you includes:

- National broker dealers (e.g., Morgan Stanley, Merrill Lynch)
- Bank broker dealers (e.g., Bank of America, Wells Fargo)
- Independent financial planners (e.g., LPL, Commonwealth Financial Network)
- Insurance agents (e.g., New York Life, Metropolitan Life)
- Certified public accountants and attorneys

Years ago people were concerned about buying a nonbank product from a bank or a noninsurance product from an insurance company. The financial services industry has undergone extensive contraction over the past several years. This includes all combinations of banks, brokerage firms, mutual funds companies, and insurance companies that have consolidated and merged. With these mergers and the heightened oversight of both the SEC and the National Association of Securities Dealers (NASD), you really needn't worry too much about the fact that your banks, brokerage firms, and insurance companies may own one and other.

The logical concern is that they would show preferential treatment to the products they manufacture. I haven't found this to be the case. They may offer their product first and they may sell more of their products than others, but the SEC and the NASD will not allow them to be presented in an inappropriate manner. This means that they cannot favor their products by paying greater commissions or offering them if they are not appropriate. A good case in point would be the independent financial planning firms that are owned by major insurance companies. Even though the insurance company owns the planning firm, the advisors are fiercely independent and are not employees of the insurance company; they are truly independent and sell a wide variety of products. Table 13–1 can help you pick and choose the services required to achieve your goal. You would simply decide which areas you want to take ownership of and which areas would be better suited to working with a professional.

Table 13–1   Retirement Planning Stages and Steps

	Ownership	
Stage and Step	**You**	**Professional**
Collect data		
Budget	✓	
Statement of assets	✓	
Statement of liabilities	✓	
Insurance review	✓	
Tax returns	✓	✓
Wills and estate information	✓	
Employee benefit information	✓	
Goal setting	✓	✓

Table 13–1   Retirement Planning Stages and Steps *(Continued)*

	Ownership	
Stage and Step	**You**	**Professional**
Analyze and evaluate		
Cost of goals	✓	✓
Characteristics of goals	✓	✓
Implement plan		
Evaluation investment options	✓	✓
Investment selection and purchase	✓	✓
Maintain and modify	✓	✓

As you seek out assistance, Table 13–2 explains the various methods used to compensate those professionals who help you.

Table 13–2   How Advisors Are Paid

Areas of outside expertise	Type of professional	How services are provided
Tax	CPA, Tax Attorney	hourly or fee based
Estate	Estate Attorney	hourly or fee based
Investments	Financial Planner, Stockbroker, Insurance Agent, CPA, Attorney	commissions, fee based (typically percentage of assets)
Financial and retirement planning	Financial Planner, Stockbroker, Insurance Agent, CPA, Attorney	hourly or fee based
Insurance	Financial Planner, Insurance Agent or Broker	Commissions

Finding the Right Planner for *You*   I've seen all types of planners throughout my career in the financial services industry. I've seen good planners and bad planners, and I've seen some who call themselves planners but are nothing more than product salespeople with the singular purpose of generating as much in commission as possible. The free enterprise system is not perfect, and selling can be ugly. That's why there are oversight mechanisms like self-regulation and government regulatory bodies to protect consumers.

Be Careful

Unfortunately, most major stock brokerage firms, banks, and independent financial planning firms are interested in working only with "high-net-worth" customers. Although some define these as individuals who have $500,000 in available investable assets, most require over $1 million. This makes it very challenging for those with more modest assets to invest to get the help that they need. Some of the no-load mutual fund companies do have programs for investors who aren't millionaires.

Within the financial services industry are several professional designations earned by planners and other professionals. In addition, a number of standards-setting organizations ensure that your interests are protected. The most popular designation, and the one that gets the most press, is the certified financial planner (CFP) designation. Two organizations that work closely with the CFP designation are the Financial Planning Association (FPA) and the National Association of Personal Financial Advisors (NAPFA).

Some in the presses have suggested that the CFP designation and the coursework is a sham, but this is hardly the case. Although anyone can memorize information and pass a test, the CFP designation is widely respected in the industry, not just because it's an industry designation but because of the integrity that the organization brings to the industry. As a former CFP who gave up the designation only because I wasn't doing any client financial planning, I was proud to have the designation for many years. That doesn't mean that you can't find CFPs who don't deserve the designation, but the CFP Board wants to be the first to hear about it that so that it can preserve the integrity of the association for all planners.

The other major industry designation is offered by the American College. The American College is home to the chartered life underwriter (CLU) and charter financial consultant (ChFC) designations. These designations have traditionally been associated with insurance services, though the ChFC designation is more of a traditional CFP designation with a greater emphasis on risk management.

Both of these organizations have codes of ethics and self-regulate their industries. To view the CFP code of ethics, go to *www.cfp.net/ learn/ethics.asp*. For the CLU and ChFC designations offered by the American College, you can review their statement of canons found at *www.amercoll.edu/Ethics/canons.asp*. While at the CFP Web site, you can submit a complaint against a CFP for unethical conduct. That doesn't mean bad advice; it means unethical business practices. To register a complaint, follow the process online at *www.cfp.net/learn/complaint.asp*.

In the end, your best mechanism to protect yourself from associating with the wrong planner is to do your research. I'm convinced that when many people say that a planner is bad, they are most likely saying, "The planner and I don't work well together" or "The planner is not a good communicator." One of the things you need to do is set the tone of any relationship by clearly defining your expectations and hearing what the planner has to say about the sales process.

My definition of the "objective of selling" is to properly match the characteristics of the needs of the consumer with the characteristics of the product. If properly executed, the sale results in a win-win-win situation in which the consumer, the salesperson, and the product manufacturer all feel that the transaction has been fair in terms of price and value. Unfortunately, in the real world, something happens to upset the balance of this equation, and the system can break down at all levels, so assigning guilt should be done not universally, but selectively.

As consumers, we sometimes discount the value of knowledge and abuse the salesperson. Have you ever knowingly worked with an experienced salesperson to gain product insight only to then turn around and buy the product elsewhere, having searched for the lowest price? Although we all do this at some level, you can well appreciate how that practice impacts the sales process and trust.

We expect the salesperson to trust us, but at the same time, we don't trust the salesperson. You can avoid this confusion by clearly stating your objectives when you establish the relationship. I tell salespeople up front that I'm beginning to research the product. If they are willing to take the time to educate me honestly and impartially, I'll consider them when I purchase the item or service as long as their pricing is competitive.

My philosophy is to trust and verify. I'll trust what they say unless it feels intuitively incorrect or until I have further evidence to suggest they are wrong. And if what they tell me is a one-sided sales pitch, I certainly won't do business with them. If, on the other hand they prove to be a valuable resource, I feel obligated to give them the business if the price is competitive, but it doesn't have to be the lowest price. I also believe in the old adage, "Fool me once, shame on you; fool me twice, shame on me."

Key Point

Financial and retirement planning seminars are offered all the time. These are typically free seminars sponsored by either the brokerage house or the mutual fund or insurance companies offering their products. Do they have an ulterior motive? They do. They want to sell you something. That doesn't mean that you can't get value from the seminar; just get value on your terms and treat it as a data point. A number of very good speakers conduct these seminars for advisors.

I also know salespeople who let personal and selfish sales goals and financial needs interfere with what is best for the customer. I was once working for an insurance company, and we found that one of our independent advisors was moving millions of dollars of annuity business off the books (this was in 1987 when the company was paying a very high rate of return guaranteed for 10 years). The prevailing interest rates at the time were much lower than the rate being credited to customers, so very few people were moving their money. And yet, we were getting these requests from one producer weekly. As we investigated, we found out that the advisor was going through a nasty divorce and was moving the business against the best interests of the clients for a new commission. We immediately terminated the agreement with the producer, contacted the clients affected, and reported the advisor to the state authorities.

Not all financial planners, insurance agents, or other finance professionals are bad. In fact, in most cases, they are just people who are trying to do their job. I have read a number of books that suggest that you should deal with only independent financial planning firms because representatives from banks or stockbrokerage firms will try to sell you a product being pushed by the company that employs them. I can tell you from experience this is an unfair statement, and I'll tell you why.

I had a friend who worked as a stockbroker for years in the 1980s for a major brokerage firm. As the industry changed, he decided to go off on his own and become an independent. For the most part, the difference between working for a major bank or brokerage firm and working for an independent firm is the difference between being employed and being self-employed.

Be Careful

Although the way products are sold by the major banks and broker-age houses has changed significantly, you still need to ask the right questions and be comfortable in the product choices that are recommended to you. You should always ask for more than one product choice and document the differences.

When an advisor is working for someone else, the company provides benefits, a salary, and an office environment. It also tends to spend a lot of money on advertising so that its advisors can more easily establish a relationship with prospective clients based on name recognition and the safety of a large corporate name backing the advisor. This makes it easier for some salespeople to be effective. Conversely, they pay a price for those benefits in lower commissions than independent producers who must pay all of their own costs associated with running their business.

My friend went out on his own and started an independent practice. After one year, he went back to working for the same brokerage house because he couldn't deal with being on his own. He didn't like the feeling that he didn't have anyone behind him and didn't like prospecting without the name of the big stockbrokerage firm. He was the same person providing the same advice, but the environment of being his own boss wasn't for him. I can tell you for certain that he was an excellent planner and loved people.

The moral of the story is to judge people for who they are and not for where they work. You simply don't know why people choose to work where they do, and what should matter is their ability to perform to meet your needs, not the reputation of the company they work for.

Designations and Their Significance   Here's some background on the designations that you are likely to run into as you look at securing professional help:

- **Accredited estate planner (AEP).** An AEP is an estate planning specialist who passes the exam and meets the stipulated educational requirements.
- **Chartered financial analyst (CFA).** This is a very difficult designation to earn and is awarded by the Association for Investment Management and Research, which offers an in-depth financial, investment, and accounting curriculum.

- **Certified financial planner (CFP).** Licensed by the Certified Financial Planner Board, a CFP requires initial testing and continuing education.

- **Certified fund specialist (CFS).** This is a mutual fund designation offered by the Institute of Certified Fund Specialists that requires certain educational and experience requisites be met, along with passing an exam.

- **Certified public accountant (CPA).** This designation is licensed by the state after the accountant passes a uniform examination administered by the American Institute of Certified Public Accountants, which follows completion of its coursework.

- **Certified retirement planner (CRP).** Offered by the American Institute of Retirement Planners, this designation requires both an exam and continuing education.

- **Chartered financial consultant (ChFC).** Offered by the American College, this designation requires exams as part of a 10-course curriculum to meet experience requirements and continuing education.

- **Chartered life underwriter (CLU).** Also offered by the American College, this designation is focused more on forms of risk management and requires members to pass an exam, have experience, and receive continuing education.

- **Chartered mutual fund consultant (CMFC).** Similar to the CFS, this designation is offered by the National Endowment for Financial Education. A prerequisite for this designation is the completion of a course by the Investment Institute Company, as well as passing an exam.

- **Enrolled agent (EA).** This is a designation offered by the IRS to income tax specialists who pass an exam and have five years of audit experience with the IRS.

- **Juris doctorate (JD).** This is an attorney who has earned a *juris doctorate* degree in post-graduate studies.

- **Personal financial specialist (PFS).** This designation is awarded specifically to CPAs who take and pass an exam and meet certain experience requirements.

- **Registered investment advisor (RIA).** Individuals with this designation are registered with the Securities Exchange Commission. There is no exam required; they must only pay a fee.

◆ **Registered financial consultant (RFC).** This designation is awarded by the International Association of Registered Financial Consultants and requires minimum education and experience. It is available only to those who have earned a securities license or an insurance license of another form of certification, such as the CPA designation.

The Interview Process—This Is *Your* Retirement   Once you decide that you want to find an advisor, you'll need to determine what your process will be for selecting one. You will need to collect both quantitative and qualitative information before you select an advisor. The quantifiable information is fairly easy and is really just like filling out a basic form. The qualitative information is what will make the difference. That is how you will ultimately determine which advisor might be best suited to meet your needs.

I think you need to begin by setting the ground rules for the interview. This isn't about dominance; it's about your being able to clearly articulate not only what your goals are but also who you are and what you expect. If you scare the advisor off, so be it. It's important that your advisor view you as someone who will be an active participant in the process. Remember—you're the client.

Key Point

Make certain that you understand what you are buying. Ask questions and get terms in writing—you won't regret it.

Consider that this will be a person you will be working very closely with for a long time, so it's a relationship worth spending some time researching. Ask your friends about the advisors they use and whether they would recommend them. But be careful—just because a friend has a good relationship with an advisor does not mean that you'll have a good relationship with that advisor. There are plenty of very competent advisors who would be a bad match for your personality. Try to meet your candidates more than once and see how they operate under a variety of circumstances.

Lets talk about the topics that you'll need to cover in your interview. Start by asking about experience:

- Years in the business and type of experience
- Years with the firm or their own practice
- Average number of years your clients utilize your services
- Number of clients you serve
- References
- Reprimands or disciplinary action by the NASD, any state, or the SEC

Next, ask about qualifications:

- Education
- Designations
- Ongoing education
- Licenses and regions in which they are registered

You will want to know about services offered and experience in each category:

- Planning
- Insurance
- Tax
- Estate
- Investment

To learn about their approaches to financial planning, ask your potential advisors to provide an overview of their philosophy on planning.

Method of compensation is another issue to clarify:

- Commission
- Percentage of assets
- Fee only
- Combination of methods
- Business affiliation with a company whose products they are offering or recommending
- Preferred relationships with manufacturers whose products might involve higher compensation than others

On the qualitative side of the equation, you are looking for someone who you can click with. You don't have to be friends, and you don't even have to like the person, though it may make it easier to spend time together if you do. What you are looking for first and foremost is someone you can trust and communicate with. I've found that most people have pretty good intuition, and gut feelings are important, so trust yours.

You also need to make certain that your spouse or partner is comfortable with the advisor you choose because both of you should be active participants in this process. I have seen too many couples run into trouble when one partner buys a product or takes some action without the other's consent or acknowledgment.

How the Professional Is Compensated   Compensation can vary, but it is based fundamentally in one of three categories or some combination of them: commission, hourly rate or fee, or assets.

In the commission-based world, much has changed over the past 15 years, and most of it works to the benefit of the consumer. Most of the major distributors have gone to models under which all products in a given category pay the same commission, regardless of the product selected. There's nothing wrong with commissions as long as one product is not favored over another unreasonably and you know what you are paying.

An increasing number of the large brokerage houses are trying to get their clients to utilize their consulting services by charging clients a percentage of their assets for their services and applying a minimum fee for clients without large assets. This can be a good choice if you look at how much you are paying for the services provided. Additionally, this usually includes an advisor who will provide you with a comprehensive financial plan.

Most fee-based planners are independent financial planners, CPAs, or attorneys. They may charge by the hour or charge a flat amount to set up a plan on an hourly basis for their ongoing services. Some fee-based planners will charge an ongoing monthly fee and provide you with a certain number of consulting hours each month.

A very popular investment strategy used by major full-service brokerage firms and banks is wrap accounts or separate managed accounts. These accounts are designed to provide highly customized asset management from a professional money manager. They are being marketed as personal mutual funds. They are also relatively expensive, running in cost between 2 percent of assets and 3 percent of assets on an annual basis.

Checking on Your Advisor Through Industry Watchdogs   The NASD and the North American Securities Administrators Association (NASAA) work together to provide consumers with reports on advisors.

The NASD, a private nonprofit organization, was created in 1938 by the Maloney Act amendments to the Securities Exchange Act of 1934. Even though the NASD is not a government agency, it broadly represents the federal government. NASAA represents the 50 state security departments. The resulting product of this cooperative effort is the Central Registration Depository (CRD). You can request a report on a particular advisor by contacting either organization. The NASD can be contacted on the Web at *www.nasdr.com* or by phone at 800 289-9999. NASAA can be contacted on the Web at *www.nasaa.org* or by phone at 202 737-0900. The NASAA will not generate the report but will tell you how to contact your state securities department directly.

The Distribution of Products Today and Tomorrow

The Internet is changing the way many industries distribute their products, and the financial services industry is no different. Take a look at the short list of online brokerage services in Table 13–3. You'll see that the range for a stock trade is a low of just under $10 to a high of just under $30. In 1999, the average cost was more than twice the average cost today. Most of the major banks, stockbrokerage. and financial planning firms are migrating away from traditional stock and bond trading and trying to gather assets to help people manage.

Table 13–3   Online Brokerage Services and Their Average Stock Trades

Online brokerage firms	Stock trade
Ameritrade	$10.99
Charles Schwab	$29.95
E-Trade	$12.99
JB Oxford	$9.50
ShareBuilder	$15.95
TD Waterhouse	$29.00

As the trend shifts more toward consultative selling in which the driver is the fulfillment of the needs of the consumer, products are likely to change as well. For example, there are very few true no-load insurance products available. Even the cheap term you see advertised on the Web and through direct mail has a commission equal to 25–40 percent of the first year's premium. Interestingly enough, there are no-load, no-commission annuity products. But in general, the current model of distribution simply doesn't support the new evolving manner in which products are being purchased.

The likely result of this trend will be a clear differentiation between the cost of receiving advice and the cost of buying the product. In my opinion, financial planners will shift their business model to a pay-for-advice relationship with clients that will be based on a fixed fee, an hourly fee, or a percentage of assets under management. That will leave the actual process of acquiring the investment to the consumer or the planner, but on a much lower cost basis.

Summary

Regardless of your decision about which path to take, what I care about is that you achieve your goals and that you do so with the least amount of wasted time and energy. Over the years, the financial services industry has gotten a reputation for caring more about the money it makes than the solutions it offers the consumer. Granted, some of that reputation has been earned by those who care only about their bottom line and not their customers' needs. However, I have found that the financial services industry is really not that different from any other industry in America—it has its good guys and its bad guys. And just as in other industries, the good guys don't like the bad guys any more than you do.

I'll share with you what I feel is most sad about the sales process in general. It simply doesn't breed enough diversification in the variety of sales reps people have to choose from. Only a certain breed of person can survive the rigors and the pressure of sales. Unfortunately, in the dog-eat-dog sales environment, we lose a very necessary force—the less aggressive sales reps who want only to do good by making sure their clients gets the best possible information, even at the cost of losing a sale.

Once again, I'm running dangerously close to getting folks angry with me. I'm not suggesting that good salespeople don't care about their clients and I'm not suggesting that all aggressive salespeople are not interested in their clients' wellbeing. I'm just saying that we need more people like Joe in the sales business.

Joe is a young man who worked for me several years ago in the marketing department of a company that I ran. Joe is the nicest guy you would ever want to meet. He genuinely loves the human race and would be a great Secret Service agent; he'd take a bullet for anyone. But he isn't a good salesperson because he won't force the sale and he gets a bit intimidated by other salespeople. Joe treats people with respect and with dignity, but is rarely rewarded with the sale. It's too bad because Joe would be the greatest financial planner; he cares, he's smart, and he puts his clients' interest first. So keep your eyes out for the Joes of the world because they're loyal, they won't let you down. and they are few and far between.

Power Checklist

✔ Do you have the time to define your goals, research your options, implement your strategy, and do all the ongoing research to maintain and fine-tune your plan?

✔ Are you qualified enough to do all this legwork without the perspective of advisors who makes these issues their profession?

✔ Most people who engage in their own financial planning will either knowingly or unknowingly compromise their goals, their investments, or both.

✔ Most of us don't think we need any help with anything until someone or something proves otherwise.

✔ Failure to succeed at any step of the planning process can lead to the overall risk of failure to achieve the goal.

✔ Rather than seek assistance, some people assume they can carry the load only to find out at some point that the load is too heavy and the road too long and difficult. By the time they seek help, valuable time that cannot be recaptured is no longer available.

✔ Butch Harmon probably does not tell Tiger Woods how to play golf; rather, he coaches him on ways he could improve his game with minor adjustments.

✔ Although the way products are sold by the major banks and brokerage houses has changed significantly, you still need to ask the right questions and be comfortable in the product choices that are recommended to you. You should always ask for more than one product choice and you should document the differences.

✔ My definition of the concept of "objective of selling" is to properly match the characteristics of the needs of the consumer with the characteristics of the product. If properly executed, the sale will result in a win-win-win situation in terms of price and value for the consumer, the salesperson, and the product manufacturer.

✔ The five steps to creating and managing your way to retirement gathering data about your goals, analyzing and evaluating your financial status, developing your own list of recommendations, implementing your recommendations, and monitoring and modifying your plan regularly.

✔ You may need an advisor for only certain aspects of your plan. The professionals who can help you include an investment advisor, a tax advisor, an estate planner, and an insurance advisor.

✔ Look for advisors experienced in the industry who have a CFP designation and a clean record. Ask them a lot of questions to get comfortable with them.

✔ Make certain that you understand what you are buying, ask for details, and get terms in writing—you won't regret it.

CHAPTER 14

Summiting the Mountain and Beating the Clock

It's so hard to make and so easy to lose!

As we draw to a close in our efforts to prepare you for retirement, you should know that I desperately want you to succeed. Part of that is selfish—writing this book will be a hollow success for me if you aren't better equipped to face the issues on your way to achieve your retirement lifestyle of choice. The other part is the genuine faith that I have in people to handle the challenges and adapt their lives to conquer adversity or adjust to its reality. As I said earlier, failing is not an option when it comes to your retirement. You deserve to retire and enjoy life in a manner that you can define and attain through proper saving and investing.

If the process of retirement planning were a recipe, it would be three parts emotion to one part action. When you break the process down, there is nothing that is so difficult to cause you to stop short of completing the process. If this were the late 1990s, you could argue that there wasn't sufficient information or resources available to the average consumer to engage in this process. Not so today. Today the challenge is too much information and too little time.

If you were to ask me which chapters of this book are the most important, I would easily answer chapters 1–6 and 12–15. I say this because I think you can find any number of books to cover the topics in chapters 7–11 equally as well if not better than I have here. But you will not likely reach your goals if you simply understand the investment products and the laws that govern your retirement saving. You have to understand the importance of identifying and managing retirement goals. That is by far the more difficult of the two aspects we are comparing here.

The markets will rise and fall and governments will change. All these factors will define periods when it is easier to save and periods when it is harder to save. You need to take advantage of those periods when all the stars align and be cautious when they aren't aligned. Regardless, you must create the inertia to move you in the right direction—neutral is the wrong speed! You have to get in the proper mindset so that you are always thinking about your financial goals and always doing something about them. Nothing will keep you from saving except you. Let me repeat that: Nothing will keep you from saving except you. This is not someone else's problem; it's yours, and there are always compromises if you look hard enough.

Where Do We Go from Here?

Of the critical issues confronting you, some are obvious and some are more subtle. Let's review a checklist:

- Sit down with your spouse or partner and discuss the big goal of saving for retirement and commit to the need for a plan.
- Determine whether you will climb the mountain with or without a guide. Are you going to seek professional coaching through an advisor?
- Take inventory of your assets and liabilities.
- Develop your list of the small goals that need to be achieved to reach the big goal.
- Take stock of the risks that might get in your way and determine what you'll do to minimize them.
- Match your goals with your assets to establish a gap, if any.
- Close the gap by determining how much more you need to save.
- Choose the path that you will take by selecting the various investment components of your plan.
- Continually monitor the plan for necessary changes. The wind and the weather on a mountain can change in an instant, and so can your life.
- Reach the summit and take a deep breath.

The less obvious issues that you'll face are those found in the "third dimension" that we have spoken about several times in the book. The third-dimension issues are the wild cards—things that come out of the blue to take the air out of your lungs or put wind in your sail. They could be life events, they could be market events, or they could just be the slow ebbing of time and the resulting emotional changes that seem to creep up on us as we age. Regardless of what they are, they can impact achievement of our goals or cause us to change our goals. All of this brings focus on the fact that we must be diligent in saving for retirement.

Your Choices

As I see it, you have two choices: do nothing or do something. If you do nothing, you face the prospect of being like 20 percent of the people in this country today who retire on only Social Security. That's right—one in five Americans lives solely on Social Security checks.

For those who retire in 2003, the maximum Social Security benefit is just under $21,000. Imagine what your life would look like if you had to live on $21,000 per year. The average check per couple in 2003 is roughly $1,500 per month or $18,000 per year. About the only good news is that you wouldn't have to pay taxes on the benefit. Before you decide to do nothing, do the math on it. Calculate your cost of living today, adjust as necessary for children leaving home, and other events, and see how far $18,000–21,000 will take you.

Obviously, the more practical choice is to do something. Develop your plan and start saving today while you still have a choice of retirement options. The longer you wait, the more quickly your options drop off until you're back to looking Social Security square in the eyes.

Spending Versus Investing

President Bush and the Congress took a number of actions to create an environment that fostered spending to boost the economy in 2003. Tax rebates and income tax bracket reductions were sweetened with a reduction in the capital gains tax. All of this was to promote spending. Although it was incredibly important for our economy to get the boost that it needed with markets in such a "bear" state, I also think that it's important for consumers not to confuse spending with investing.

Consider investing in something that can be leveraged, not consumed. Support the type of retirement reform proposed by Rob Portman and Ben Cardin that will allow consumers to save more for retirement.

This is an easy point to express but a much harder point to take action on. It revolves around keeping balance in your life. Without balance, you are out of control, and without control, it's difficult to own your own course of action. When you have a spouse and two kids and you all go to a ballgame, how much money do you spend? You'll spend at least $25 per ticket to get in, probably $15 to park, and another $35 for food and beverages. You've spent $150 before you get home, and what you got was family time and enjoyment. The *business* at the ballpark got your money. Do that four times a year and you've spent $600.

You used to be able to also argue that your children could learn from the athletes and develop role models for their lives. I'm sorry to say it, but the role models today seem few and far between. Most of the lessons that you can teach your children from professional athletes are how not to act, not how to act. Maybe what we see on TV and read in the newspapers doesn't fairly portray today's athletes, but unfortunately, those are the images and the words that our children drink into their impressionable minds and hearts. If you don't agree, you'll continue to speak with your wallet and go to as many events as you do now. I'm just suggesting that there is an alternative, one that can bring value to your retirement plan.

The alternative is to go to the ballpark twice a year and put $25 per month into a 529 plan for your child's education—now that's an investment. If you start when your child is three years old and continue for 15 years at 8 percent interest, you will have an extra $8,500 to use for college. Instead, take the additional time and play ball with your kids or go to the park and fly a kite and have a picnic.

There are so many ways that you can choose to save and invest more. Remember that when you invest, you're also helping to build America; you just don't usually have as much fun, and the results may not be as tangible. At a certain level, I am making a value judgment that I'm not entitled to make. In this case, I'm suggesting that the return you're getting on your investment in professional sports by supporting professional athletes does not provide a big enough return. You may not feel that way, and I'm certain that George Steinbrenner does not, but you get the point. Every dollar is a valuable asset that must be put to good use. You vote every day with your dollars, and no one can make these decisions in your life but you. The actions that you take today will have a long-term impact on tomorrow, so try to find balance in all aspects of your life.

Procrastination: Your Time Is Your Money

We talked earlier about procrastination, the biggest obstacle that you'll face on the road to retirement. When you get stuck, you need to get unstuck as quickly as you can (remember the concept of inertia that we covered in Chapter 1 and earlier in this chapter). A body at rest will stay at rest until moved by an outside force. You cannot afford to be stuck in your retirement planning, saving, and management.

The key reason, of course, is that our second greatest enemy is time. The previous moment is a commodity that we cannot get back, the current moment is one that we must use to plan, and the next moment is one in which we must take action. One of the principal reasons I suggested that you get a coach is that the amount of time it takes to define, execute, and manage your goals is considerable.

The final point that I want to make about procrastination relates one of the principal reasons that we procrastinate, and that is fear. Fear paralyzes us to the point where doing nothing is less of a fear than is doing something. It isn't just general fear that stops us cold; it's the fear of failure. If you're a procrastinator, and fear of failure is the emotion that is keeping you from your goals, you have to conquer those fears.

You must learn to look beyond failure to succeed. J. Wallace Hamilton once said, "People are trained for success when they should be training for failure. Failure is far more common than success; poverty is more prevalent than wealth; and disappointment is more normal than arrival." Understanding failure and how to overcome the fear of failing that results in procrastination is well beyond the scope of this book. There are, however, some wonderful books on the subject; one in particular that you might want to read is *Failing Forward: Turning Mistakes into Stepping Stones for Success* by John C. Maxwell.

The Importance of Communication and Trust

Once you are unlocked and putting yourself to work on your retirement, you need to be sure that you're communicating at every level. You need to be communicating with your spouse or partner, whether you are managing the process yourself or working with an advisor. And if you're working with an advisor, those communication lines must remain open and allow for a two-way dialogue for you to achieve the greatest result.

One tip for you to consider is to learn how the person you are trying to communicate with processes information. In general, we each process information using one of three senses: auditory, visual, or kinesthetic. How do you determine which process you or others use? You have to listen closely and often frequently. A good simple test will cost you a dollar. Here's how.

> Take out a dollar and hold at arm's length in front of you. Now simply rip it in half. As you reflect back on this experience, which sense was most evident: your ears, your eyes, or your stomach? If the sound of the dollar bill stood out most, you might be more auditory. If you pictured the dollar bill in your head most, you may be more visual. Finally, if you got sick to your stomach, you're likely to be a kinesthetic. And here's the best news—you can still tape the dollar back together.

In all seriousness, if you can determine how a person processes information, you can truly affect your level of communication. This process is called Neuro Linguistic Programming, and it's been around for many years. When people speak, do they use an auditory language? If so, they are likely to say things like: "I hear what you're saying." On the other hand, a visual person would likely say, "I see what you're saying," and a kinesthetic person would talk about feeling your message.

The way that you use this to better your communication is by conversing with someone at his or her level. If you're speaking with an auditory person, you need to focus on language; when you're speaking with someone who has a visual lens, you're best advised to use pictures to illustrate your point; and with kinesthetics, let them hold the picture. I know that these sound like small items, but the next time you're stuck trying to communicate with someone, listen closely and see if you can catch a tip that will allow you to rephrase your point in a manner better suited to his or her senses.

Once you establish communication, it is far easier to develop trust in that relationship. Trust is yet another critical part of the journey. If you don't trust your advisor, if you don't trust your spouse or partner, you're likely to get in big trouble. I hope that over the course of this book, I have earned your trust, which has clearly been my goal. Trust is an important part of retirement planning because the process is such a long one.

Perseverance

The more challenging the goal, the more important it is for us to find the strength to see the project through to the end. Perseverance has many names and faces and is exemplified by many famous and not so famous people. Coaches such as Vince Lombardi evidenced an incredibly strong will and demanded the same from his players. I remember my football days in the early 1970s when my coach told me repeatedly, "You have to want it bad enough, Shapiro. You just don't want it bad enough. "

I think that's a common theme for most of us. I wish that I had learned that lesson earlier in my life. Like most people, I have moments when I look back and say, "I could have done this," or "I could have done that." My list of "could haves" included sports like football (I was heavily recruited out of high school) and the theater (I was a theater voice major for two years in college). But I eventually gave up at both of these, and I really can't even tell you why except that apparently I didn't want it bad enough.

In my adult life, I have been fortunate, and I have refused to give up at anything that I do. As a result, I'm happy not only with my success but, more important, the road that I traveled to get there. I sincerely believe that the road you travel is just as important as the final destination. A victory tastes far less sweet if you haven't earned it. For me, that has meant following a simple formula:

- **Follow the Golden Rule.** Do unto others as you would have others do unto you. This speaks to the earlier comment that I made—the road you take is as important as the goal. I have always believed that when there is a high road and there is a low road, you have but one choice: Take the high road. The low road is exemplified by people who will do anything or pay any price to get something, including compromising what we as a society hold ethically and morally appropriate.

- **Use your head to manage your heart.** I love the Kenny Rogers line from The Gambler, "You've got to know when to hold them, know when to fold them." By the way, I define "fold them" as losing a battle, not the war. You have to maintain the balance between your head and your heart. This isn't a science, but an art. Your heart can take you great places, and it can take you to lousy places; it's your mind that you have to use to make the difference. In this case, I'm using the heart as a metaphor for emotion.

- **Use your heart to stimulate your drive.** I use my heart to push myself toward each goal. I'm also using the heart as a metaphor here—in this case, for spirit. Your drive will have to give you the fortitude to push forward when you don't think you can.

It's time for you to ask yourself, what are your "could haves"? Don't make "I could have retired with more money" one of your "could haves"; make it happen! The stories that follow are what I think are tremendous examples of courage and perseverance.

The Endurance

In 1914, an English explorer by the name of Sir Ernest Shackleton set out with a crew of 27 men, 69 Canadian sledging dogs, one cat, and an Argentine stowaway. Their expedition goal was to be the first to cross the Antarctic continent on foot. Years earlier, Shackleton had been denied that trophy by Roald Amundsen, a Norwegian explorer, and shortly after that, by Shackleton's nemesis, Sir Robert Scott. The voyage in 1914 claimed Shackleton's place in history, albeit not as he had envisioned.

This was Shackleton's third expedition to the Pole region, the second one having brought him within 100 miles of the Pole. On that trip,

Shackleton chose not to risk the lives of his crew and turned back because of a lack of supplies and for the health of some crew members.

Shackleton had run an ad in the English newspapers, to which he received over 3,000 responses. The ad was a simple one:

> MEN WANTED: FOR HAZARDOUS JOURNEY. SMALL WAGES, BITTER COLD, LONG MONTHS OF COMPLETE DARKNESS, CONSTANT DANGER, SAFE RETURN DOUBTFUL. HONOUR AND RECOGNITION IN CASE OF SUCCESS. SIR ERNEST SHACKLETON

He and his crew set out aboard The Endurance from England, making several stops before reaching Buenos Aires to load up on supplies for the journey. The Endurance was a 300-ton ship equipped with both sails and a steam engine, which was fired by coal. Interestingly, the original name for the boat was Polaris, but Shackleton didn't like the name and changed it to the Endurance to name the ship in the spirit of his family motto, "by endurance we conquer.' Little did he know at the time that the name of the ship would stand for the very men who sailed her.

The ship made its way to South Georgia Island, the southernmost port inhabited by humans. From this point, the Endurance headed toward the South Pole, navigating through the Weddell Sea. The ice packs were the worst that shippers had seen in years, and Shackleton waited as long as he could but finally headed out to sea.

In December of 1914, the ship became trapped in the slush of the Weddell Sea. After the crew's repeated attempts to break through what had become ice, the ship became totally glued to the ice in January 1915. Shackleton and the crew realized that the ship would be frozen there until the summer, some nine months away.

Unfortunately for Shackleton and the crew of the Endurance, the winter chose not to allow them to wait for a thaw. An enormous ice pack broke free and eventually crushed the Endurance in August 1915. With their ship crushed, the 28 men, the dogs, and the cat took up residence on the ice pack itself. Shackleton showed his loyalty to his men by giving the sailors warm reindeer skins while he and the officers wore less protective woolen ones. They slept in sleeping bags in tents whose linen was so sheer that the moon shown brightly through them. And perhaps worst of all, in 1915, there were no means of communication by which to notify anyone of their distress.

By March of 1916, the food had run out, and there were no more seals to kill and eat. The crew was left with no alternative other than to shoot and eat the dogs to survive. All they had left were some supplies from the boat and three lifeboats salvaged from the decimated hull of what was once the Endurance. To keep up the morale of the crew, Shackleton became a cheerleader and guaranteed each man his full pay for every day that they were lost at sea.

Shackleton made the decision to cross the ice pack, hoping to find land some 300 miles northwest of their position. The crew had to load their belongings into the three lifeboats, which, fully loaded, weighed over a ton each. Again to set the example, Shackleton took his personal Bible and his gold watch, laid them on the ice to lighten his load, and encouraged his men to do the same so that they could travel to safety. This effort came to no avail either, because the terrain on the ice pack proved too difficult for the crew to navigate. They were left hoping that the ice pack would drift them into land sometime soon.

In April 1916, the ice began to melt so thin that Shackleton and his crew had to board the life boats and endure treacherous seas for over 100 miles to reach the uninhabited Elephant Island. Miraculously, the entire crew made it to the island alive.

Shackleton was well aware of the fact that reaching Elephant Island would prolong their lives, but it would not necessarily result in their rescue. Upon arrival, Shackleton announced that he and five of his toughest sailors would take the largest of the three lifeboats, a 22.5-footer called the James Caird, on a journey back to the Whaling Station at South Georgia, over 800 miles away. They would do this by navigating with a single sextant across one of the most treacherous stretches of ocean in the world. With cloud cover for a prolonged period of time, their doom would have been certain.

Frank Worsley, the captain of the Endurance, would navigate the boat during the course of the 17-day, 800-mile sail. A one degree error would have caused the James Caird to miss the island entirely, and during that time, Worsley was able to take only four sextant readings. With a shortage of drinking water and the ill health of one of the crew members, the ship finally put to ground on the western side of South Georgia on May 10, 1916. The help they needed, unfortunately, lay 22 miles on the other side of the island, and this was no simple 22-mile trek. It spanned an uncharted mountain range that had never been crossed by men, and its peaks were just under 10,000 feet. Ten days after arriving on South Georgia Island, and in the dead of winter, they were off again.

Shackleton and two other men took a supply of food for no more than three days, a 50-foot length of rope pieces tied together, two compasses, a stove and matches, and a pair of binoculars. They had screws from the James Caird placed in their shoes for traction but did not take sleeping bags on their journey. Thirty-six hours later, having endured the nights' freezing temperatures and huge crevasses almost impossible to cross, Shackleton led the way to the whaling village where the men were met with disbelief and surprise.

It took Shackleton several months to get back to Elephant Island to rescue his remaining crew. The winter's ice was plaguing him again as he made numerous attempts to break through the ice and rescue his men. On his fourth rescue attempt, four months after leaving Elephant Island in that small lifeboat, Shackleton succeeded in returning to rescue his men and found that not one man had died. Miraculously, 28 men survived incredible odds for 18 months. This story of Sir Ernest Shackleton truly shows a level of perseverance that few human beings could ever match.

Imagine the perseverance it took to survive both emotionally and physically in those extreme conditions. How can we apply this lesson to using *Retirement Countdown* and achieving your goals? The longer it takes to see results in anything we do, the more difficult it is to maintain concentration and focus. Vince Lombardi was once quoted as saying, "The harder you work, the harder it is to surrender." Each time you consider your retirement too difficult a task to complete, think of Ernest Shackleton and take the next step forward.

It Ain't Over Until the Fat Lady Sings

I have always believed that success should be measured over a period of time, not at a point in time. I'll give you two examples. A personal goal of mine was to find a partner to share the rest of my life with. I failed at that on two attempts. My first and second wives weren't bad people; we just learned that we weren't meant for each other, and fortunately, we didn't have any children. Then I met my soul mate, Judy, and for me, the search was over. If I looked at this goal as a point in time and used my previous two marriages as the measuring point, I would have considered the achievement of my goal a failure. Instead, I look at it today as a brilliant success.

A much more famous example is the story of a man whose achievements we know all too well. Although his place in history is secure today, it wasn't so secure prior to the achievement of his goals. Do you know whose life I am referring to? If you think you've had rough times, read on:

- ◆ He lost his job in 1832.
- ◆ He was defeated for the legislature in1832.
- ◆ He failed in business in 1833.

- He was elected to the legislature in 1834.

- His sweetheart died in 1835.

- He suffered a nervous breakdown in 1836.

- He was defeated for speaker in 1838.

- He was defeated for nomination for Congress in 1843.

- He was elected to Congress in 1846.

- He lost his renomination for Congress in 1848.

- He was rejected for land officer in 1849.

- He was defeated for the Senate in 1854.

- He was defeated for the nomination for vice president of the United States in 1856.

- He was again defeated for the Senate in 1858.

- Abraham Lincoln was elected President of the United States in 1860.

Reading about perseverance doesn't ensure that you'll succeed, but it does provide you with the perspective that you have company on your journey. You're not alone in your struggle to balance all of the challenges in life that make if difficult to invest for your future. Sometimes you have to make compromises today for the sake of tomorrow. I read a terrific quote by Tony Robbins that I'll share with you here: "It's in moments of decision that your destiny is shaped."

A business associate of mine always used to say that if you don't know where you're going, any path will get you there. I disagree. I believe that's a good way to get yourself even more lost and sometimes killed. I'd much rather know where I'm going, and if I don't know, I'd rather stop and think through my options than boldly going where no one has gone before.

Retirement Countdown, the Web Site

The Internet is a wonderful resource for you to use, but not without its limitations. Be careful when you take advice from sources on the Internet unless you are comfortable that the source is reputable. You are often well advised to stick to brick-and-mortar establishments that have built a presence on the Web. Obviously, there are notable exceptions to that rule, including discount brokerage firms like E-TRADE and others that have made their home on the Web and developed a loyal following. Another such source is the Motley Fool, at *www.fool.com.*

You can visit the Retirement Countdown Web site at *www.retirement-countdown.com* and find lots of information related to the book and retirement. You can also get a kick in the butt if you're feeling that you need one. I'm always happy to put things into perspective for you. Here's what you'll find waiting for you:

- ◆ Retirement facts and statistics

- ◆ Retirement tools and calculators

- ◆ Personal monitoring tools

- ◆ Retirement discussion groups, both hosted and unhosted

- ◆ Product education area

The Next Step Is Yours

Almost every book starts with a working title, and as the thoughts and images form into a body of work, the author settles on the final title. The working title for this book was *Empower Your Retirement*. I hope you're empowered to take the next step, the next step, and the next step leading you closer to the summit, however you are defining it. When you eliminate all the obstacles, your path to success is clear and achievable. Just be certain that one of the obstacles is not you. Do you have the time to define

your goals, research your options, implement your strategy, and conduct all the ongoing research to maintain and fine-tune your plan?

One final note before you move into the last chapter on taking action: Enjoy the journey because life is too short not to enjoy every aspect of it as you start your Retirement Countdown.

Power Checklist

The Power Checklist for this chapter is a number of quotes that I thought you might benefit from. They are on target, inspirational, motivational, poignant, and most of all, empowering.

- ✔ "I find that the harder I work the more luck I seem to have."—Thomas Jefferson

- ✔ "Do, or do not. There is no 'try.'"—Yoda (in *The Empire Strikes Back)*

- ✔ "The previous moment is a commodity that we cannot get back; the current moment is one that we must use to plan; and the next moment is one in which we must take action."—David Shapiro

- ✔ "Security is an illusion. Life is either a daring adventure or it is nothing at all."—Helen Keller

- ✔ "It is your attitude more than your aptitude that will determine your altitude!"—Dr. Gary V. Carter

- ✔ "I don't measure a man's success by how high he climbs but how high he bounces when he hits bottom."—General George S. Patton

- ✔ "I have not failed. I've just found 10,000 ways that won't work."—Thomas Edison

- ✔ "We didn't lose the game; we just ran out of time."—Vince Lombardi

- ✔ "The optimist proclaims that we live in the best of all possible worlds, and the pessimist fears this is true."—James Branch Cabell

- ✔ "Be nice to people on your way up because you'll meet them on your way down."—Jimmy Durante

- ✔ "The true measure of a man is how he treats someone who can do him absolutely no good."—Samuel Johnson

✔ "Success should be measured over a period of time, not at a point in time."—David Shapiro

✔ "Obstacles are those frightful things you see when you take your eyes off your goal."—Henry Ford

✔ "Success usually comes to those who are too busy to be looking for it."—Henry David Thoreau

✔ "Far better it is to dare mighty things, to win glorious triumphs, even though checkered by failure, than to take rank with those poor spirits who neither enjoy much nor suffer much, because they live in the gray twilight that knows not victory nor defeat.—Theodore Roosevelt

✔ "The harder you work, the harder it is to surrender."—Vince Lombardi

✔ "When you eliminate all the obstacles, your path to success is clear and achievable; just make certain that one of the obstacles is not you."—David Shapiro

CHAPTER 15

Developing an Action Plan

In this final chapter, we will put together an action plan. This chapter is all about action and nothing else. We'll look at Dennis and Mary Glover's current financial position and develop a plan for achieving or modifying their retirement goals to illustrate the concepts we have discussed in *Retirement Countdown*. Keep in mind that there are dozens of ways to attack these issues. Ultimately, you will have to determine which alterative or alternatives feel most comfortable. Let's start by taking a closer look at the Glovers.

Current Status for the Glovers

Here are the statistics on Dennis Glover:

Age: 58.

Occupation: Foreman for a local machinist company. He has worked for the same company for over 28 years and participates in the company's health and retirement plans.

Salary: $45,000 per year, and he currently invests only 3 percent into the company 401(k) plan. His company matches 50 cents on the dollar up to 6 percent.

Health: Relatively good, though he is a bit overweight. His family medical history is good, and there is no reason to suspect he will not live out his normal life expectancy.

Risk tolerance: Average.

Targeted retirement age: 67.

Here's are the facts on Mary Glover:

Age: 56.

Occupation: High school English teacher. She has been with her current employer for over 10 years and participates in the school system's health plan.

Salary: $40,000 per year. She participates in the district's 403(b) program, contributing 6 percent each year. (She would like to contribute more, but their budget is so tight that she is afraid to make the commitment.)

Health: Excellent. With her strong family medical history, she will likely outlive the normal life expectancy for her age and gender.

Risk tolerance: Conservative to moderate.

Targeted retirement age: 65.

As we review this critical information, we can already see some areas of concern. The first is that Dennis and Mary have differing views on risk tolerance. They need to decide on an investment strategy that is consistent with their "couples" risk-tolerance desires and establish the basis for compromise. Regardless of the manner in which they resolve the issue, they must address it up front to mitigate any hard feelings down the road.

The second area of concern is that they have no will and no healthcare directive to carry out their wishes if they become incapacitated. They can create these documents with or without an attorney. Hospitals and health-care providers can usually provide generic forms to complete. The Glovers' will must clearly state their intentions for the distribution of their assets at the time of death, and their healthcare directive will provide direction to their children and any healthcare provider in case decisions regarding their lives need to be made. They may also want to consider ways to avoid probate by using a family trust.

Once Dennis and Mary have agreed on their couples approach to risk tolerance, they can begin to collect the information they will need to analyze their current financial condition. This will require Dennis and Mary to prepare a budget, something very few people do. But without a budget, it's very difficult to see where your problems are. Table 15–1 is a snapshot of the Glovers' current budget.

Table 15–1   The Glovers' Current Budget

	Preretirement		
	Dennis	**Mary**	**Total**
Income and Assets			
Gross Salary	$45,000	$40,000	$85,000
Net Salary	$33,750	$30,000	$63,750
Bonus			
Outside Consulting			
Pension Benefits			
Social Security Benefits			
Rental Property			
Tax Refund			
Unemployment			

Table 15–1 The Glovers' Current Budget *(Continued)*

	Preretirement		
	Dennis	**Mary**	**Total**
Interest Income			
CD			$300
Savings Account			$2
Money Market			$4
Loan Interest Received			
Dividend Income			
Mutual Fund			
Stock Dividends			$110
Earned Income			
Annuity Income			
Trust Income			
Alimony/Child Support			
Systematic Liquidations			
Reverse Mortgage			
IRA/401 Distributions			
Other Income			
Total Income			**$64,166**
Expenses			
Automobile			
Fuel			$2,500
Loan			$1,800
Registration			$200
Maintenance			$1,200
Bad Debt			
Bank Charges			
Monthly Fee			
Late Fees			
Credit Card Interest			$150

Table 15–1   The Glovers' Current Budget *(Continued)*

	Preretirement		
	Dennis	**Mary**	**Total**
Cash Withdrawals			$3,000
Charity			
Cash			$3,500
Non-cash			
Clothing			$3,000
Books and Magazines			$250
Education			
Entertainment			
Dining			$2,000
Movies			$500
Sporting Events			$300
Concerts			$100
Gifts Given			$500
Groceries			$4,000
Housing Costs			
Mortgage			$13,800
Equity Line			
Second Home Mortgage			
Association Fees			
Property Taxes			$3,500
Maintenance			$1,500
Insurance			
Life			$800
Health			$1,200
Medicare			
MediGap			
Long Term Care			
Automobile			$600

Table 15–1   The Glovers' Current Budget *(Continued)*

	Preretirement		
	Dennis	**Mary**	**Total**
Insurance *(Continued)*			
Homeowners			$500
General Liability			$100
Disability			
Deductables Paid			$200
Retirement Plan Contributions	$1,350	$4,800	$6,150
Legal and Accounting Fees			$250
Major Purchases			$150
Office and Home Supplies			$50
Personal Care			$750
Postage			$30
Rental			
Repairs			
Taxes (over and above those withheld)			
Utilities			
Cable or Satelite			$300
Garbage and Recycling			$150
Gas and Electric			$1,800
Internet Access			$120
Telephone			$540
Water			$100
Vacation			$2,500
Total Expenses			**$58,090**
Net Income			**$6,076**

A cursory review shows there is little room for additional savings. Dennis and Mary have a mere $6,076 in net income to add to achieving retirement goals and only eight years to supplement their current assets.

Insurance Review

Dennis and Mary have a $75,000 life insurance policy on Dennis that was purchased over 20 years ago. In addition, his employer provides $10,000 through a group life insurance policy. Dennis and Mary have health insurance through their respective employers. They have no other coverage.

Tax Documents

Dennis and Mary have never been in a high enough tax bracket to worry much about tax planning. They have their standard deductions for their mortgage interest, retirement plan contributions, and property taxes. Table 15–2 and Figure 15–1 show the Glovers' current assets.

Table 15–2   The Glovers' Current Assets

Asset	Value ($)
House	350,000
Dennis's 401(k)	79,000 (stock mutual funds)
Mary's TSA	57,000 (fixed annuity)
Money market account	30,000
CD	10,000
Stocks	11,000
Equity mutual fund	5,000
Government bonds	30,000
Total	**574,004**

As we look at the Glovers' assets, we can see that over 60 percent are in their home. This is likely to cause problems for Dennis and Mary because they will probably not achieve their retirement goal without selling their house. Let's look at the value of their investments between now and retirement. As Table 15–3 shows, the value of their investment will be $736,316 when they retire. In addition, saving another $5,000 per year would add $50,000, assuming a 5 percent growth rate, leaving the Glovers with $786,316 to fund their retirement goals.

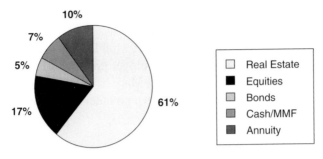

Figure 15–1   The Glovers' Current Assets

Goal Setting and Costs

Dennis and Mary Glover need to address the topics in the following sections as they prepare for their retirement.

Emergency Fund

Although we haven't yet addressed the Glovers' budget in retirement, we'll assume that their expenses will be about the same as they are now for purposes of this projection. Today's expenses are roughly $58,000, which will be inflation adjusted to $71,000 at retirement. That means the Glovers require at least $35,500 to provide for up to six months of necessary cash flow in the event of an emergency. This can be applied to their extended life-expectancy goal. They need to look at the following:

- ◆ Goal cost calculation: Nonrequired.
- ◆ Asset assignment: Dennis and Mary will assign their money market fund to meet this goal. To the extent that the return on this investment fails to at least match the rate of inflation, other assets will need to be targeted to maintain this goal.

Long-Term Care Insurance Fund

Dennis and Mary want to reduce their risk of having to pay for any extended healthcare costs in retirement. Their goal is to buy a joint LTC policy with a 90-day elimination period and a $175-per-day benefit for five years. By going with a 90-day elimination period, they can reduce the

Table 15–3 The Glovers' Assets, 2004–2012

Year	Age	Primary House	Dennis's 401(k)	Mary's TSA	Money Market	CD	Stocks	Equity MF	Gov't Bonds	Total Investments
2004	58	350,000	79,000	57,000	30,000	10,000	11,000	5,000	30,000	$574,062
2005	59	360,500	83,740	60,420	30,600	10,300	11,770	5,250	31,200	$564,644
2006	60	371,315	88,764	64,045	31,212	10,609	12,594	5,513	32,448	$586,118
2007	61	382,454	94,090	67,888	31,836	10,927	13,475	5,788	33,746	$608,528
2008	62	393,928	99,736	71,961	32,473	11,255	14,419	6,078	35,096	$631,919
2009	63	405,746	105,720	76,279	33,122	11,593	15,428	6,381	36,500	$656,341
2010	64	417,918	112,063	80,856	33,785	11,941	16,508	6,700	37,960	$681,845
2011	65	430,456	118,787	85,707	34,461	12,299	17,664	7,036	39,478	$708,484
2012	66	443,370	125,914	90,849	35,150	12,668	18,900	7,387	41,057	$736,316

cost significantly. They don't want to purchase the policy now; they want to purchase it in five years. The specifics are as follows:

- ◆ Goal cost calculation: Calculate the number of years to funding, the duration of the goal, and the inflation-adjusted cost of the goal; then calculate the present value of achieving that goal at the specified time. See *www.retirementcountdown.com* for assistance with goal cost calculations.
- ◆ Retirement goal: Fund long-term care.
- ◆ Category: Insurance.
- ◆ Years to goal: 5.
- ◆ Cost of goal today: $4,200.
- ◆ Inflation adjusted for when needed: $6,171.
- ◆ Amount need to fund: $55,722.
- ◆ Asset assignment: $30,000 from government bonds and $26,000 from Mary's retirement plan. Dennis and Mary have scant assets to work with, and this goal is best suited to the government bonds that they currently own. They will need to supplement this with other assets, such as Mary's retirement plan or Dennis's retirement plan because they have such limited investments. The duration of this investment is moderate in term and requires a high level of safety. Another alternative would be to completely revamp Dennis and Mary's existing portfolio of investments and then reassign the proper resulting asset to this goal.

Ninety-Day Elimination Period Fund

Funding the 90-day elimination period will cover the $15,750 required for the first 90 days of nursing care and can be taken from the emergency fund if needed. The cost calculation and assignment are as follows:

- ◆ Goal cost calculation: None required
- ◆ Asset assignment: Money market fund

Extending Life Expectancy Fund

Dennis and Mary want to make certain they have enough income to survive 10 years beyond their joint life expectancy of 23 years. Specifics are the following:

◆ Goal cost calculation: Inflate living expenses for years 31–41, which covers the 10-year period beyond their expected life expectancy. Then discount that back to today's dollars for funding. See *www.retirementcountdown*.com for assistance with goal cost calculations.

◆ Retirement goal: Extended life expectancy.

◆ Category: Income.

◆ Years to goal: 31.

◆ Cost of goal today: $415,000.

◆ Cost of goal at retirement: $547,000.

◆ Asset assignment: Insufficient to achieve this goal.

Income Insurance Fund

Dennis and Mary's goal is to retire on 90 percent of their preretirement income. Remember that $33,528 of the $92,266 (assumes inflation-adjusted income at the last year of employment) they will require will come from Social Security payments if Dennis retires at age 67 Mary takes an early retirement at age 65, and benefits are not reduced by the government before they retire. Specifics are as follows:

◆ Goal cost calculation: Look at the income required to fund their annual expenses, inflate those expenses to cover life expectancy, and then do a present value calculation to determine the cost of the goal. See *www.retirementcountdown.com* for assistance with goal cost calculations.

◆ Retirement goal: Income insurance.

◆ Category: Income.

◆ Years to goal: 8.

◆ Cost of goal today: Based on the 10-year average for inflation and assuming a blended interest rate of 3.81% on their investments (heavily weighed down by their home), close to $1,000,000.

◆ Result: Failure to achieve their goal.

Some possible solutions would be for the Glovers to:

◆ Deposit an additional lump sum of $419,000 today or save an additional $60,000 per year until retirement.

◆ Reduce the percentage of income required postretirement, which means cutting back on expenses, reducing their standard of living, or modifying their existing goals.

Dennis and Mary's plight is clear: They must start making decisions that will ultimately affect their postretirement lifestyle. They will need to mix and match trade-offs to achieve their goal. For example, if they choose not to buy LTC insurance, they will have an additional $55,700 to invest toward their retirement income and can reduce the amount required to achieve their goal of 90 percent of preretirement income to $323,000. If they consider tightening their belts on the expense side after retirement and reduce the 90 percent goal to 55 percent, they can also achieve their goal.

Tough Decisions

Dennis and Mary also have to deal with the fact that their largest asset, their house, does not spin off income. When they retire, their home will be worth roughly $445,000. If Dennis and Mary sell their home and move into a less expensive home, or simply rent, they will be able to dedicate that asset to generating an income. One option they may want to consider is using their home to generate insured income for the rest of their lives. For example, they can earn $28,000 a year for the rest of both of their lives by selling their home and using the assets to purchase income insurance. If their Social Security payments are kept intact, the combination would provide over $61,000 in income.

A similar approach would be to consider a reverse mortgage, which is a reverse loan. In this case, Dennis and Mary would borrow money from the bank in a lump sum, a monthly payment, or a line of credit using the house as collateral. The advantage is that the income is not taxed; the problem is that most reverse mortgages would offer only 25 percent of the equity in the home. In this case, the Glovers would be able to generate only $100,000 in income from the reverse mortgage.

If the Glovers purchase income insurance, they would still have $343,000 in other assets to increase their postretirement income and achieve their goals. If we further assume that the Glovers allocate $35,000 to their emergency fund and another $55,700 to purchase LTC insurance, they would have just over $250,000 left to generate additional income. If they utilized systematic withdrawals of 4 percent each year, they would generate another $10,000 in income, bringing their total predictable income to $71,000. Let's look at Table 15–4 for the Glovers' revised budget that reflects these changes.

Table 15–4   The Glovers' Revised Budget

	Preretirement			Post-Retirement
	Dennis	**Mary**	**Total**	
Income and Assets				
Gross Salary	$45,000	$40,000	$85,000	
Net Salary	$33,750	$30,000	$63,750	
Bonus				
Outside Consulting				
Pension Benefits				
Social Security Benefits				$33,528
Rental Property				
Tax Refund				
Unemployment				
Interest Income				
CD			$300	
Savings Account			$2	
Money Market			$4	
Loan Interest Received				
Dividend Income				
Mutual Fund				
Stock Dividends			$110	
Earned Income				
Annuity Income				$28,000
Trust Income				
Alimony/Child Support				
Systematic Liquidations				$10,000
Reverse Mortgage				
IRA/401 Distributions				
Other Income				
Total Income			**$64,166**	**$71,528**

Table 15–4   The Glovers' Revised Budget *(Continued)*

	Preretirement			Post-Retirement
	Dennis	**Mary**	**Total**	
Expenses				
Automobile				
Fuel			$2,500	$3,075
Loan			$1,800	$955
Registration			$200	$246
Maintenance			$1,200	$1,476
Bad Debt				
Bank Charges				
Monthly Fee				
Late Fees				
Credit Card Interest			$150	$184
Cash Withdrawals			$3,000	$1,000
Charity				
Cash			$3,500	$1,845
Non-cash				
Clothing			$3,000	$2,460
Books and Magazines			$250	$246
Education				
Entertainment				
Dining			$2,000	$3,075
Movies			$500	$922
Sporting Events			$300	$369
Concerts			$100	$123
Gifts Given			$500	$1,230
Groceries			$4,000	$3,690
Housing Costs				
Mortgage			$13,800	$26,500
Equity Line				

Table 15–4   The Glovers' Revised Budget *(Continued)*

	Preretirement			Post-Retirement
	Dennis	**Mary**	**Total**	**Retirement**
Housing Costs (*Continued*)				
Second Home Mortgage				
Association Fees				
Property Taxes			$3,500	$4,305
Maintenance			$1,500	$1,845
Insurance				
Life			$800	$800
Health			$1,200	
Medicare				$800
MediGap				$3,600
Long Term Care				
Automobile			$600	$738
Homeowners			$500	$615
General Liability			$100	$123
Disability				
Deductables Paid			$200	$984
Retirement Plan Contributions	$1,350	$4,800	$6,150	
Legal and Accounting Fees			$250	$307
Major Purchases			$150	$184
Office and Home Supplies			$50	$92
Personal Care			$750	$922
Postage			$30	$37
Rental				
Repairs				
Taxes (over and above those withheld)				

Table 15–4   The Glovers' Revised Budget *(Continued)*

	Preretirement			Post-Retirement
	Dennis	**Mary**	**Total**	
Utilities				
Cable or Satelite			$300	$369
Garbage and Recycling			$150	$184
Gas and Electric			$1,800	$2,214
Internet Access			$120	$148
Telephone			$540	$664
Water			$100	$123
Vacation			$2,500	$3,075
Total Expenses			**$58,090**	**$69,525**
Net Income			**$6,076**	**$2,003**

The Glovers will punctuate their retirement by analyzing trade-offs and managing expenses. In addition to modifying their goals, the Glovers could take these steps to improve their chances of meeting their retirement goals:

◆ They could sell their home now and invest the proceeds more aggressively than the growth rate assumed on their home.

◆ They could be more aggressive in their overall investing. Each percentage point of increased return yields an additional $7,000 that can be compounded over the remaining eight years until their retirement.

◆ They could start reducing expenses now, enabling them to save more for their retirement.

◆ Dennis could elect to work to age 70 and enjoy increased Social Security benefits. His delay would also allow Mary to enjoy the better benefits at her normal retirement age and give the Glovers more time to save.

Retirement on Your Terms

Retirement is a process, not an event, and the more you do every day to save more and spend less improves your chances of being able to retire on *your* terms.

APPENDICES

APPENDIX A

The "Uniform Lifetime Table"

For calculating lifetime required distributions[1]

Table A–1   Table for Determining the Divisor

Age	Divisor	Age	Divisor	Age	Divisor
70	27.4	86	14.1	102	5.5
71	26.5	87	13.4	103	5.2
72	25.6	88	12.7	104	4.9
73	24.7	89	12.0	105	4.5
74	23.8	90	11.4	106	4.2
75	22.9	91	10.8	107	3.9
76	22.0	92	10.2	108	3.7
77	21.2	93	9.6	109	3.4
78	20.3	94	9.1	110	3.1
79	19.5	95	8.6	111	2.9
80	18.7	96	8.1	112	2.6
81	17.9	97	7.6	113	2.4
82	17.1	98	7.1	114	2.1
83	16.3	99	6.7	115+	1.9
84	15.5	100	6.3		
85	14.8	101	5.9		

As an example, if you have $300,000 in your IRA at age 70 you must take a distribution no less than $300,000 ÷ 27.4, which equals $10,549.

Single Life Expectancy Table for Inherited IRAs[2]

For use by designated beneficiaries, this is the single life expectancy table based on the beneficiaries age in the year after the IRA owner's death.

---

[1] Certain exceptions apply such as a spouse who is greater than 10 years younger than the participant and who is the sole beneficiary of the plan.

[2] To be used for calculating post-death required distributions to beneficiaries

Table A–2   Single Life Expectancy Table for Inherited IRAs

0	82.4	38	45.6	76	12.7
1	81.6	39	44.6	77	12.1
2	80.6	40	43.6	78	11.4
3	79.7	41	42.7	79	10.8
4	78.7	42	41.7	80	10.2
5	77.7	43	40.7	81	9.7
6	76.7	44	39.8	82	9.1
7	75.8	45	38.8	83	8.6
8	74.8	46	37.9	84	8.1
9	73.8	47	37.0	85	7.6
10	72.8	48	36.0	86	7.1
11	71.8	49	35.1	87	6.7
12	70.8	50	34.2	88	6.3
13	69.9	51	33.3	89	5.9
14	68.9	52	32.3	90	5.5
15	67.9	53	31.4	91	5.2
16	66.9	54	30.5	92	4.9
17	66.0	55	29.6	93	4.6
18	65.0	56	28.7	94	4.3
19	64.0	57	27.9	95	4.1
20	63.0	58	27.0	96	3.8
21	62.1	59	26.1	97	3.6
22	61.1	60	25.2	98	3.4
23	60.1	61	24.4	99	3.1
24	59.1	62	23.5	100	2.9
25	58.2	63	22.7	101	2.7
26	57.2	64	21.8	102	2.5
27	56.2	65	21.0	103	2.3
28	55.3	66	20.2	104	2.1
29	54.3	67	19.4	105	1.9
30	53.3	68	18.6	106	1.7
31	52.4	69	17.8	107	1.5
32	51.4	70	17.0	108	1.4
33	50.4	71	16.3	109	1.2
34	49.4	72	15.5	110	1.1
35	48.5	73	14.8	111+	1.0
36	47.5	74	14.1		
37	46.5	75	13.4		

Life Expectancy[3]

Table A–3   Single Life

Age	Male	Female	Age	Male	Female	Age	Male	Female
0	73.63	78.92	31	44.49	49.06	62	17.86	20.95
1	73.19	78.42	32	43.56	48.10	63	17.14	20.15
2	72.23	77.46	33	42.62	47.13	64	16.44	19.37
3	71.26	76.48	34	41.69	46.17	65	15.75	18.60
4	70.28	75.50	35	40.77	45.21	66	15.07	17.84
5	69.29	74.51	36	39.84	44.26	67	14.40	17.09
6	68.31	73.52	37	38.92	43.30	68	13.75	16.35
7	67.32	72.53	38	38.00	42.35	69	13.11	15.62
8	66.33	71.54	39	37.08	41.41	70	12.49	14.91
9	65.35	70.55	40	36.17	40.46	71	11.89	14.21
10	64.36	69.56	41	35.27	39.52	72	11.30	13.52
11	63.36	68.57	42	34.36	38.58	73	10.73	12.84
12	62.37	67.58	43	33.47	37.65	74	10.17	12.17
13	61.38	66.59	44	32.58	36.72	75	9.62	11.53
14	60.40	65.60	45	31.69	35.79	76	9.09	10.90
15	59.43	64.62	46	30.82	34.87	77	8.57	10.28
16	58.47	63.64	47	29.95	33.95	78	8.06	9.68
17	57.52	62.66	48	29.09	33.04	79	7.57	9.09
18	56.58	61.69	49	28.23	32.13	80	7.09	8.52
19	55.64	60.72	50	27.39	31.22	81	6.64	7.98
20	54.71	59.74	51	26.54	30.33	82	6.21	7.45
21	53.78	58.77	52	25.71	29.43	83	5.80	6.95
22	52.85	57.80	53	24.87	28.55	84	5.42	6.47
23	51.93	56.83	54	24.05	27.67	85	5.06	6.03
24	51.01	55.85	55	23.24	26.80	86	4.72	5.60
25	50.08	54.88	56	22.43	25.93	87	4.39	5.20
26	49.15	53.91	57	21.64	25.08	88	4.08	4.82
27	48.22	52.94	58	20.86	24.23	89	3.79	4.45
28	47.29	51.97	59	20.09	23.39	90	3.52	4.11
29	46.36	51.00	60	19.34	22.57			
30	45.42	50.03	61	18.59	21.75			

[3] Based on the United States Life Tables, 2000. Courtesy of Milliman.

Table A–4 Joint Life

Male	Female											
	45	46	47	48	49	50	51	52	53	54	55	56
45	40.66	40.08	39.53	38.99	38.47	37.96	37.47	37.00	36.53	36.07	35.61	35.15
46	40.29	39.69	39.12	38.57	38.03	37.51	37.01	36.52	36.05	35.58	35.12	34.67
47	39.91	39.33	38.73	38.17	37.61	37.08	36.56	36.06	35.57	35.10	34.64	34.18
48	39.55	38.95	38.37	37.78	37.21	36.66	36.13	35.61	35.11	34.63	34.16	33.70
49	39.20	38.59	38.00	37.41	36.83	36.26	35.71	35.18	34.67	34.17	33.69	33.22
50	38.85	38.24	37.64	37.04	36.46	35.88	35.32	34.77	34.24	33.73	33.23	32.76
51	38.50	37.89	37.29	36.68	36.09	35.51	34.93	34.37	33.83	33.30	32.79	32.30
52	38.16	37.55	36.94	36.33	35.73	35.15	34.57	33.99	33.43	32.89	32.36	31.86
53	37.80	37.20	36.59	35.99	35.39	34.79	34.20	33.63	33.05	32.50	31.95	31.43
54	37.43	36.84	36.25	35.64	35.04	34.44	33.85	33.26	32.69	32.12	31.56	31.03
55	37.05	36.48	35.89	35.30	34.70	34.10	33.50	32.91	32.33	31.76	31.19	30.64
56	36.66	36.10	35.53	34.94	34.35	33.76	33.16	32.56	31.97	31.40	30.83	30.26
57	36.24	35.70	35.15	34.58	34.00	33.41	32.82	32.22	31.63	31.05	30.47	29.91
58	35.80	35.29	34.75	34.20	33.64	33.06	32.48	31.88	31.29	30.71	30.12	29.55
59	35.33	34.85	34.34	33.81	33.26	32.70	32.13	31.54	30.96	30.37	29.78	29.21
60	34.84	34.38	33.90	33.39	32.87	32.32	31.77	31.20	30.62	30.03	29.45	28.87
61	34.32	33.89	33.43	32.95	32.45	31.93	31.39	30.84	30.27	29.70	29.12	28.54
62	33.77	33.37	32.94	32.49	32.01	31.52	31.00	30.46	29.91	29.35	28.78	28.21
63	33.20	32.82	32.42	32.00	31.55	31.08	30.59	30.07	29.54	28.99	28.44	27.87
64	32.60	32.25	31.88	31.48	31.06	30.62	30.15	29.66	29.15	28.62	28.08	27.53
65	31.97	31.65	31.30	30.93	30.54	30.13	29.69	29.22	28.74	28.23	27.71	27.17
66	31.31	31.02	30.70	30.36	29.99	29.61	29.20	28.76	28.30	27.82	27.32	26.81
67	30.64	30.36	30.07	29.76	29.42	29.06	28.68	28.27	27.84	27.39	26.91	26.42
68	29.94	29.69	29.42	29.13	28.82	28.48	28.13	27.75	27.35	26.92	26.47	26.01
69	29.22	28.99	28.74	28.47	28.19	27.88	27.55	27.20	26.83	26.43	26.01	25.57
70	28.48	28.27	28.04	27.79	27.53	27.25	26.95	26.63	26.28	25.91	25.52	25.11
71	27.72	27.53	27.32	27.09	26.85	26.60	26.32	26.02	25.71	25.37	25.00	24.62
72	26.94	26.77	26.58	26.37	26.15	25.92	25.66	25.39	25.10	24.79	24.46	24.10
73	26.15	25.99	25.81	25.63	25.43	25.21	24.98	24.74	24.47	24.18	23.88	23.55
74	25.33	25.19	25.03	24.87	24.69	24.49	24.28	24.05	23.81	23.55	23.27	22.97
75	24.51	24.38	24.24	24.09	23.92	23.75	23.55	23.35	23.13	22.89	22.64	22.36
76	23.67	23.55	23.43	23.29	23.14	22.98	22.81	22.62	22.42	22.21	21.98	21.73
77	22.82	22.71	22.60	22.47	22.34	22.20	22.04	21.87	21.69	21.50	21.29	21.07
78	21.95	21.86	21.75	21.64	21.53	21.40	21.26	21.11	20.94	20.77	20.58	20.38
79	21.07	20.99	20.90	20.80	20.69	20.58	20.45	20.32	20.17	20.02	19.85	19.67
80	20.18	20.11	20.03	19.94	19.85	19.75	19.64	19.52	19.39	19.25	19.09	18.93
81	19.28	19.22	19.15	19.07	18.99	18.90	18.80	18.69	18.58	18.46	18.32	18.18
82	18.38	18.32	18.26	18.19	18.12	18.04	17.95	17.86	17.76	17.65	17.53	17.40
83	17.46	17.41	17.36	17.30	17.24	17.17	17.09	17.01	16.92	16.82	16.72	16.61
84	16.54	16.49	16.45	16.40	16.34	16.28	16.22	16.14	16.07	15.98	15.89	15.79
85	15.60	15.57	15.53	15.48	15.44	15.38	15.33	15.27	15.20	15.13	15.05	14.96
86	14.66	14.63	14.60	14.56	14.52	14.48	14.43	14.38	14.32	14.26	14.19	14.11
87	13.72	13.69	13.66	13.63	13.60	13.56	13.52	13.48	13.43	13.37	13.32	13.25
88	12.76	12.74	12.72	12.69	12.67	12.63	12.60	12.56	12.52	12.48	12.43	12.38
89	11.81	11.79	11.77	11.75	11.73	11.70	11.67	11.64	11.61	11.57	11.53	11.49
90	10.84	10.83	10.81	10.80	10.78	10.76	10.73	10.71	10.68	10.65	10.62	10.58

Table A–4   Joint Life *(Continued)*

Male	Female											
	57	58	59	60	61	62	63	64	65	66	67	68
45	34.69	34.23	33.75	33.27	32.77	32.25	31.72	31.16	30.59	30.00	29.39	28.75
46	34.21	33.75	33.29	32.82	32.33	31.83	31.32	30.78	30.23	29.66	29.07	28.45
47	33.73	33.27	32.82	32.35	31.88	31.40	30.90	30.39	29.86	29.30	28.73	28.14
48	33.24	32.79	32.34	31.89	31.43	30.96	30.47	29.98	29.46	28.93	28.38	27.81
49	32.76	32.31	31.86	31.41	30.96	30.50	30.03	29.55	29.06	28.55	28.02	27.46
50	32.29	31.83	31.38	30.94	30.49	30.04	29.58	29.12	28.64	28.14	27.63	27.10
51	31.82	31.36	30.91	30.46	30.02	29.57	29.12	28.67	28.20	27.73	27.23	26.72
52	31.37	30.90	30.44	29.99	29.54	29.10	28.66	28.21	27.76	27.29	26.82	26.33
53	30.93	30.45	29.98	29.52	29.07	28.63	28.19	27.75	27.31	26.85	26.39	25.92
54	30.51	30.01	29.53	29.06	28.61	28.16	27.72	27.28	26.85	26.41	25.96	25.50
55	30.10	29.59	29.10	28.62	28.15	27.70	27.26	26.82	26.39	25.95	25.51	25.06
56	29.72	29.19	28.68	28.19	27.71	27.25	26.80	26.36	25.93	25.50	25.06	24.63
57	29.35	28.81	28.28	27.77	27.28	26.81	26.36	25.91	25.47	25.04	24.61	24.18
58	29.00	28.44	27.90	27.38	26.87	26.39	25.92	25.47	25.03	24.60	24.17	23.74
59	28.64	28.09	27.53	27.00	26.48	25.98	25.50	25.04	24.59	24.15	23.72	23.30
60	28.30	27.74	27.19	26.64	26.11	25.60	25.10	24.63	24.17	23.72	23.29	22.86
61	27.96	27.40	26.84	26.29	25.75	25.23	24.72	24.23	23.76	23.30	22.86	22.43
62	27.63	27.06	26.50	25.95	25.41	24.87	24.35	23.85	23.36	22.90	22.44	22.01
63	27.30	26.73	26.17	25.61	25.07	24.53	24.00	23.48	22.99	22.51	22.04	21.60
64	26.97	26.41	25.84	25.28	24.73	24.19	23.67	23.14	22.63	22.13	21.66	21.20
65	26.63	26.07	25.52	24.96	24.41	23.86	23.33	22.81	22.28	21.78	21.29	20.82
66	26.28	25.74	25.19	24.64	24.09	23.54	23.00	22.47	21.96	21.44	20.94	20.46
67	25.91	25.38	24.85	24.31	23.76	23.22	22.68	22.15	21.63	21.12	20.60	20.11
68	25.52	25.02	24.50	23.97	23.44	22.90	22.36	21.83	21.30	20.79	20.29	19.78
69	25.11	24.63	24.13	23.62	23.10	22.58	22.05	21.52	20.99	20.47	19.96	19.47
70	24.68	24.22	23.75	23.26	22.76	22.24	21.73	21.20	20.68	20.16	19.65	19.15
71	24.21	23.79	23.34	22.87	22.39	21.90	21.39	20.88	20.37	19.85	19.34	18.84
72	23.72	23.33	22.91	22.47	22.01	21.54	21.05	20.55	20.05	19.54	19.04	18.53
73	23.20	22.83	22.44	22.03	21.60	21.15	20.69	20.21	19.72	19.23	18.73	18.23
74	22.65	22.31	21.95	21.57	21.17	20.75	20.31	19.85	19.38	18.90	18.41	17.92
75	22.07	21.76	21.43	21.08	20.70	20.31	19.90	19.47	19.02	18.56	18.09	17.61
76	21.46	21.18	20.88	20.56	20.21	19.85	19.46	19.06	18.64	18.20	17.75	17.29
77	20.83	20.57	20.30	20.00	19.69	19.35	19.00	18.62	18.23	17.82	17.39	16.95
78	20.16	19.93	19.68	19.42	19.13	18.83	18.50	18.16	17.79	17.41	17.01	16.59
79	19.47	19.26	19.04	18.80	18.54	18.27	17.97	17.66	17.32	16.97	16.60	16.20
80	18.76	18.57	18.37	18.16	17.93	17.68	17.41	17.13	16.83	16.50	16.16	15.79
81	18.02	17.86	17.68	17.49	17.28	17.06	16.82	16.57	16.29	16.00	15.69	15.35
82	17.26	17.12	16.96	16.79	16.61	16.41	16.20	15.97	15.73	15.46	15.18	14.88
83	16.49	16.36	16.22	16.07	15.91	15.73	15.55	15.35	15.13	14.90	14.64	14.37
84	15.69	15.57	15.45	15.32	15.18	15.03	14.87	14.69	14.50	14.29	14.07	13.83
85	14.87	14.77	14.67	14.55	14.43	14.30	14.16	14.00	13.84	13.66	13.47	13.26
86	14.04	13.95	13.86	13.76	13.66	13.54	13.42	13.29	13.15	12.99	12.82	12.64
87	13.19	13.11	13.04	12.95	12.86	12.77	12.66	12.55	12.43	12.29	12.15	11.99
88	12.32	12.26	12.19	12.12	12.05	11.96	11.88	11.78	11.68	11.57	11.45	11.31
89	11.44	11.39	11.33	11.27	11.21	11.14	11.07	10.99	10.90	10.81	10.71	10.60
90	10.54	10.50	10.46	10.41	10.36	10.30	10.24	10.18	10.11	10.03	9.94	9.85

Table A–4　Joint Life *(Continued)*

Male	Female											
	69	70	71	72	73	74	75	76	77	78	79	80
45	28.10	27.43	26.74	26.03	25.30	24.56	23.80	23.02	22.22	21.41	20.58	19.74
46	27.82	27.17	26.50	25.81	25.10	24.37	23.63	22.86	22.08	21.28	20.47	19.64
47	27.53	26.90	26.24	25.57	24.88	24.17	23.44	22.70	21.93	21.15	20.35	19.54
48	27.22	26.61	25.98	25.32	24.65	23.96	23.25	22.52	21.77	21.00	20.22	19.42
49	26.89	26.30	25.69	25.06	24.41	23.73	23.04	22.33	21.60	20.85	20.08	19.30
50	26.55	25.98	25.39	24.78	24.15	23.49	22.82	22.13	21.41	20.68	19.93	19.16
51	26.19	25.64	25.07	24.48	23.87	23.24	22.58	21.91	21.21	20.50	19.77	19.01
52	25.82	25.29	24.74	24.17	23.58	22.97	22.33	21.68	21.00	20.31	19.59	18.86
53	25.43	24.92	24.39	23.84	23.27	22.68	22.07	21.43	20.78	20.10	19.40	18.69
54	25.02	24.53	24.02	23.50	22.95	22.38	21.79	21.17	20.54	19.88	19.20	18.51
55	24.61	24.13	23.65	23.14	22.61	22.06	21.49	20.90	20.29	19.65	18.99	18.31
56	24.18	23.72	23.25	22.77	22.26	21.73	21.18	20.61	20.02	19.41	18.77	18.11
57	23.75	23.31	22.85	22.38	21.89	21.39	20.86	20.32	19.74	19.15	18.53	17.90
58	23.31	22.88	22.44	21.99	21.52	21.03	20.53	20.00	19.45	18.88	18.29	17.67
59	22.88	22.45	22.02	21.58	21.13	20.66	20.18	19.67	19.15	18.60	18.03	17.43
60	22.44	22.02	21.60	21.17	20.73	20.28	19.82	19.33	18.83	18.30	17.75	17.18
61	22.01	21.59	21.17	20.75	20.33	19.89	19.44	18.98	18.50	17.99	17.47	16.92
62	21.58	21.16	20.75	20.33	19.92	19.50	19.06	18.62	18.15	17.67	17.17	16.64
63	21.16	20.74	20.33	19.92	19.51	19.09	18.67	18.24	17.80	17.34	16.86	16.35
64	20.76	20.33	19.91	19.50	19.10	18.69	18.28	17.87	17.44	16.99	16.53	16.05
65	20.37	19.93	19.51	19.10	18.69	18.29	17.89	17.48	17.07	16.64	16.20	15.74
66	19.99	19.55	19.12	18.70	18.29	17.89	17.49	17.09	16.69	16.28	15.85	15.41
67	19.63	19.18	18.74	18.31	17.90	17.49	17.10	16.70	16.31	15.91	15.50	15.08
68	19.29	18.82	18.37	17.93	17.51	17.11	16.71	16.32	15.93	15.54	15.14	14.74
69	18.96	18.49	18.02	17.58	17.15	16.73	16.33	15.94	15.55	15.17	14.78	14.39
70	18.66	18.16	17.69	17.23	16.79	16.37	15.97	15.57	15.19	14.80	14.43	14.04
71	18.34	17.86	17.37	16.91	16.46	16.03	15.61	15.21	14.82	14.44	14.07	13.69
72	18.04	17.55	17.08	16.60	16.14	15.70	15.27	14.87	14.47	14.09	13.72	13.35
73	17.73	17.25	16.77	16.30	15.83	15.38	14.95	14.53	14.13	13.75	13.37	13.00
74	17.43	16.95	16.47	16.00	15.54	15.08	14.64	14.22	13.81	13.41	13.04	12.67
75	17.13	16.65	16.17	15.70	15.24	14.80	14.34	13.92	13.50	13.10	12.71	12.34
76	16.82	16.35	15.88	15.41	14.95	14.50	14.07	13.62	13.20	12.79	12.40	12.02
77	16.50	16.04	15.58	15.12	14.66	14.21	13.77	13.35	12.91	12.50	12.10	11.72
78	16.16	15.72	15.27	14.82	14.37	13.92	13.48	13.06	12.64	12.22	11.82	11.43
79	15.80	15.38	14.95	14.51	14.07	13.63	13.20	12.77	12.36	11.96	11.54	11.15
80	15.41	15.02	14.61	14.19	13.77	13.34	12.91	12.49	12.08	11.68	11.29	10.88
81	15.00	14.63	14.25	13.86	13.45	13.04	12.62	12.21	11.80	11.40	11.01	10.64
82	14.56	14.22	13.87	13.50	13.11	12.72	12.32	11.92	11.53	11.13	10.74	10.37
83	14.08	13.78	13.45	13.11	12.75	12.38	12.01	11.63	11.24	10.86	10.48	10.11
84	13.57	13.30	13.00	12.69	12.36	12.02	11.67	11.31	10.94	10.57	10.21	9.84
85	13.03	12.78	12.52	12.24	11.94	11.63	11.31	10.97	10.63	10.27	9.92	9.57
86	12.45	12.23	12.00	11.75	11.49	11.20	10.91	10.60	10.28	9.95	9.62	9.29
87	11.83	11.64	11.44	11.22	10.99	10.74	10.48	10.20	9.91	9.61	9.30	8.99
88	11.17	11.01	10.84	10.66	10.45	10.24	10.00	9.76	9.50	9.23	8.94	8.66
89	10.48	10.35	10.20	10.05	9.88	9.69	9.49	9.28	9.05	8.81	8.55	8.29
90	9.75	9.65	9.53	9.40	9.26	9.10	8.93	8.75	8.55	8.34	8.12	7.89

Table A–4   Joint Life *(Continued)*

					Female				
Male	81	82	83	84	85	86	87	88	89	90
45	18.89	18.03	17.15	16.26	15.36	14.46	13.54	12.61	11.68	10.74
46	18.80	17.95	17.08	16.20	15.31	14.41	13.50	12.58	11.66	10.72
47	18.71	17.86	17.01	16.14	15.26	14.37	13.46	12.55	11.63	10.70
48	18.60	17.77	16.93	16.07	15.20	14.32	13.42	12.52	11.60	10.67
49	18.49	17.68	16.84	16.00	15.14	14.26	13.38	12.48	11.57	10.65
50	18.37	17.57	16.75	15.91	15.06	14.20	13.32	12.43	11.53	10.62
51	18.24	17.45	16.65	15.83	14.99	14.13	13.27	12.39	11.49	10.59
52	18.10	17.33	16.54	15.73	14.90	14.06	13.21	12.34	11.45	10.55
53	17.95	17.19	16.42	15.62	14.81	13.98	13.14	12.28	11.40	10.51
54	17.79	17.05	16.29	15.51	14.71	13.90	13.07	12.22	11.35	10.47
55	17.61	16.89	16.15	15.39	14.61	13.81	12.99	12.15	11.30	10.42
56	17.43	16.73	16.00	15.26	14.49	13.71	12.90	12.08	11.24	10.38
57	17.23	16.55	15.85	15.12	14.37	13.60	12.81	12.00	11.17	10.32
58	17.03	16.37	15.68	14.97	14.24	13.49	12.71	11.92	11.10	10.27
59	16.81	16.17	15.50	14.81	14.10	13.37	12.61	11.83	11.03	10.20
60	16.58	15.96	15.32	14.65	13.96	13.24	12.50	11.74	10.95	10.14
61	16.34	15.74	15.12	14.47	13.80	13.10	12.38	11.63	10.86	10.07
62	16.09	15.52	14.91	14.29	13.64	12.96	12.25	11.53	10.77	9.99
63	15.83	15.27	14.70	14.09	13.46	12.80	12.12	11.41	10.67	9.91
64	15.55	15.02	14.47	13.89	13.28	12.64	11.98	11.29	10.57	9.82
65	15.26	14.75	14.22	13.67	13.08	12.47	11.83	11.16	10.46	9.73
66	14.96	14.47	13.97	13.44	12.88	12.29	11.67	11.02	10.34	9.63
67	14.64	14.18	13.70	13.19	12.66	12.10	11.50	10.87	10.22	9.53
68	14.32	13.88	13.42	12.94	12.43	11.89	11.32	10.72	10.08	9.41
69	13.99	13.57	13.13	12.67	12.19	11.68	11.13	10.56	9.94	9.30
70	13.65	13.25	12.84	12.40	11.94	11.45	10.94	10.38	9.80	9.17
71	13.32	12.93	12.53	12.12	11.68	11.22	10.73	10.20	9.64	9.04
72	12.98	12.61	12.22	11.83	11.41	10.97	10.51	10.01	9.47	8.90
73	12.64	12.28	11.91	11.53	11.14	10.72	10.28	9.80	9.29	8.75
74	12.31	11.95	11.59	11.23	10.85	10.46	10.04	9.59	9.10	8.58
75	11.98	11.63	11.28	10.92	10.56	10.19	9.79	9.36	8.91	8.41
76	11.66	11.31	10.97	10.62	10.27	9.91	9.53	9.13	8.70	8.23
77	11.35	11.00	10.66	10.32	9.98	9.63	9.27	8.89	8.48	8.04
78	11.06	10.70	10.36	10.02	9.69	9.35	9.01	8.64	8.26	7.84
79	10.77	10.41	10.07	9.73	9.41	9.08	8.74	8.40	8.03	7.63
80	10.51	10.14	9.79	9.45	9.13	8.81	8.48	8.15	7.80	7.42
81	10.25	9.89	9.53	9.19	8.87	8.55	8.23	7.91	7.57	7.21
82	10.01	9.63	9.29	8.94	8.62	8.30	7.99	7.67	7.35	7.01
83	9.75	9.41	9.05	8.72	8.39	8.07	7.76	7.45	7.14	6.81
84	9.49	9.15	8.83	8.48	8.17	7.85	7.54	7.24	6.93	6.61
85	9.23	8.90	8.58	8.27	7.95	7.65	7.34	7.04	6.73	6.42
86	8.96	8.64	8.32	8.03	7.75	7.43	7.15	6.85	6.55	6.25
87	8.67	8.37	8.06	7.78	7.50	7.24	6.94	6.67	6.37	6.08
88	8.37	8.08	7.79	7.51	7.25	7.00	6.76	6.47	6.21	5.91
89	8.03	7.76	7.50	7.24	6.99	6.74	6.51	6.29	6.02	5.76
90	7.65	7.41	7.17	6.93	6.70	6.47	6.25	6.04	5.84	5.58

APPENDIX B

Social Security Income

The formula that the Social Security Administration uses to calculate your benefit is designed to give you credit for your 35 highest paying years. Here's how it works:

1. Your lifetime earnings (to age 60) are adjusted for inflation.

2. Your total earnings are divided by the number of months you worked to determine what is known as your average indexed monthly earnings.

3. Your base benefit is based upon your average indexed earnings.

The chart below shows the maximum annual benefit at different retirement ages based upon current factors. This will help you to estimate your potential annual benefit. For example, the average annual individual benefit in 2003 was $899 while the maximum benefit was $1,348.

The normal retirement age is 65 for people born after 1938 and increases to 67 for people born in 1960 and after. These tables assume that one individual has maximized their benefit and the other retiree qualified for the maximum of 50 percent spousal benefit,

If you haven't done so recently, you should request a Personal Earnings and Benefits Estimate Statement from the Social Security Administration

(SSA) by calling 1–800–772–1213 and asking for Form 7004 (Request for Statement of Earnings). Or, if you prefer, you can submit the *request for an estimate statement* online (www.ssa.gov)

Individual (retirement age)	40	45	50	55	60
62	$41,208	$34,080	$29,448	$23,628	$18,636
67	$68,772	$56,268	$44,520	$36,168	$28,752
70	$94,728	$78,372	$67,596	$55,152	$44,424

Individual (retirement age)	40	45	50	55	60
62	$61,812	$51,120	$44,172	$35,442	$27,954
67	$68,772	$84,402	$66,780	$54,252	$43,128
70	$94,728	$117,558	$101,394	$82,728	$66,636

APPENDIX C

Compound Interest Table

Use this table if you don't have access to a calculator to determine the value of a sum of money over a specific period of time. Let's say you want to see what $10,000 will be worth in twenty years assuming a six percent growth rate. All you need to do is multiply the factor for twenty years and six percent by $10,000. In this case, the factor is 3.20714, so $10,000 will be worth $32,071 in twenty years.

Table C–1 Compound Interest Table

Number of Years						Annual Percentage						
	1%	2%	3%	4%	5%	6%	7%	8%	9%	10%	11%	12%
1	1.01000	1.02000	1.03000	1.04000	1.05000	1.06000	1.07000	1.08000	1.09000	1.10000	1.11000	1.12000
2	1.02010	1.04040	1.06090	1.08160	1.10250	1.12360	1.14490	1.16640	1.18810	1.21000	1.23210	1.25440
3	1.03030	1.06121	1.09273	1.12486	1.15763	1.19102	1.22504	1.25971	1.29503	1.33100	1.36763	1.40493
4	1.04060	1.08243	1.12551	1.16986	1.21551	1.26248	1.31080	1.36049	1.41158	1.46410	1.51807	1.57352
5	1.05101	1.10408	1.15927	1.21665	1.27628	1.33823	1.40255	1.46933	1.53862	1.61051	1.68506	1.76234
6	1.06152	1.12616	1.19405	1.26532	1.34010	1.41852	1.50073	1.58687	1.67710	1.77156	1.87041	1.97382
7	1.07214	1.14869	1.22987	1.31593	1.40710	1.50363	1.60578	1.71382	1.82804	1.94872	2.07616	2.21068
8	1.08286	1.17166	1.26677	1.36857	1.47746	1.59385	1.71819	1.85093	1.99256	2.14359	2.30454	2.47596
9	1.09369	1.19509	1.30477	1.42331	1.55133	1.68948	1.83846	1.99900	2.17189	2.35795	2.55804	2.77308
10	1.10462	1.21899	1.34392	1.48024	1.62889	1.79085	1.96715	2.15892	2.36736	2.59374	2.83942	3.10585
11	1.11567	1.24337	1.38423	1.53945	1.71034	1.89830	2.10485	2.33164	2.58043	2.85312	3.15176	3.47855
12	1.12683	1.26824	1.42576	1.60103	1.79586	2.01220	2.25219	2.51817	2.81266	3.13843	3.49845	3.89598
13	1.13809	1.29361	1.46853	1.66507	1.88565	2.13293	2.40985	2.71962	3.06580	3.45227	3.88328	4.36349
14	1.14947	1.31948	1.51259	1.73168	1.97993	2.26090	2.57853	2.93719	3.34173	3.79750	4.31044	4.88711
15	1.16097	1.34587	1.55797	1.80094	2.07893	2.39656	2.75903	3.17217	3.64248	4.17725	4.78459	5.47357
16	1.17258	1.37279	1.60471	1.87298	2.18287	2.54035	2.95216	3.42594	3.97031	4.59497	5.31089	6.13039
17	1.18430	1.40024	1.65285	1.94790	2.29202	2.69277	3.15882	3.70002	4.32763	5.05447	5.89509	6.86604
18	1.19615	1.42825	1.70243	2.02582	2.40662	2.85434	3.37993	3.99602	4.71712	5.55992	6.54355	7.68997
19	1.20811	1.45681	1.75351	2.10685	2.52695	3.02560	3.61653	4.31570	5.14166	6.11591	7.26334	8.61276

Table C–1 Compound Interest Table *(Continued)*

Annual Percentage

Number of Years	1%	2%	3%	4%	5%	6%	7%	8%	9%	10%	11%	12%
20	1.22019	1.48595	1.80611	2.19112	2.65330	3.20714	3.86968	4.66096	5.60441	6.72750	8.06231	9.64629
21	1.23239	1.51567	1.86029	2.27877	2.78596	3.39956	4.14056	5.03383	6.10881	7.40025	8.94917	10.80385
22	1.24472	1.54598	1.91610	2.36992	2.92526	3.60354	4.43040	5.43654	6.65860	8.14027	9.93357	12.10031
23	1.25716	1.57690	1.97359	2.46472	3.07152	3.81975	4.74053	5.87146	7.25787	8.95430	11.02627	13.55235
24	1.26973	1.60844	2.03279	2.56330	3.22510	4.04893	5.07237	6.34118	7.91108	9.84973	12.23916	15.17863
25	1.28243	1.64061	2.09378	2.66584	3.38635	4.29187	5.42743	6.84848	8.62308	10.83471	13.58546	17.00006
26	1.29526	1.67342	2.15659	2.77247	3.55567	4.54938	5.80735	7.39635	9.39916	11.91818	15.07986	19.04007
27	1.30821	1.70689	2.22129	2.88337	3.73346	4.82235	6.21387	7.98806	10.24508	13.10999	16.73865	21.32488
28	1.32129	1.74102	2.28793	2.99870	3.92013	5.11169	6.64884	8.62711	11.16714	14.42099	18.57990	23.88387
29	1.33450	1.77584	2.35657	3.11865	4.11614	5.41839	7.11426	9.31727	12.17218	15.86309	20.62369	26.74993
30	1.34785	1.81136	2.42726	3.24340	4.32194	5.74349	7.61226	10.06266	13.26768	17.44940	22.89230	29.95992
31	1.36133	1.84759	2.50008	3.37313	4.53804	6.08810	8.14511	10.86767	14.46177	19.19434	25.41045	33.55511
32	1.37494	1.88454	2.57508	3.50806	4.76494	6.45339	8.71527	11.73708	15.76333	21.11378	28.20560	37.58173
33	1.38869	1.92223	2.65234	3.64838	5.00319	6.84059	9.32534	12.67605	17.18203	23.22515	31.30821	42.09153
34	1.40258	1.96068	2.73191	3.79432	5.25335	7.25103	9.97811	13.69013	18.72841	25.54767	34.75212	47.14252
35	1.41660	1.99989	2.81386	3.94609	5.51602	7.68609	10.67658	14.78534	20.41397	28.10244	38.57485	52.79962
36	1.43077	2.03989	2.89828	4.10393	5.79182	8.14725	11.42394	15.96817	22.25123	30.91268	42.81808	59.13557
37	1.44508	2.08069	2.98523	4.26809	6.08141	8.63609	12.22362	17.24563	24.25384	34.00395	47.52807	66.23184
38	1.45953	2.12230	3.07478	4.43881	6.38548	9.15425	13.07927	18.62528	26.43668	37.40434	52.75616	74.17966

Table C-1 Compound Interest Table *(Continued)*

<table>
<tr><th rowspan="2">Number of Years</th><th colspan="12">Annual Percentage</th></tr>
<tr><th>1%</th><th>2%</th><th>3%</th><th>4%</th><th>5%</th><th>6%</th><th>7%</th><th>8%</th><th>9%</th><th>10%</th><th>11%</th><th>12%</th></tr>
<tr><td>39</td><td>1.47412</td><td>2.16474</td><td>3.16703</td><td>4.61637</td><td>6.70475</td><td>9.70351</td><td>13.99482</td><td>20.11530</td><td>28.81598</td><td>41.14478</td><td>58.55934</td><td>83.08122</td></tr>
<tr><td>40</td><td>1.48886</td><td>2.20804</td><td>3.26204</td><td>4.80102</td><td>7.03999</td><td>10.28572</td><td>14.97446</td><td>21.72452</td><td>31.40942</td><td>45.25926</td><td>65.00087</td><td>93.05097</td></tr>
<tr><td>41</td><td>1.50375</td><td>2.25220</td><td>3.35990</td><td>4.99306</td><td>7.39199</td><td>10.90286</td><td>16.02267</td><td>23.46248</td><td>34.23627</td><td>49.78518</td><td>72.15096</td><td>104.21709</td></tr>
<tr><td>42</td><td>1.51879</td><td>2.29724</td><td>3.46070</td><td>5.19278</td><td>7.76159</td><td>11.55703</td><td>17.14426</td><td>25.33948</td><td>37.31753</td><td>54.76370</td><td>80.08757</td><td>116.72314</td></tr>
<tr><td>43</td><td>1.53398</td><td>2.34319</td><td>3.56452</td><td>5.40050</td><td>8.14967</td><td>12.25045</td><td>18.34435</td><td>27.36664</td><td>40.67611</td><td>60.24007</td><td>88.89720</td><td>130.72991</td></tr>
<tr><td>44</td><td>1.54932</td><td>2.39005</td><td>3.67145</td><td>5.61652</td><td>8.55715</td><td>12.98548</td><td>19.62846</td><td>29.55597</td><td>44.33696</td><td>66.26408</td><td>98.67589</td><td>146.41750</td></tr>
<tr><td>45</td><td>1.56481</td><td>2.43785</td><td>3.78160</td><td>5.84118</td><td>8.98501</td><td>13.76461</td><td>21.00245</td><td>31.92045</td><td>48.32729</td><td>72.89048</td><td>109.53024</td><td>163.98760</td></tr>
<tr><td>46</td><td>1.58046</td><td>2.48661</td><td>3.89504</td><td>6.07482</td><td>9.43426</td><td>14.59049</td><td>22.47262</td><td>34.47409</td><td>52.67674</td><td>80.17953</td><td>121.57857</td><td>183.66612</td></tr>
<tr><td>47</td><td>1.59626</td><td>2.53634</td><td>4.01190</td><td>6.31782</td><td>9.90597</td><td>15.46592</td><td>24.04571</td><td>37.23201</td><td>57.41765</td><td>88.19749</td><td>134.95221</td><td>205.70605</td></tr>
<tr><td>48</td><td>1.61223</td><td>2.58707</td><td>4.13225</td><td>6.57053</td><td>10.40127</td><td>16.39387</td><td>25.72891</td><td>40.21057</td><td>62.58524</td><td>97.01723</td><td>149.79695</td><td>230.39078</td></tr>
<tr><td>49</td><td>1.62835</td><td>2.63881</td><td>4.25622</td><td>6.83335</td><td>10.92133</td><td>17.37750</td><td>27.52993</td><td>43.42742</td><td>68.21791</td><td>106.71896</td><td>166.27462</td><td>258.03767</td></tr>
<tr><td>50</td><td>1.64463</td><td>2.69159</td><td>4.38391</td><td>7.10668</td><td>11.46740</td><td>18.42015</td><td>29.45703</td><td>46.90161</td><td>74.35752</td><td>117.39085</td><td>184.56483</td><td>289.00219</td></tr>
<tr><td>51</td><td>1.66108</td><td>2.74542</td><td>4.51542</td><td>7.39095</td><td>12.04077</td><td>19.52536</td><td>31.51902</td><td>50.65374</td><td>81.04970</td><td>129.12994</td><td>204.86696</td><td>323.68245</td></tr>
<tr><td>52</td><td>1.67769</td><td>2.80033</td><td>4.65089</td><td>7.68659</td><td>12.64281</td><td>20.69689</td><td>33.72535</td><td>54.70604</td><td>88.34417</td><td>142.04293</td><td>227.40232</td><td>362.52435</td></tr>
<tr><td>53</td><td>1.69447</td><td>2.85633</td><td>4.79041</td><td>7.99405</td><td>13.27495</td><td>21.93870</td><td>36.08612</td><td>59.08252</td><td>96.29514</td><td>156.24723</td><td>252.41658</td><td>406.02727</td></tr>
<tr><td>54</td><td>1.71141</td><td>2.91346</td><td>4.93412</td><td>8.31381</td><td>13.93870</td><td>23.25502</td><td>38.61215</td><td>63.80913</td><td>104.96171</td><td>171.87195</td><td>280.18240</td><td>454.75054</td></tr>
<tr><td>55</td><td>1.72852</td><td>2.97173</td><td>5.08215</td><td>8.64637</td><td>14.63563</td><td>24.65032</td><td>41.31500</td><td>68.91386</td><td>114.40826</td><td>189.05914</td><td>311.00247</td><td>509.32061</td></tr>
<tr><td>56</td><td>1.74581</td><td>3.03117</td><td>5.23461</td><td>8.99222</td><td>15.36741</td><td>26.12934</td><td>44.20705</td><td>74.42696</td><td>124.70501</td><td>207.96506</td><td>345.21274</td><td>570.43908</td></tr>
<tr><td>57</td><td>1.76327</td><td>3.09179</td><td>5.39165</td><td>9.35191</td><td>16.13578</td><td>27.69710</td><td>47.30155</td><td>80.38112</td><td>135.92846</td><td>228.76156</td><td>383.18614</td><td>638.89177</td></tr>
</table>

Table C–1 Compound Interest Table *(Continued)*

Number of Years						Annual Percentage						
	1%	2%	3%	4%	5%	6%	7%	8%	9%	10%	11%	12%
58	1.78090	3.15362	5.55340	9.72599	16.94257	29.35893	50.61265	86.81161	148.16202	251.63772	425.33661	715.55878
59	1.79871	3.21670	5.72000	10.11503	17.78970	31.12046	54.15554	93.75654	161.49660	276.80149	472.12364	801.42583
60	1.81670	3.28103	5.89160	10.51963	18.67919	32.98769	57.94643	101.25706	176.03129	304.48164	524.05724	897.59693
61	1.83486	3.34665	6.06835	10.94041	19.61315	34.96695	62.00268	109.35763	191.87411	334.92980	581.70354	1005.30857
62	1.85321	3.41358	6.25040	11.37803	20.59380	37.06497	66.34286	118.10624	209.14278	368.42278	645.69093	1125.94559
63	1.87174	3.48186	6.43791	11.83315	21.62349	39.28887	70.98686	127.55474	227.96563	405.26506	716.71693	1261.05906
64	1.89046	3.55149	6.63105	12.30648	22.70467	41.64620	75.95595	137.75912	248.48253	445.79157	795.55579	1412.38615
65	1.90937	3.62252	6.82998	12.79874	23.83990	44.14497	81.27286	148.77985	270.84596	490.37073	883.06693	1581.87249

Index

A

A shares, mutual fund, 251

AARP (American Association of Retired Persons), 18

Absolute analysis, 26–27

Accidental death rider, 217

Accredited estate planner (AEP), 296

Action plan case study (the Glovers), 17. *See* Goal Oriented Retirement Planning (GORP) case study

Active management, 268

Administrative fees, variable annuities, 210

ADRs. *See* American Depository Receipts (ADRs)

Aggressive growth mutual funds, 241

Alpha, investment, 271

Alternative Minimum Tax (AMT), 185

A.M. Best insurance company ratings, 221

American Association of Retired Persons (AARP), 18

American College, 293, 294

American Depository Receipts (ADRs), 134, 172

American Express, 73

American Savings Education Council, 51

Annual reports, corporate, 168

Annuitant, 200

Annuities, 116–117, 145–146, 199–214, 215

1035 tax-free exchanges, 214

403(b) plans and, 79–80

benefits of, 200–201

costs of, 202, 203, 209–210

criticisms of, 215–216

fixed, 57, 79–80, 200, 202–205, 209

guaranteed income from, 57–58, 116–117, 143, 145–146, 211–213

life expectancy and, 213–214

origins of, 200

parties in contract of, 200

probate process, exemption from, 202

safety of, 220–221

subaccount transfers within, 209

tax-deferred growth and, 200, 201–202

tax implications of, 52, 200, 269

terminal funded, 49–50

variable, 57, 200, 202, 205–210

withdrawal features, 208

Annuitization (insured income), 54–58, 116–117, 143, 145–146, 199, 211–214

fixed, 57, 211

life expectancy and, 213–214

popular forms of, 212

retirement income from, 54–58, 211–213

variable, 57–58, 208, 211

Art investments, 110, 157, 232, 234

Asset allocation, 260–262. *See also* Diversification

Asset allocation funds, 242

Assets

distribution of during retirement, 38

gifting of, 122

insuring, 198

leaving as a legacy, 40

liquidity of, 109–110

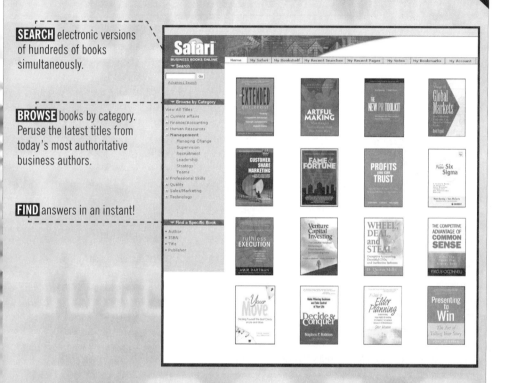

8 reasons why you should read the Financial Times for 4 weeks RISK-FREE!

To help you stay current with significant developments in the world economy ... and to assist you to make informed business decisions — the Financial Times brings you:

 Fast, meaningful overviews of international affairs ... plus daily briefings on major world news.

 Perceptive coverage of economic, business, financial and political developments with special focus on emerging markets.

 More international business news than any other publication.

 Sophisticated financial analysis and commentary on world market activity plus stock quotes from over 30 countries.

 Reports on international companies and a section on global investing.

❻ Specialized pages on management, marketing, advertising and technological innovations from all parts of the world.

❼ Highly valued single-topic special reports (over 200 annually) on countries, industries, investment opportunities, technology and more.

❽ The Saturday Weekend FT section — a globetrotter's guide to leisure-time activities around the world: the arts, fine dining, travel, sports and more.

FT FINANCIAL TIMES
World business newspaper

The *Financial Times* delivers a world of business news.

Use the Risk-Free Trial Voucher below!

To stay ahead in today's business world you need to be well-informed on a daily basis. And not just on the national level. You need a news source that closely monitors the entire world of business, and then delivers it in a concise, quick-read format.

With the *Financial Times* you get the major stories from every region of the world. Reports found nowhere else. You get business, management, politics, economics, technology and more.

Now you can try the *Financial Times* for 4 weeks, absolutely risk free. And better yet, if you wish to continue receiving the *Financial Times* you'll get great savings off the regular subscription rate. Just use the voucher below.